Shakespeare's Speaking Pictures

SHAKESPEARE'S SPEAKING PICTURES

Studies in Iconic Imagery

John Doebler

UNIVERSITY OF NEW MEXICO PRESS

Albuquerque

1909633

*To Ruth and Mark
for whom there can be no future
without a past*

Contents

Illustrations

Preface

Few lovers of the theater are insensitive to the symbolic use of stage effects. When the pregnant Hedda commits suicide under the portrait of General Gabler we are instantly aware of Ibsen's emphasis on three generations united in death. When Strindberg's Father bursts through a wallpapered door, after stripping away all hypocrisy by hurling a lighted lamp at his wife, we know that Adolf is now both fully mad and fully sane. When the portraits of the Marchioness Matilda and Henry IV suddenly spring to life we literally see Pirandello's ambiguities of life and art, the past and the present, truth and fiction. Yet Shakespeare's symbolic stagecraft, surely as creative as that found among the most distinguished of modern playwrights, seems largely to have escaped the interest of scholars and critics in the twentieth century. His plays have often been regarded as literary artifacts rather than living action for the stage. In recent decades, however, increasing weight has fallen on both Shakespeare's stage and his dramaturgy. By relating Renaissance iconography to stagecraft, *Shakespeare's Speaking Pictures* adds its own modest contribution to a further redressing of the imbalance.

Shakespeare lived in a world saturated with visual tropes conveyed by paintings, stained-glass windows, tapestries, household objects, and even armor, as well as by widely distributed books and graphics. Thread, printer's ink, and paint were the media for an enormously rich storehouse of conventional motifs, emblems, and impresas. Formerly a Rosetta stone, this visual vocabulary has been in large part deciphered by intellectual historians: Émile Mâle, Erwin Panofsky, and many others. The symbolism such men have so brilliantly recovered in medieval and Renaissance art can also be applied to an understanding of Shakespeare's plays.

Many symbols are common to both the plastic arts of the sixteenth century and the images chosen by Shakespeare for his dramatic verse, but my major emphasis falls upon his iconic stage imagery. When at the end of *King Lear* the defeated Edmund is flat on his back, after his defeat in the lists by Edgar, the bastard brother makes the choric observation that "The wheel is come full circle; I am here" (V. iii. 174). The verbal allusion to Fortune's wheel has a particular visual association for those familiar with the innumerable representations of that wheel in the Renaissance. As most students of Shakespeare know, a blindfolded Dame Fortune was frequently shown turning her wheel, with perhaps four small figures attached to equidistant points on the rim. At the zenith might be a king; at the nadir a beggar on his back in the mire. Edmund, who has risen from bastard younger son to virtual king of England, is now literally on his back, fatally wounded. Thus iconic stage imagery covers details of production—props, gestures, blocking, even sound effects—which had a conventional symbolic meaning for an Elizabethan audience, a meaning since lost. And yet a modern audience will also have a powerful response to Edmund's line and to his helpless posture on the stage. They can easily see the justice of Edgar, who has been forced by his brother's guile into the lowest of social positions, now standing over his fallen enemy. What we have here is a symbolic stage image partly created and partly reinforced by verbal allusion to Fortune's wheel. These compatible verbal and stage images operate on several levels of meaning, at least one of them iconic and thus only understood by those familiar with the conventions of medieval and Renaissance symbolism and art. As for staging, the term can still cover all details of production, whether symbolic or mimetic; for Shakespeare often moves back and forth between the emblematic and the mimetic within a single play, even within a particular scene. A further attempt on my part to clarify terminology is the consistent use of *iconographic* for conventional symbolism in the graphic and plastic arts and *iconic* for comparable visual and aural symbolism on stage.

Because the iconic approach to Shakespeare emphasized in this book is comparatively new, a definition of terms is called for. The newness of the iconic interpretation of his imagery also helps to account for the limited scale of *Shakespeare's Speaking Pictures*. It makes no attempt to be exhaustive, but only to offer tentative scholarly and critical suggestions about the different ways in which the tool of iconography can be used to enrich our understanding of verbal and especially stage imagery. Particularly interesting is the way in which a visual image could communicate to a Renaissance audience a concentrated pattern of associations summarizing the inner meaning of many dramatic events, all the more so if the meaning were in turn a union of seeming opposites, such as love and chastity or free will and fate. The iconic is one of Shakespeare's many forms of ellipsis. In the same spirit I have chosen to render Latin mottoes, many of them integral parts of emblems, in a literal form conveying the telegraphic style of the original, and thus without the variations on the verb *to be* usually supplied by a translator. The Neoplatonic ideal was for the soul to supply intuitively the connectives linking juxtaposed (but seemingly unrelated) events, images, and concepts.

I have from time to time even taken the liberty of guessing about possibilities of iconic staging. Hopefully, the reader will indulge these occasional guesses as I move with hesitation along the length of unstable limbs. Much remains to be done in the way of confirmation and refutation, and "essays" (in Montaigne's sense of the word) might have been a better choice of diction than "studies" for some of my chapters when it came to choosing a subtitle for this book. We all recognize the stark dramatic clarity and amplitude of meaning when Lear stands a bare forked animal amid the storm, despite the verbal economy accompanying one of the most poignant stage images in all of Shakespeare; but countless other understated moments constantly teased my curiosity about the intended stage effect. It often seemed to me that a partially informed guess was at least a way of pointing to my instinctive feelings about many of these less-recognized moments.

The quotations from Shakespeare illustrating the use of the tool of iconography are all drawn from the second edition of *The Complete Works,* edited by Peter Alexander (New York: Random House, 1952), unless indicated otherwise. Virtually all the quoted stage directions, for instance, are taken from the substantive quarto or First Folio texts.

An appendix on *Othello,* written by my wife, provides detailed historical background for the ars moriendi, the craft of holy dying that is so ubiquitous a theme both in Shakespeare and in much Renaissance art and literature. The ars is extensively referred to in many of my chapters; conversely, the appendix applies the visual conventions of the ars to the iconic verbal and stage imagery of *Othello.* Both Mrs. Doebler and I thank the Johns Hopkins University Press and the editors of *ELH* for permission to print a revised version of what first appeared as an article in that journal, 34 (1967):156–72. Other portions of this book which have appeared publicly in earlier form are sections of the *As You Like It* and *Hamlet* chapters, in *Shakespeare Survey* 26 (1973):111–17; and *Shakespeare Quarterly* 23 (1972):161–69, respectively. Both articles were, in turn, based on papers presented at scholarly conventions: the *As You Like It* at the World Shakespeare Congress (Vancouver, 1971); and the *Hamlet* at the Modern Language Association annual meeting (Chicago, 1967). A portion of the chapter on *The Tempest,* having to do with Ariel as harpy, was the basis of a paper presented at the Central Renaissance Conference (Lincoln, 1973).

I also welcome this opportunity to thank my wife and many others for their great generosity in assisting the completion of this book: in particular my former colleague and esteemed friend William Bowden; my research assistant and tolerant companion Robert Nordlie; Martha Hester Fleischer, whose scholarly suggestions were helpful in countless ways; Elizabeth Heist, for her editorial knowledge and patience; and the librarians and staff of the Folger Shakespeare Library, the Boyd Lee Spahr Library of Dickinson College, the British Museum, the Warburg Institute, the Hayden Memorial Library of Arizona State University, and the library of the University of California at San Diego. For grants-in-aid used to support research on this book I am grateful to the Folger Shakespeare Library, Dickinson College, and Arizona State University. The original debt, however, is owed my teachers of many years past: Madeleine Doran, Mark Eccles, and Allan H. Gilbert. Their continuing influence combines with the work of innumerable scholars and critics, many cited, most not, to create the foundation for this book. Where it endures they should be recalled; where the fabric is weak I am responsible.

John Doebler
Arizona State University

Introduction: Iconic Imagery

Mine eye hath play'd the painter and hath stell'd
Thy beauty's form in table of my heart;
My body is the frame wherein 'tis held,
And perspective it is best painter's art.
For through the painter must you see his skill
To find where your true image pictur'd lies,
Which in my bosom's shop is hanging still,
That hath his windows glazed with thine eyes.
Now see what good turns eyes for eyes have done:
Mine eyes have drawn thy shape, and thine for me
Are windows to my breast, where through the sun
Delights to peep, to gaze therein on thee;
    Yet eyes this cunning want to grace their art;
    They draw but what they see, know not the heart.

Shakespeare's famous Sonnet 24 begins with an implied comparison between poet and painter and concludes with the superiority of the former to the latter—the painter, like the eye, sees; the poet, like the heart, understands. The sonnet begins with three quatrains of witty comparison, concludes with a couplet of judgmental contrast. Most of *Shakespeare's Speaking Pictures* is devoted to comparison, for the art of the Renaissance is applied to several of Shakespeare's plays distributed among his comedies, his histories, his tragedies, and his romances. Drawing connections between the literary and plastic arts is certainly far from new. Horace's famous

1

dictum about poetry resembling painting, "ut pictura poesis," along with the notion attributed to Simonides that painting is silent poetry and poetry a speaking picture, remained a commonplace of literary criticism well into the eighteenth century.[1] The subsequent interest of German intellectual historians in a zeitgeist has remained strong until the present, despite the tendency within this approach toward facile generalizations about a spirit of the times uniting all the arts of a stylistic period.[2]

At many points in Western history a renewed distrust of Aristotelian categories has produced a Platonic yearning for continuum. International Neoplatonism, centered at the fifteenth-century Florentine academy of Marsilio Ficino, appealed to humanists with a broad range of educated talents. Certain intellectual and artistic movements of the twentieth century have also been hostile to the traditional categories of genre. The urge to combine poetry and music, so popular in Renaissance madrigal and Romantic lieder, reemerged in the cool jazz and poetry of the West Coast. And, more recently, mixed media has rapidly moved from innovation to cliché. Far less faddish is the movement among modern European intellectuals that has made us deeply suspicious of thought based on the categories of nationality and race, so common as models in the nineteenth century. Some of the most distinguished work opposed to these categories has been centered at the Warburg Institute, founded in Hamburg in 1921. Moved to London in 1933, the Institute has been affiliated with the University of London since 1945 and is a well-known gathering point for many of the most distinguished intellectual historians of our century. Fritz Saxl, Gertrud Bing, E. H. Gombrich, and others have sought the unity and continuity of symbolic forms throughout the history and range of Indo-European civilization. The Institute grew out of Aby Warburg's admiration of Jacob Burckhardt's monumental discoveries about neoclassical Renaissance Italy, and its work stresses a humanistic unity in all human experience.[3] Furthermore, the publications sponsored by the Institute illustrate the archetypal forms of symbolic expression uniting all the arts. The temporal modes vary and conflate, but the eternal substance and many of the forms remain one. Jean Seznec's *The Survival of the Pagan Gods,* for instance, shows how false was our view that classical mythology almost totally disappeared during the centuries between the fall of Rome and the Renaissance. As Seznec asserts in his introduction:

> Above all, it is now recognized that pagan antiquity, far from experiencing a "rebirth" in fifteenth-century Italy, had remained alive within the culture and art of the Middle Ages. Even the gods were not *restored* to life, for they had never disappeared from the memory or imagination of man.[4]

The breaking down of national and historical categories has been aided from another and quite different quarter. Many historians of English literature have been anxious to answer the opinion of the so-called Whig historians, and those who have pressed Jacob Burckhardt into that point of view, that the highest achievement of the Renaissance was the overthrow of medieval religious superstition, which had enslaved mind and body for many centuries. E. M. W. Tillyard's *The Elizabethan World Picture*[5] and the contribution of C. S. Lewis to the Oxford History of English Literature,[6] although both subsequently qualified by their authors, have been two famous rebuttals. These books present the English Renaissance in the context of a medieval background, almost to the point of there being no Renaissance at all, simply modification of the Gothic.[7] The stressing of the medieval religious character of what is best in even the apparently secular English literature of the sixteenth and seventeenth centuries has been the work of many scholars since Tillyard and Lewis, but Rosemond Tuve was certainly among the most distinguished of these. In her *Elizabethan and Metaphysical Imagery*[8] she opposed the antihistorical and largely Freudian interpretation of the English Metaphysical poets by the fashionable New Criticism. In her later study of George Herbert she drew upon one body of secondary material in particular: the writings of Émile Mâle, whose investigations into the symbolism of medieval French cathedrals are encyclopedic. One of Mâle's special concerns is the typological prefiguration of the New Testament in the Old. An interest in the iconography of medieval illuminations, paintings, garments, and stained glass remained Tuve's strong concern in the posthumously published *Allegorical Imagery*.[9] A culture largely based upon a common store of biblical symbols and images, shared by the plastic arts and literature, became for her a tradition sweeping out of the Middle

Ages, across Spenser, and into Milton. A consideration of the contributions of iconography is now a standard tool for students of the Middle Ages and the nondramatic English Renaissance.[10] An example of the degree to which the application of what we now know about the conventions of medieval and classical visual symbolism has filtered down is the excellent student edition of Spenser selections prepared by Robert Kellogg and Oliver Steele.[11] The iconography of the legend of St. George and the Dragon is elaborately applied to the first book of the *Faerie Queene*, and that of the myth of Mars and Venus to the second. A careful study of the introduction and footnotes of this edition suggests the full relevance of Renaissance iconography to Renaissance literature.[12]

Surprisingly, the conventions of Renaissance visual symbolism have been more slowly applied to our understanding of English drama. Drama is obviously one of the most comprehensive artistic forms, uniting as it does language and spectacle. Comparatively little has been done, nevertheless, with iconography and Renaissance drama as poetry, to say nothing of the even more important consideration of drama as drama, as Aristotelian spectacle. Yet students of medieval drama have begun to point the way. As might be expected, Mâle's biblical typology, so often given visual expression in the Middle Ages, is found pertinent to the medieval craft cycles in V. A. Kolve's *The Play Called Corpus Christi*.[13] Kolve draws our attention to how the Fall of Lucifer prefigures the Fall of Man and the Temptation of Christ, and how the story of Abraham and Isaac is mankind's foretaste of both the Crucifixion and the Resurrection. These theological parallels inform the juxtaposition of both the carved scenes in a reredos and the selection, sequence, and imagery of dramatized episodes in the mystery cycles.[14] Mary D. Anderson has reversed the emphasis by regarding drama as the inspiration for church carvings and paintings, in her *Drama and Imagery in English Medieval Churches*.[15] As for the subsequent Renaissance drama, most of the work has been the identification of ideas common to both poetic imagery and visual symbolism—especially the symbolism found in the emblem books of the period. A pioneering book is Henry Green's century-old *Shakespeare and the Emblem Writers*.[16] Of more recent interest are Mario Praz, *Studies in Seventeenth-Century Imagery*,[17] and Russell Fraser, *Shakespeare's Poetics*.[18]

The approach of Praz and Fraser can clearly enrich our understanding of Shakespeare's art. My own investigations have turned up an example of a Shakespearean verbal image still powerful today, but without its traditional source of iconic stage impact, in Edgar's memorable comment on the mad Lear, fantastically dressed with wild flowers: "O thou side-piercing sight!" (IV. vi. 85). Critics have said much about the sight-blindness-learning pattern of imagery in *King Lear,* as well as about the images of horrible physical suffering, with both patterns combined here in Edgar's statement. These patterns of language within the play are undoubtedly reinforced by those events in an audience's experience which have taught them the suffering that inevitably awaits us all. Perhaps even the physical sensation of stabbing pain in the region of the heart which can accompany the sudden recognition of a horrible fact is part of their response to that line. The play and experience make the images here powerful still, but the Elizabethans probably also would have seen an historical allusion in Edgar's statement. Familiar to them would have been the stylized pictures of the Crucifixion in which Mary is shown with a spear entering her side as she watches by her son hanging on the Cross.[19] Additionally familiar might have been the frequent religious poems on the same subject—as the spear enters Christ's side a sympathetic one enters the side of Mary. Mary came to be the very type of compassion of all men, and Edgar, with Kent and Cordelia, and occasionally Albany, embodies this virtue. Furthermore, this image can now be seen as one of several in the play alluding to the life of Christ, and thus part of a third pattern of imagery, in addition to those related to sight and to suffering. Yet my analysis is confined to the verbal, or spoken, imagery. No sword is literally brought on stage.

More than one book has stressed the appearance of a play in production, especially the famous *Prefaces* of Harley Granville-Baker and more recently the studies of John Russell Brown; but in *Shakespeare's Roman Plays,* Maurice Charney made widely familiar the concept of "presentational" imagery,[20] the visual action on the stage in contrast to verbal imagery.[21] Charney made extensive explicit use of Caroline Spurgeon's work on Shakespeare's "iterative" imagery, but he insisted on the emphasis created by what is characteristically seen or heard in performance in contrast to her seeming regard for mere quantity of verbal images.[22] Charney did

not make use, however, of the findings of modern students of
iconography.[23] His concern is with presentational images conveying symbolism apparent to any audience sensitive to artistic form,
whether it has Renaissance learning or not. For instance,

> . . . it is Cleopatra's suicide by the asp which brings the
> serpent theme of the play to a culmination. . . . the serpent
> image has suggested evil and death, but . . . now . . .
> becomes a presentational image of life, or a kind of life-in-
> death. . . .[24]

For any further interpretation of the asps in the climax of *Antony
and Cleopatra* we must turn to those students who have chosen to
stress the conventional contemporary implications of what I will
consistently refer to as iconic stage images, details of staging
carrying conventional symbolic meanings for the Renaissance. The
average Renaissance Englishman knew a language of images, an
iconography, whether he encountered those images in graphic
form, in literature, or on a stage. Samuel Chew was certainly
among the first scholars to bring this knowledge to the study of
Shakespeare. Two of his books extremely important to the student
of iconic stage images are *The Virtues Reconciled* and *The Pilgrimage
of Life.* In both Shakespeare was defended against the charge of
ignorance of the arts.[25] In his earlier book Chew made the
now-famous suggestion that Falstaff's cushion, mockingly used as a
crown in Act II, scene iv, of *1 Henry IV,* was ironically intended by
the playwright to be an emblem of sloth and lechery. Among
many parallels in the arts Chew cited "Father Jan David's design
showing the assault of the Infernal Trinity upon the Christian
Knight. . . . [where] Flesh wears upon her head a large, square,
tasselled cushion."[26] Also in *The Virtues Reconciled* is Chew's
definition of Bassanio as Mercy, Portia as Sapience, and Shylock as
Justice. But when in the trial scene Shylock holds in his hands
scales and a knife (symbol of treachery), instead of scales and a
sword (the proper attribute of Justice), he is revealed to the
audience as a travesty of the virtue he declares,[27] as I will further
elaborate in my chapter on *The Merchant of Venice.*

A few scholars have followed Chew's lead, but surprisingly little
has been published, despite the quality of a number of excellent
articles published along the lines of iconic stage imagery in recent
years.[28] Incorporating a knowledge of such imagery into his

doctoral dissertation on a Christian *Othello,* Lawrence J. Ross, for instance, later published an article about iconic strawberries in Shakespeare.[29] The most important instance, that of Desdemona's embroidered handkerchief, unites in a complex way the two traditions of symbolic meaning embodied in strawberries: emblems of the Virgin expressing perfect goodness, and "any 'show of goodness,' pleasurable to man's corrupt nature, which can spiritually damage him through unwary moral choice."[30] In a paper delivered before the 1962 meeting of the Modern Language Association Conference on Research Opportunities in Renaissance Drama, a paper later published, Ross made a repeated invitation for greater study of iconic staging.[31] He gave a number of helpful suggestions based on the obvious continuity in the three levels of action characterizing medieval and Renaissance art and theater: "the most important convention shared by art and drama was the idea of a cosmic building. The church, the original theatre for the religious drama, was conceived as a model of the cosmos. . . . ," a model symbolizing heaven, earth, and hell.[32]

More recently, Martha Hester Fleischer, who began her work in this area with a doctoral dissertation on the iconic in English history plays, has contributed an article on "stage imagery" to *The Reader's Encyclopedia of Shakespeare.*[33] Her definition seems to make all stage action symbolic, and perhaps she is also inclined to overemphasize the static and the didactic in the dramatist's use of such imagery. Yet she does point toward a valid approach to Shakespeare still largely uninvestigated:

> Stage imagery is created by the persons, properties, and actions visible or audible on stage when a play is in production. Its function is analogous to that of the allegorical picture in the emblem books of the Renaissance: to present the truth for instantaneous comprehension by the eye; while the dialogue, like the emblem book's verses, explicates and elaborates the image for the benefit of methodical, discursive reason.

Among the stage devices she goes on to cite are those serpents of Cleopatra:

> We have been prepared by Enobarbus' description to perceive the Queen in state as an entrancing quean, or Voluptas;

a woman with vipers at her breasts is the sign of Luxuria; and the serpents' teeth seem to bring only drowsy pleasure. At the same time Cleopatra becomes maternal at last, speaking to the creatures as babes nursing at her breasts, transforming herself into a Madonna or Charity. In this one obstinately ambivalent scene, as throughout the play, Cleopatra remains faithful to all the contradictory extremes of her own nature and of human love itself.[34]

In recent years Dieter Mehl has extended the interests expressed in his well-established book on the dumb show into the whole range of critical and scholarly problems raised by his awareness of the emblematic in Elizabethan and Jacobean stagecraft.[35] In an article subsequent to his book he classified several ways in which the emblem books of the period (and thus Renaissance iconography in general) can be applied to the form and content of Renaissance drama.[36] His divisions are valuable in their own right but also because they describe the different kinds of iconic imagery emphasized in *Shakespeare's Speaking Pictures*. First, the dramatist may simply quote an emblem in the spoken text, a device frequent and undramatic in Chapman, but subordinated to the action in other dramatists, especially Shakespeare. A clear example of the dramatic use of such an image in Shakespeare is one already cited in my introduction, the mad Lear as a "side-piercing sight." We may not see a sword, but we do see Lear. Second, an allegorical scene or tableau is often inserted for the purpose of commenting on its mimetic context, as with the dumb shows. The tableau becomes the emblem picture and the dramatic text the emblem poem, although dumb shows themselves probably owe more to civic pageantry than they do to emblem books.[37] Bassanio's choice of the correct casket at the midpoint of *The Merchant of Venice* is among the examples discussed in this book, with the added qualification that this "dumb show" is more commented upon by its mimetic context than the other way around. Thirdly, conventional mimetic action, such as a seemingly digressive scene or subplot, may be the emblem poem glossing the main line of action. The subplot of *The Changeling,* for instance, exposes the love of DeFlores and Beatrice-Joanna as madness. Another well-known example of dramatic glossing is the garden scene at Langley, on which I will make some additional comment in my chapter on

Richard II. Finally, the staging throughout the play may often suggest emblem pictures, quickly explained by dialogue, aside, and soliloquy.[38] This last possibility partially expresses the sense in which Fleischer made her encyclopedia definition of "stage imagery." Emblematic staging is illustrated in my own text by a host of examples, from Hymen's costume in *As You Like It* to Prospero's "airy charm," made with his magician's staff. Another aspect of such staging is the way it can draw a character into the role of personification. The way Cleopatra's serpents draw her, for a moment at least, into the ambiguous roles of both Madonna and Luxuria has just been mentioned above. Many other instances occur in the course of this book: Orlando as an athlete of virtue, Shylock as false Justice and then possibly Penance, and Richard II as both persecuted Christ and fallen Adam, to name but a few examples.

Beyond Mehl's categories is one not easily described. It includes Renaissance works of art as analogues to issues shared with the drama. One scholar to have developed this possibility with sophistication is once again Lawrence J. Ross, in a fully documented monograph which draws careful critical parallels between a Michelangelo marble statue of an old man being defeated by a young one and the rejection of Falstaff by Hal in *2 Henry IV*.[39] In this book I have made similar attempts to identify clarifying analogues, ones my readers will recognize in discussions of Donatello's bronze *David,* Holbein's "Genius" title-border, and Giorgione's *Tempesta.*[40]

For the most part, however, *Shakespeare's Speaking Pictures* confines imagery to its traditional application in English studies. Imagery in general has now become one of the oldest and one of the newest approaches to Shakespeare, while the critical emphasis has shifted from quantitative verbal images to qualitative stage images. Traditionally included among verbal images are metaphors and words or phrases appealing not only to sight but to any of the five senses; yet sound effects,[41] props, gestures, and costumes are also now seen to be as much the imagery of a play as its words. The sights and sounds produced on the stage, furthermore, invite the critic to a consideration of their function within both the particular and the full dramatic and artistic context of the play. The scholar, for his part, has the responsibility of putting verbal and stage images into their historical context. Both critical and scholarly is the classification of images as mimetic, symbolic, or iconic, or as combinations. All iconic imagery is obviously symbolic, whether verbal or what Fleischer means by "stage imagery." But Charney's "presentational" imagery can communicate symbolic meaning to an audience completely unaware of the conventions of Renaissance iconography.

My own emphasis in *Shakespeare's Speaking Pictures* is upon the critical reinterpretation of an entire play assisted by an historical awareness of the conventions of Renaissance iconography, especially as those conventions affect our understanding of stage event. I am also concerned in some measure with theater symbolism independent of Renaissance iconography.

Each of my chapters turns the Shakespearean prism to a new angle. The recognition of the iconic meaning of the wrestling match staged in *As You Like It* makes of Orlando a far more central character than he is usually thought to be. The casket scene in *The Merchant of Venice* more easily regains the pivotal place given it by Shakespeare when the caskets are seen as expressing the theme of justice and mercy echoed in the trial scene, and reechoed in the rings faithlessly surrendered as legal fees. A full response to the iconic language and staging of *Richard II* underscores the title character as a sanctified monarch whose human personality undergoes a kinetic growth it is often denied in production. The trope of the mousetrap in *Hamlet* is based upon a medieval iconographic commonplace that unifies the seemingly disparate themes of deception, madness, and maturation in a play confusing to everyone but theater audiences. The supernatural realism of *Macbeth* demands literal details of staging that have been abandoned over the centuries. As for *The Tempest,* the storm, the banquet, and the magic circle are iconic stage devices drawing the entire play into a vortex of spiritual crisis never fully resolved, making of Shakespeare's "farewell to the stage" a less mellow but deeper play than it is often described as being.

An investigation of Renaissance symbolism and the symbolism of Shakespeare's staging will, I hope, open windows into his plays and create a more informed sense of where the dramatic emphasis and balance of meaning come to rest. Beyond this hope is the reminder of Shakespeare's full complexity. Despite his repeated use of commonplace symbolism in the language and stagecraft of his plays, this symbolism is dramatically contained within the living presence of fully drawn stage personalities. The symbols are never merely conventional nor are the plays to be read as didactic allegories, ". . . as the painting of a sorrow, /A face without a heart." Shakespeare's art is always complex, his conclusions about the human condition in large measure open-ended, provoking the beginning, not the end, of analysis. The paradoxical tension he repeatedly creates is between the initial conventional response and his refusal to allow the more thoughtful members of his audience to be fully satisfied with that response.

Great art often stimulates such paradoxes. The face-to-face encounter has the clarity of intuition. Retrospective analysis exposes mysteries dimly perceived in the dark reflection of the intellectual's discursive glass. Readers of Shakespeare have constantly been reminded that many of these mysteries will disappear if we trust our first encounter, that the plays were written for the stage and not the study, that he never particularly intended them to be read. Indeed, we would not have so strong an urge to interpret and reinterpret Shakespeare's works were they not so remarkably successful on the stage many centuries after the virtual disappearance of the culture that nourished them, and in front of such diverse audiences. Many distinguished critics have studied the factors behind this amazing phenomenon. And many scholars have tried to recover the responses of Shakespeare's audiences in his own day. Yet the issue here is not so much the difference between seen action and printed action as it is the difference between initial experience and retrospective experience, with the printed page offering an ideal opportunity for recollection. We are not moving away from the work of art; we are simpy allowing the aesthetic experience to have its full effect. Among the appreciative audience in the retrospective phase of their experience may be scholars and critics; their controversy is but one symptom of the mysterious complexity that lies at the heart of the human experience rendered by great art. That mystery in Shakespeare is persuasively argued by Norman Rabkin in *Shakespeare and the Common Understanding.*[42] Even here, however, qualifications must be made. The Renaissance understanding of mystery was more precise than ours. Not only did they accept its right to exist, but Renaissance philosophers gave mystery an epistemology. Even the presence of mystery could be known with some care and precision.

In his brilliant and definitive article on Neoplatonic symbolism,

E. H. Gombrich outlined the Renaissance controversy over the meaning and purpose of visual symbols.[43] Is Dame Fortune a symbol of life's uncertainty or does her image stand for a conscious supernatural power which delights in surprising us? If the latter, do her conventional attributes of globe, wheel, and forelock originate in the forms assumed by her in visions of inspiration or are these merely tokens of her fickle behavior? The Neoplatonic synthesis assigned to Dionysius Areopagita (one of the traditional converts of Paul) regarded symbolic images as the starting points of meditation. Our fallen understanding of the transcendent truth lying behind appearances in the visible world requires arresting images. These frequently esoteric and thus fascinating images enable minds obscured by the flesh to focus on a bridge between the two worlds, a bridge quickly abandoned. The Neoplatonic Renaissance synthesis of Pico della Mirandola, however, saw such images as fully satisfying the highest form of human cognition. His transcendent images were neither mere symbols nor crutches for man's fallen understanding. For Pico the esoteric image was the incarnation of the cosmic world, comparable to God's fusion of heaven and earth in his person as Christ. Both sense perception, shared with the beasts, and reason, unique to man, are exceeded by the intuitive and instantaneous perception of divine truth shared by man with the angels and communicated by occult symbols. In other words, the popular Renaissance debate between the poet and the painter can conclude with the plastic arts as the superior of the discursive and ratiocinative verbal arts because visual images produce instantaneous and intuitive understanding of divine truth.[44] No wonder Shakespeare could not resist entering the debate in the first act of *Timon of Athens*

Clearly, the verbal monument of Shakespeare's works cannot be used to illustrate Pico's conclusion, but a fuller historical sense of the meaning and substance visual images could have for the Renaissance may give us fresh insights into the importance his staging may have had. We no longer suffer from the early nineteenth-century limitation of needing Aristotle to tell us that a play is not fully a play until actors are speaking lines on a stage. But we are still very much inclined to see Shakespeare's superiority to his contemporaries in the sufficiency of his lines and a consequent minimum of stage effects, especially those having to do

with creaking thrones and dismembered bodies. The very economy
of Shakespeare's reliance on staging, however, makes of what he
does use an emphatic theatrical device. When an important detail
of blocking, prop, or costume is combined with surprise, furthermore, we may come very near to Pico della Mirandola's concept of
the visual image as offering instant and intuitive recognition of
transcendent reality.

Consider the sudden appearance of Hymen at the end of *As You
Like It*. This detail is apparently disturbing to modern directors
because of the incongruity of an allegorical personification in the
midst of "real people," with the standard for them no doubt set by
the characters found in the later Ibsen and commended by
William Archer. But toward what level of "reality" is *As You Like It*
designed to point if not the one of ideal love, honor, and virtue?
The sudden introduction of Hymen throws the entire play into his
world, at least for a moment of recognition in which many mythic
and psychological elements coalesce: Antaeus, the Nemean Lion,
instant conversion, athletic virtue, and married chastity, to list a
few. These elements are often in turn paradoxical combinations of
seeming opposites. The transcendent world here is not one of pat
and moralistic truths; rather, it is a mysterious world fleetingly
glimpsed behind the surface of "real" action, and only partially
subject to the language of discursive reason.

Another surprise is Richard's dashing of the mirror to the floor
of Westminster Hall. Taken by surprise are the theater audience,
the assembled lords on stage, and perhaps even Richard himself.
The event is given emblematic meaning by Richard's moralizing
explanation, but the explanation is dramatic in context because it
is a refutation of Bolingbroke's caustic observation. The mirror
symbolizes many things, but primarily the recognition of truth,
and ideally the audience will perceive the public exposure of
Bolingbroke as a "vile politician," paradoxically served by
Richard's public confession of his own royal and human fallibility. The effect on several of the assembled lords is to galvanize
sympathy for Richard and opposition to Bolingbroke. The Bishop
of Carlisle, the Abbot of Westminster, and Aumerle see perfectly
both Richard's gross incompetence as a ruler and Bolingbroke's
very considerable ability; yet the lords temporal and spiritual
reach paradoxical conclusions about the course of action that
should be taken by virtuous men. Great art continually returns to

similar complexities. Tolstoy's Karenin is both repulsive to the reader and known to be right.

Finally, the sudden appearance of Ariel as harpy is alarming to the "men of sin," and all the more shocking because it interrupts a lovely and relaxing banquet. The device is a tour de force of surprise, designed to bring conversion. The emblematic harpy speaks its own explanation, but its dramatic purpose is more fully served by its unexpected and frightening appearance. In *King Lear,* similarly, when Edgar converts his father from despair by leading him through the process of suicide, the experiences of leaping off the "cliff" and losing consciousness a moment later are what temporarily realign Gloucester, far more than the disguised Edgar's explanation of an intervening supernatural agency. In *The Tempest* the existential process of conversion is caused by the combining of the sudden promise of a tantalizing banquet offered starving men and the equally sudden frustration provided by the harpy as an emblem of greed.

The number of associations a Renaissance audience might have had with this stage image depends on many variable factors. That the harpy proverbially stood for greed was probably almost universally known. Molière was relying on a commonplace when he called his miser Harpagon, and today we still call a greedy person a harpy. Those in the Renaissance who knew Virgil's *Aeneid,* then surely the most famous of classical epics, were aware of the appropriateness of travelers shipwrecked on an island having their food snatched away by a bird with the head of a woman. A familiarity with the tradition of allegorizing the epics, which began at least as early as the Stoic commentators and was widely distributed in the Renaissance, partly through emblem books, would be another level of educated response for those able to see a connection between Alonso's suicidal grief-stricken guilt and the harpy as an emblem of avarice destroying itself. We should probably devote more critical attention to distinguishing the associations a given historical period *might* have had with a given symbol and those actually intended by the artist, despite the so-called intentional fallacy, even though the task is made especially difficult in the case of the Neoplatonic image by its inclination to speak for itself in eternal language, out of time, beyond the temporal limits of discursive understanding. Pico's symbol depends upon concentrated perception in an age when a full Shakespearean production required but two hours. Is it possible that men once talked and thought faster? Certainly the density of meaning in a Shakespearean line is already astonishing without the added knowledge that it was probably spoken at nearly twice the modern rate. The pace of art may be decelerating. Compare, for instance, Bach to Mahler.

Shakespeare also appears to decelerate in some ways within the confines of his own career. In the case of the three sudden stage images of Hymen, the broken mirror, and the harpy, Shakespeare is increasingly moving in the direction of the emblem book tradition, where esoteric images are explicitly interpreted. Hymen's rhymed speeches and song are little more than ritualistic greeting, exposition, and blessing; the mirror is moralized in a highly dramatic context; and Ariel is very explicit about his symbolic meaning. Shakespeare does not abandon surprise, but he relies less and less on the understanding of his audience. He is increasingly inclined to tell us what associations he wants us to make, but even toward the end of his career both his images and his concepts, like his words, require a glossary for the modern student concerned with historical accuracy and a fuller understanding of his art.

Also, it is clear that Shakespeare binds some of the associations very closely to his stage images, while leaving others on the periphery of consciousness, especially in the earlier plays. In *The Merchant of Venice* the appearance and contents of the three caskets at Belmont are emphatically presented as tests of male character and as objects of meditation on death. The associations with death would be especially apparent to an audience imbued with popular tracts on the ars moriendi. Both the skull of Yorick and the caskets are memento mori. Whether the caskets also suggested the well-known legend of the Three Living and the Three Dead is conjecture. Nothing in the text of the play brings the legend to mind. Here we are in the area of pure speculation, yet of a sort that has an obvious historical validity absent from the speculations of critics who see in Shakespeare a proto-Freudian or proto-Marxist. At least his audience carried around in their heads concepts such as this legend, and thus we are closer to the range of Renaissance audience response, whatever precisely it may have been. After all, the rings in the play are never specifically cited as emblems of chastity even though several passages remain obscure

without our knowledge of that convention, a convention repeated
both throughout Shakespeare and in the works of many other
Elizabethan dramatists. The difference here is that the symbolism
of the rings is less tenuous because it is repeated elsewhere, it is
necessary to a clarification of dialogue, and it provides a greater
structural unity to the play, whereas the legendary interpretation
of the caskets makes little difference. With or without it the play is
appreciably neither more nor less. At most it is only an iconic
possibility awaiting fuller verification within the play.

Neoplatonic controversy over the meaning of symbols also points
up another issue central to Shakespeare's use of stage images, one
closely related to range of associations. At what level of Neoplatonic reality, or "abstraction" if you prefer, is a given stage image
designed to operate? When Orlando wrestles Charles we are still
absorbed in the vital dramatic situation of a handsome and
untried young man in the presence of his beloved and threatened
with death by a beefy professional. How additionally conscious
was Shakespeare's audience of the parallels with Hercules and
Antaeus stimulated by the blunted allusions? Even if audiences at
the original production of the play might have understood these
allusions, to what extent did staging reinforce the parallel?
Assuming that an audience can hold both levels of action, the one
mimetic and the other mythical, fully in mind, how adequately
will the myth convey a conventional allegorical meaning having to
do with the defeat of vice by virture? It may even seem by now
that the higher levels of abstraction idealized by the Neoplatonists
are the enemies of drama, that Orlando defeating Charles has far
more dramatic value than virtue defeating vice, especially when
Charles is not even particularly vicious. But Pico, as opposed to
Dionysius, probably helps us to draw the correct emphasis. The
iconic stage image in Shakespeare is not the bridge to another
world, leaving this one behind. It is the point at which all worlds
meet in a single moment of action. The amplitude of meaning will
depend on our interests, education, and cognitive abilities. Furthermore, the topmost level of abstraction, good against evil,
circles around to the simplest level of audience response. Only the
perverse or the outright stupid would think Charles the good guy
and Orlando the bad.

Older medieval habits of mind seem preserved in Shakespeare's
handling of what might be called additional dimensions of reality,

having to do with heaven and hell, the past and the future, and eternity. The witches in *Macbeth* are ugly and malevolent old women practicing magic, but they are also demonic tempters and iconic stage images of fate, however contradictory these concepts may appear to us. Banquo's ghost, like the air-drawn dagger, is both an illusion born of Macbeth's guilty conscience and a vision undoubtedly meant to be seen by character and audience alike—in other words, seen by all those aware of the unified psychological and supernatural realities here being given palpable form. I justify these coexistent dimensions of reality extensively in my chapter on *Macbeth*.

The style of presentation for iconic stage images, particularly those crucial to the psychological or supernatural tone of a play, is especially challenging to a modern director. Should the head of Macbeth be a realistic prop from Madame Tussaud's, held forth by Macduff as Perseus holds at arm's length the head of Medusa, or should it be tastefully concealed in a sanitary blood-proof sack? Jonas A. Barish, speaking before a general session of the World Shakespeare Congress (August 1971), described two productions he had recently seen of John Ford's *'Tis Pity She's a Whore*. In the naturalistic London production Giovanni displayed on the point of his sword what appeared to be the literal bloody heart of his sister Annabella. When Barish saw the same play in Paris, the foil of the incestuous brother bore a beautifully stylized heart made of lavender crepe, ornamented with delicate streamers representing blood. The question of style of production, both in Shakespeare's day and in our own, remains one of the most challenging and perplexing of issues. This question is certainly one over which emotions run high, perhaps because it addresses most directly the tone and thus the purposes of the play as a theater experience.

Another disturbing question is, what can the conventions of Renaissance iconography, no matter how fully recovered by scholarship, possibly mean to a modern audience? Daniel Seltzer has commented, "It was easier for Shakespeare to write Prince Hal into the center of his plays than it is for any modern actor or director to keep him there; . . . his . . . stage life exists often in terms of stage conventions we no longer perceive as conveying reality."[45] In like manner, many of Shakespeare's theatrical intentions regarding iconic stage imagery obviously rely on extinct conventions. Certainly the survival rate in this area is far lower than in the area of character. As C. Walter Hodges has observed, *"Enter* Rumour, *painted full of tongues,"* is perfectly clear only in print.[46] The personification would probably mystify most audiences were it suddenly shown to them on a modern stage. Seltzer, however, does go on to offer some reassurance to the scholar who is concerned that his research have some value for modern production:

> It can be most useful to the modern director or actor when there exists in the text a conventional gesture—a speech, an action, the use of a property—that we sense, or that research tells us, would have been immediately understood by an Elizabethan audience, but the significance of which is lost for us; . . . we may discover . . . that human psychology provides a behavioral answer that is not so distant from the Shakespearean intention, so far as we can know it.[47]

The critic's task is to assist the director in translating as many ideas as possible into the modern language of the stage, while at the same time preserving as much as he can of the original image. Reconsider Falstaff's cushion. Samuel Chew has identified it as an emblem of sloth and lust, of Luxuria. Even a modern audience could perceive this meaning were Falstaff to fondle and kiss it, to hold it lovingly against his body, in short to do what the original actor playing Falstaff probably did with the cushion in the Renaissance before it ended up on his head as a crown.

Iconography can, of course, address itself to the interpretation of action other than stage images seen by the audience. Orlando's killing of the lion is no less an emblem of Herculean virtue than the wrestling match with Charles, yet it is reported as offstage action. Nor are offstage sound effects, such as the music in *The Tempest* or in the last act of *The Merchant of Venice,* any the less emblematic for being heard, although emblematic music can also be both heard and "seen," as in the case of the song played while Bassanio makes his choice. The howling winds threatening Alonso's ship in the first act of *The Tempest* illustrate how a symbolic effect—the storm—can be created both onstage and off. The ship, furthermore, is a setting suggesting the mutability of a world ruled by Fortune, and setting can create a very broad emblematic context for action, even if the setting is only suggested by the permanent architecture of the stage or merely described.

Macbeth's hellcastle probably drew its substance, at least in public performances, largely from the theater's doorways, windows, and upper stage, as did Richard's Castle of Fortune. The cell in which Richard is finally imprisoned, elaborate symbol though it is, undoubtedly relied entirely for its stage effect upon Richard's description of it.

Verbal imagery in general is a vast field for iconic interpretation. I keep such interpretation to a strict minimum, primarily because so much excellent work is being done in this area, but it is often difficult to draw a careful line. Not only are iconic stage images frequently underlined verbally—indeed we are on much firmer scholarly ground when they are—but we can never be entirely sure that what appears to be a verbal image alone was not given further stage expression. Ophelia's famous speech to Laertes about the primrose path, for instance, appears to confine the iconography of Hercules at the Crossroads entirely to the verbal. But if a director of *Hamlet* instructs his Ophelia to gesture in one direction toward the steep and thorny way and in another toward the primrose path as she speaks her lines, then the actor's movements convert the verbal image into a stage image as well. A similar possibility is Hamlet's title for his play within the play—"The Mouse-trap." One wonders if the trope remained a trope, or if the original production staged "The Murder of Gonzago" in something resembling a Renaissance mousetrap. Putting aside critical opinion about whether or not this would be an improvement, the possibility cannot but tantalize the scholar.

Lastly, the scholarly study of the storehouse of symbols preserved in the plastic arts of the Renaissance can provide us with tools helpful in the critical analysis of dramatic structure. Hamlet's "Mouse-trap" gives us an opportunity for the investigation of a long-forgotten religious symbol of self-destruction, but this once commonplace iconographic trope also works as a touchstone for our understanding of the consistent pattern of surprise and mystification in this most ambiguous of Shakespeare's plays. The use of iconography for structural analysis can work from the outside in, as well, in the sense that we can bring visual materials to bear that are not specifically suggested by references in the Shakespearean text. Donatello's bronze *David,* Holbein's "Genius" title-border, and Giorgione's *Tempesta* are not necessarily related to *As You Like It, Hamlet,* and *The Tempest.* Yet the Renaissance topoi of the athlete of virtue, the pilgrimage of life, and the union of Fortezza and Carita are thematic structures in a culture shared by Shakespeare and his contemporaries in the plastic arts. The Elizabethan world picture was just as frequently expressed visually as verbally. Art can clearly draw us back into the frame of Renaissance culture, and in a way at least as closely related to Shakespeare's genius as political theory or natural history.[48]

1

As You Like It: Herculean Virtue

In the late 1960s, that rebellious youth Orlando made *As You Like It* at least briefly contemporary again. Crowds of the Colorful Generation flocked to mod musical-comedy productions of the play. There is enough, especially at the beginning of the play, to explain why. Orlando's first speech is a shout of protest. He tells Adam, the old family servant, about his exploitation by the older generation in the person of an eldest brother. Ever since the death of their father, Oliver has treated Orlando shamelessly, denying him a relevant education by setting him to mindless tasks. We suddenly know ourselves to be in the Renaissance rather than the twentieth century, however, when Orlando claims as the spring of his rebellion a noble spirit inherited from his father, not the superior moral sense of youth. The combination of blood and manhood—Orlando's beard is just emerging—makes his servitude intolerable. His new personality is expressed dramatically in two decisive ways. After quarreling violently with Oliver, Orlando leaves home and stays away when he learns of his brother's plan to burn him alive. A public declaration of manhood is the wrestling match with the lethal professional, Charles. Both statements are physical as well as verbal. In the quarrel Orlando seizes the throat of an insulting brother, and the actual contest follows the challenge to Charles. This stage image of the wrestling match is always a memorable part of the theater experience of the play, but its interest is deepened if it is seen in the older context of Renaissance iconography.

Recall that Rosalind encourages Orlando by invoking the classical prototype of strength: "Now, Hercules be thy speed, young man!" It is well known that Hercules stands for all that is manly and virtuous in innumerable emblems, epigrams, and allusions throughout the literature of Shakespeare's day. In Stephen Bateman's *Golden Booke of the Leaden Goddes* (London, 1577),[1] the descriptions of classical deities as moral allegories in their appearance and attributes predictably include Hercules:

> Hercules apparayled in a Lions skinne, signyfyeth the valiant courage of a woorthy Captayne, also the Prudencie wherewith his minde beinge furnished, he subdued his outragious affections: the Club, signifieth understanding, throughe which the motions of wicked affections are repressed and vtterly vanquished.
>
> *Hercules* was . . . a Prince of worthye Fame, a mainteiner of Vertue, and a punisher of Vice, such a one as hated those that chose to steale by policye, rather then to win by prowesse. (sigs. C4r–v)

What Orlando has lost through the "policye" of Oliver he hopes to recover by his "prowesse" over Charles.

Also familiar to students of the Renaissance is the story of the encounter of Hercules with Antaeus, son of Neptune and Earth, one of the most commonly allegorized classical myths about this hero, just as the theme of Hercules at the Crossroads is the commonplace of the later accretions.[2] The way the Renaissance read the Antaeus story, Hercules (virtue) won victory over the giant Antaeus (vice) by lifting him out of contact with his mother Earth (the base passions).[3] In *The Arte of Rhetorike* (London, 1584), Thomas Wilson saw all of Hercules' labors in this way: "What other thyng are the wonderfull labours of Hercules, but that reason should withstand affection, and the spirit for ever should fight against the fleshe" (p. 199). It is easy to see why Hercules and Antaeus were a popular subject of freestanding bronzes, the ideal medium for the expression of power and movement. The treatment of the subject by Pollaiuolo (ca. 1475) is world famous. A vigorous rendering by Franceso da Sant' Agata is of the Paduan School, first half of the sixteenth century (Plate 1).[4] These bronzes are often small, designed to grace the desk of the humanist connoisseur, were he scholar or prince, just as the skull was introduced as an object of meditation about the same time. The theme of the triumph of the soul over the body was the same in both cases, whether discovered in bone or bronze. Before Hercules found out the secret of Antaeus' strength, the giant renewed himself every time he was thrown to the ground, where his mother filled his entire body with vital energy. In other words, the soul must wrench the body away from base desires before eternal victory can be achieved. A Renaissance Italian sculpture by Vincenzo Danti (1530–76), *Honor Triumphant over Falsehood,* shows two nude athletes. According to his contemporary Vasari, Danti carved this marble sculpture after failing to produce a bronze group of Hercules and Antaeus.[5] Shakespeare, of course, is writing a play, not a sermon, and the classical allusions are lightly handled, kept almost subliminal.[6] Indeed, the relationship between "Antaeus" and the earth is even displaced, for it is Charles who boasts to Orlando: "Come, where is this young gallant that is so desirous to lie with his mother earth?" Finally, just before the Duke's wrestler is thrown by Orlando, Celia wishes she were Jove—"If I had a thunderbolt in mine eye, I can tell who should down"—thus reinforcing the classical context.

Shakespeare probably drew on Thomas Cooper's Latin-English *Thesaurus* (London, 1565), which went through five editions, the last in 1587, for his knowledge of the Hercules-Antaeus myth ("Dictionarium," sig. B5r).[7] As he does with so many details in his plays, Shakespeare is also both carrying over and changing material in one of his sources, the major one, *Rosalynde: Euphues Golden Legacie* (1590), by Thomas Lodge. There the lovers merely exchange burning looks before the contest; thus, instead of Rosalind's invoking Hercules to assist Orlando, Lodge introduces the classical allusion before anyone accepts the open invitation to fight the awesome wrestler known only as "the Norman":

> . . . the *Norman* presented himselfe as a chalenger against all commers; but he looked like *Hercules* when he advaunst himselfe against *Achelous:* so that the furie of his countenance amased all that durst attempt to incounter with him. . . .[8]

Shakespeare has applied the strength of Hercules to Orlando instead of Charles and deleted the allusion to the labor of Hercules in which he overcomes the river Achelous. It is usually safe to assume that Shakespeare's changes are made for a reason, and the reason in this case is one that may very well have originated in his imagined understanding of the visual effect of this scene in production.

The source is quite specific about the actual wrestling. Entering the lists, Orlando's original, Rosader, is so taken by his first glimpse of Rosalind that the Norman

> . . . drave him out of his *memento* with a shake by the shoulder; *Rosader* looking back with an angrie frowne . . . discovered to all by the furie of his countenance that he was a man of some high thoughts. . . . [Rosader] roughlie clapt to him with so fierce an incounter, that they both fell to the ground, and with the violence of the fall were forced to breathe: in which space the *Norman* called to minde . . . that this was hee whom *Saladyne* [Oliver] had appoynted him to kil; which conjecture made him stretch everie limb, & trie everie sinew. . . . On the contrarie part, *Rosader* while he breathed was not idle, but still cast his eye uppon *Rosalynd,* who . . . lent him such an amorous looke, as might have made the most coward desperate: which glance of *Rosalynd* so fiered the passionate desires of *Rosader,* that turning to the *Norman* hee ran upon him and braved him with a strong encounter; the *Norman* received him as valiantly, that there was a sore combat, hard to judge on whose side fortune would be prodigall. At last *Rosader* . . . roused himselfe and threw the *Norman* against the ground, falling upon his chest with so willing a waight, that the *Norman* yeelded nature her due, and *Rosader* the victorie.[9]

We can only guess at how a contemporary production of *As You Like It* might have shown the wrestling match. The dress of Elizabethan wrestlers, for instance, is suggested by one of the standard woodcuts illustrating the first edition of Raphael Holinshed's *Chronicles* (London, 1577), although Shakespeare is only known to have consulted the enlarged but unillustrated edition of 1587. In the earlier illustrated edition the woodcut (Plate 2), like most of its companions, is used more than once, to accompany the account of a match between Corineus and Gogmagog, a giant, in the time of Brute ("The Historie of Englande," p. 15); and again to illustrate the reign of King Ewin, who instructed the youth to keep fit by wrestling ("The Historie of Scotlande," p. 23). The wrestlers have cast their outer clothes aside (in the lower right-hand corner) and wear only loincloths and harnesses, while the spectators are dressed in the conventional manner of the late sixteenth century. As for what Shakespeare intended his wrestlers to do on stage, the earliest stage directions provide no more than a *"Wrastle"* at the beginning and three lines later a *"Shout"* when Charles is thrown (F1—"Comedies," p. 188).[10] The usurping Duke thereupon commands, "No more, no more," and a few lines later says, "Bear him away," after it is seen that the former champion can no longer even speak. Although the source made it clear that the Norman was dead, Shakespeare, no doubt to lighten the tone, provides us with no further information about him.

The question of what exactly occurred on the stage at the play's first production will probably always remain a mystery, but we do have Godfrey Turner's record of a theatrically successful handling of this match in a way consistent with the Hercules and Antaeus episode, at a time in the nineteenth century when the symbolic details of that myth would probably have been entirely forgotten. That the associations must have been forgotten or thought totally unimportant as early as 1723 is illustrated by an "improvement" of the play written by Charles Johnson and staged at Drury Lane in that year: a duel with rapiers is substituted for the wrestling match, presumably in order to fit the dignity and social standing of Orlando.[11] In 1883 the wrestling match was back in *As You Like It,* but Godfrey Turner reported that he had seen it done successfully on only two occasions, one of them at Sadler's Wells:

> Marston, a Lancashire lad, wrestled superbly and was as agile as a cat. . . . [He] allowed himself to be caught up by Charles so as to lean over the wrestler's shoulder, while his own feet, being lifted clear above the ground were coiled round the giant's firmly planted leg. For a few moments the statuesque position was retained; and then just as Orlando appeared in utmost peril of being thrown, he suddenly regained his footing, reversed the situation, cross-buttocked Charles, and flung him heavily to earth.[12]

This description is consistent both with the little information provided by the first publication of the play in the Folio of 1623 and with the many Renaissance representations of Hercules subduing Antaeus. The Sadler's Wells production has first Orlando and then Charles lifted "clear above the ground," as in Hercules' legendary defeat of the son of Mother Earth, and then the professional flung to the ground, as implied in the comments made about the defeated Charles, when the Duke orders the speechless wrestler borne away. The only details needed to complete the Renaissance accounts of Hercules and Antaeus would be two revivals of Charles after being pinned to the earth by Orlando, before the final lifting of Charles above the ground, his subsequent exhaustion, and the flinging of him to the stage. If the wrestling were to be staged in this way it would become an iconic stage image fulfilling the verbal allusions to Hercules and Antaeus. Shakespeare is doing something similar in the way of a Herculean context for a love test in *The Merchant of Venice* when Portia tells Bassanio to choose his casket advisedly. She then compares herself to Hesione, the sacrificial victim saved by Hercules from the sea monster. She even gives the signal for the time to choose by saying, "Go, Hercules! /Live thou, I live. With much much more dismay /I view the fight than thou that mak'st the fray" (III. ii. 60–62).

The labors of Hercules, both the originally codified twelve and later accretions, are still well known. Renaissance artists found them endlessly stimulating. Michelangelo's pastel drawing of three of them (the Nemean Lion, Antaeus, and the Hydra), at the Royal Library, Windsor, is justly famous.[13] The labors appear in innumerable commonplace and artistically insignificant places as well. See, for instance, *The Boke of Common Praier: The Psalter* (London, 1594),[14] where a capital letter *B* shows Hercules battling the Hydra (passim). The Christian relevance of these labors is explained in many sources. In Raleigh's *The History of the World* (1614), Hercules' descent into the underworld to capture Cerberus is paralleled to Christ's Harrowing of Hell.[15] In *Paradise Regained* (IV. 562–68), Milton saw, as did Spenser in the *Faerie Queene* (II. xi. 34.6–46.9), the parallel of Christ's overthrow of Satan on the third day and Hercules' defeat of Antaeus at the third attempt. Numerous examples of these and similar parallels, made in England and on the Continent, can be cited. Perhaps most famous to the Renaissance was Pierre de Ronsard's poem on the Christianized Hercules, *Hercule chrestien* (1556), one of the best-known works of the Pléiade and derived from the iconographically important *Ovide moralise.*

As for the Herculean pattern in *As You Like It*, it is completed by Orlando's last "labor," his defeat of the lioness menacing his unnatural brother in the forest. Hercules and the Nemean Lion, which he strangled with the bare hands, was a very popular subject during the Renaissance. This was one of Hercules' best-known labors, bearing as it did the parallel of the lion which is the Beast of Revelation, a familiar hellmouth second only to the whale and the cauldron as a medieval symbol of evil forces defeated by Christ in the Harrowing of Hell.[16] Once again, Shakespeare has made small and significant changes in his source in Lodge. The emblematic character of the events reported by Oliver is established by the addition of a serpent coiled around the sleeping brother's neck, about to crawl into his mouth, when Orlando approaches and frightens the creature off into the underbrush. This is the brother whose words have been so unjust, about to receive just punishment, but Orlando cannot enjoy his revenge by simply standing by. He must perform the natural offices of a brother, according to the Renaissance Cordelian bond. The Rosader of the source carries a boar spear with which he assails the hungry lion awaiting the awakening of his sibling enemy. Shakespeare, however, makes no mention of a weapon in the events reported by Oliver, the spear having been appropriated to the costume of Rosalind disguised as Ganymede. Orlando apparently, like Hercules, kills the lion with his bare hands, receiving a wound in the arm, rather than in the breast as his original, Rosader, does in Lodge's *Rosalynde.*

It is interesting to note that Shakespeare has this second Hercules parallel, the killing of the lion, reported, rather than showing it onstage as he showed the wrestling match. Clearly, it is more difficult to stage the frightening of a snake and the strangulation of a lion than a wrestling match, but Shakespeare is also a playwright capable of that most famous of all stage directions, *"Exit, pursued by a bear,"* when he really wants to convey a sense of romantic amazement. We should at least consider the possibility that Shakespeare wants to place a special emphasis upon the wrestling match, making it a thematic introduction to the role he has outlined for Orlando.

The Athlete of Virtue

The victorious athlete, according to Colin Eisler, is "one of the oldest and most powerful symbols of the triumph of virtue in Western culture."[17] Athletic contests in ancient Greece were supposedly started by Hercules, and thus physical strength and beauty were accepted as signs of divine favor, in turn sustained and earned by the efforts of gymnastic training. Exercise, the practice of order and control, represented constant striving after divine acceptance, a ceaseless struggle for virtuous self-discipline against the temptation of relaxed abandonment to evil and decay, moral and physical. This ideal, endorsed by most Greek philosophy and, of course, still alive in our own century, was adopted early by Christian theology. The most important events in the early centuries of the church were the martyrdoms of Christians in the arena and stadium. Thus the classical image of virtue found a context in the new religion. The Greek church father Chrysostom describes Christ as "the Victor of all the Olympic games, the Champion Pancratiast, the One who has run the entire course, the Athlete of eternal victory."[18] Peter Damiani even calls the eleventh-century Monastery of Cluny a "spiritual gymnasium."[19] An elaborate typology had clearly been worked out, one that applied to all heroes. Chrysostom also refers to Christ's precursor David as a divinely sustained athlete, a wrestler who rallies unexpectedly.[20] Indeed, Geoffrey Bullough, without mentioning the typological tradition, also hears the biblical echoes that would have risen to the mind of a Renaissance audience, when, in commenting on the various sources of *As You Like It,* he says: "In Shakespeare and *Gamelyn* the hero is taunted by the wrestler, who in Lodge merely takes him by the shoulder. But the taunting is more dramatic and brings out the David-Goliath element in the encounter."[21]

It is no wonder that the religiously conscious Renaissance is full of paintings, graphics, and sculptures representing a nude, athletically built hero—especially Hercules or David—overcoming the forces of evil. The bronze *David* cast by Donatello in mid-fifteenth-century Florence is one of the major examples (Plate 3). For some curious reason, perhaps because Michelangelo's genius cut off further comment, David is the subject of only three statues in the Italian Renaissance, those by Donatello, Verrocchio, and Michelangelo. The differences are a perfect insight into the full range of Renaissance art, from iconography, to literalism, to psychological realism. A baroque concluding statement is made by Bernini's *David* (1623), in the Galleria Borghese, Rome. Surprisingly, Donatello's iconographic statement helps us to draw together the various elements combined by Shakespeare in *As You Like It*. Yet the iconography of the statue has puzzled many art historians by its seeming eclecticism; the combination, for instance, of a nude athlete with a bucolic hat, worn in the fourteenth and fifteenth century for hunting and travel. H. W. Janson, the established Donatello authority, expresses the problem: "We find ourselves confronted . . . with the enigmatic qualities of the statue. What message was it meant to convey to the beholder? That it did have a message we can hardly doubt; otherwise why all the puzzling details? But the context into which these features can be fitted continues to elude us."[22] Janson finally tentatively accounts for these "puzzling details" by documenting Donatello's contemporary reputation as a homosexual. Are the details then fetishes? John Pope-Hennessy later restores the balance even though leaving the subject a mystery: "An attempt (Janson) to relate the iconography to Dontello's presumed homosexuality is an *ex post facto* interpretation which throws no light on the original intentions of the artist."[23]

Eclecticism, however, was one of the artistic elements that delighted Renaissance man the most: the true relatedness of the seemingly unrelated, revealed to the beholder in a moment of intuitive insight, often by visual means. This concept controls a great deal of what we know about late Renaissance imagery, and it is fundamental to the ideal of "discordia concors" (the union of contraries).[24]

Donatello's David is just entering manhood. Both David and Hercules were usually equated in the Renaissance mind with the issues confronting the boy turning into a man, like Orlando, whose beard has just begun to grow. Hercules as a very young man is usually associated with the choice during adolescence between self-discipline and self-gratification, exemplified by the image of Hercules at the Crossroads. A topical variant is a Renaissance illumination showing Massimiliano Sforza at the Crossroads.[25] This Italian Renaissance subject is clothed and very young indeed, though the allusion is to the nude and muscular Hercules usually

represented. Donatello's very youthful David stands with one foot
on the severed head of Goliath, foreshadowing Christ, the Second
Adam, who as Son of Man will bruise the serpent's head with his
heel and defeat the sin that defeated the First Adam. David, like
Hercules, was a common type of Christ, but with the added
advantage of centuries of biblical typology. Augustine had drawn a
parallel between David's defeat of Goliath and Christ's victory
over Satan. Cyril described David's sling as the prefiguration of
Christ's cross. And certainly the Jews had anticipated a messiah
from the House of David.[26] Donatello's bronze David, stripped for
the contest of faith as the Greek athletes stripped for the
gymnasium, is clothed merely in the boots of the warrior and the
hat of the rustic. He thus combines many ideals: the nude athlete;
Christ; David as the "Hercules" of the Old Testament; the
Christian warrior wearing the Pauline armor of God; the Arcadian
natural man uncorrupted by exposure to the City of Man; and,
ultimately, virtue itself, triumphant over evil. The bucolic hat,
betasseled and beribboned, and suggesting David the shepherd as
a biblical Arcadian who foreshadows Christ the Good Shepherd, is
wreathed in triumphant laurel. Another laurel wreath is at the
base of the statue. The generalized Triumph depicted in Goliath's
visor is probably an ironic comment by the sculptor. The giants of
this world can be defeated by mere boys with hearts divinely
inspired, the gist of a later Renaissance emblem of David and
Goliath, with the motto "quid immania corpora possunt" (what
huge bodies accomplish).[27] The wings on Goliath's helmet as
designed by Donatello may recall a common Teutonic motif of
battle dress, thus suggesting to Italians such as Machiavelli a
barbarian invasion, but the specific context also suggests the
Philistine as a type of the fallen angel Satan, for an angel was
always identified by wings, just as the superfluous stone held in the
victor's hand is his iconographic identification as David.

Orlando, too, is adolescent. He, too, defeats a giant, finds
sanctuary in the wilderness, where he leads a bucolic life, and
finally comes to represent all that is virtuous in opposition to all
that is corrupt. The conflation of the athlete and the Arcadian,
both drawn from the Golden Age of classical civilization, is the
essential connection relating the seemingly disparate elements of
As You Like It. Previous scholarship and criticism of this play have
put the emphasis either one way or another, on the pastoral or on

the mythological,[28] just as art historians have seen no traditional continuity in David's bucolic hat and his nudity. There is, however, no necessary conflict between seemingly disparate elements in either the statue or the play—quite the contrary. The iconic stage image of the wrestling match gives Orlando an emphatic position he retains throughout the play, a position in which he repeatedly unites seemingly disparate forces and thus makes a union of contraries. Shakespeare's thematic purpose throughout most of *As You Like It* seems to be the paradoxical reconciliation of apparent opposites in the context of repeated tests or contests. Orlando is the Samson Agonistes, the lion killer and enemy of evil, at the center of the play, but other characters—notably Oliver and Duke Frederick—must pass tests as well before the play can reach a satisfactory conclusion.

The theme of apparent or real contradiction is introduced almost as soon as the play begins. Orlando is treated worse than an animal by his brother—he must feed like a beast, but his nurture is inferior to that of the highly trained horse. He must endure the position of the prodigal younger brother at the hog trough, although he is by nature virtuous.[29] Shakespeare plays on the nature-nurture theme throughout the play as a means of reinforcing the gentlemanly inborn nature of Orlando and his lack of nurture in the social and moral life of the aristocracy.[30] The conflict is resolved by the nurture Orlando develops for himself by nature and in nature. The process of maturation begun in escaping the restraints of an unjust older brother, and then continued in the victory inspired by the beauty of Rosalind, is concluded in the green world of Arden. Orlando is able to accomplish the transformation by himself partly because of his own witty and vital nature but also because he had the good fortune to fall in among those who have been nurtured—the merry and courtly band of the Duke Senior, exiled to nature. These careful nature-nurture paradoxes are introduced early by a conversation between Rosalind and Celia interrupted by Touchstone. Rosalind has made a schoolbook distinction, "Fortune reigns in the gifts of the world, not in the lineaments of Nature," when the Fool intrudes and Celia replies, "No; when Nature hath made a fair creature, may she not by Fortune fall into the fire? Though Nature hath given us wit to flout at Fortune, hath not Fortune sent in this fool to cut off the argument?" (I. ii. 38–43).

Orlando also intrudes upon others, and in a way that makes him feel foolish. When in search of food for the starving Adam and himself, Orlando breaks in upon the feasting rustic courtiers and claims the argument of necessity for his rude behavior. The Duke Senior questions whether that or a simple lack of good manners be the explanation, and Orlando replies: ". . . the thorny point /Of bare distress hath ta'en from me the show /Of smooth civility; yet I am inland bred, /And know some nurture . . ." (II. vii. 94–97). The mere fact of having lived close to the court helped Orlando to enjoy nurture, despite all his brother's efforts to the contrary. Orlando is chagrined by his own behavior the moment he hears his host's gentle response; he puts up his sword, saying, in effect, let your civility, not my sword, enforce my needs. But before the famished Orlando will eat, the older Adam's needs must be served. Such are the dictates of both Orlando's gentle nature and his inland nurture. This scene illustrates how fortune, which might have undermined one aspect of Orlando's better parts by forcing him into rudeness through the necessities of a rude environment, helped him instead to preserve and further cultivate his gentle virtues, by casting him among gentlemen.[31] The paradox lies in the athletic virtue which causes Orlando to risk his life in the first place, among those he thinks to be savages, in order to serve the needs of a starving old servant. This combination of "rude" virtue among seeming brutes easily turned to civil virtue among gentlemen is the kind of complex idealism to which the play constantly returns.

We should remember, however, that not all courtliness, all nurture in the usual sense, is desirable. As we discover in the conversation between Touchstone and Corin (early in III. ii), decorum is an important qualification to nurture. What is appropriate at court is not necessarily appropriate in the country, and vice versa. When it comes to nature, once again Shakespeare's attitude is characteristically complex. First of all, there are the two fundamental senses of *nature:* that which is morally natural to the duty of a man, a brother, a subject, or a guest; and that which occurs in a state of nature away from the corrupting sophistications of the court. In the second sense of the term, nature can refresh and complete a man like Orlando, whose innocence in the making of those little parodies of Petrarchan love poems is at once unfinished and totally engaging; but nature away from the court can also cause men to lose all sense of rational proportion. Jaques, for instance, refuses to see the difference between the usurpation of the country by the wicked younger brother of the Duke Senior and the usurpation of the forest from the deer by killing them for food. The rebuttal obvious to any member of Shakespeare's audience is in the divinely ordained world where according to nature in the moral sense of the term older brothers reign ahead of younger brothers and animals are biblically appointed to serve man's needs. As in his quasi-religious meditation on dying deer (reported II. i. 45ff.), Jaques uses nature in the modern sense to come to some conclusions most unnatural in the more characteristic Renaissance sense. But then Jaques, as we all know, is a perverse melancholiac; he travels only that he may see the worst in his own country and thinks only that he may despair. His famous speech on the seven ages of man (II. vii) is a variation on one of the great common-places of the age, familiar to the audience in a thousand visual and literary instances.[32] Also obvious to them would be the way in which Jaques converts the standard descriptions of the various ages of man into the most dismal terms: the "Mewling and puking" infant, the lover "Sighing like furnace," and finally "mere oblivion." Although Thomas M. Parrot sees this passage as perhaps little more than dramatic filler, written to allow Orlando to bring in Adam from offstage, it is also very much in character.[33] But then Shakespeare has already deftly keyed us in to Jaques' ultimate limitations, for all his seeming worldly sophistication, by having him at the very first encounter with the audience mispro-nounce "stanza" as "stanzo."[34] The final refutation of Jaques' point of view is the iconic stage image concluding his seven ages speech. Orlando's entry with old Adam on his back, a "venerable burden" the exiled Duke invites him to "Set down," is surely intended by Shakespeare to recall the image of Aeneas carrying his father Anchises out of a burning Troy. This episode is the subject of numerous Renaissance works of art, and it stands in the emblem books as a touchstone of filial piety. It occurs in the first extant edition of Alciati (1531), with the motto, "pietas filiorum in parentes" (filial devotion toward parents). The same scene and the same motto is printed by Geffrey Whitney, *A Choice of Emblemes* (Leyden, 1586), with a suitable explanatory poem in English (p. 163). The woodcut and poem (Plate 4) must have been familiar to many of those in Shakespeare's audience. In 1579 Aeneas and

Anchises appear in the emblem book of Laurentius Haechtanus paired with Nero's murder of his mother, and the motto "pietatis et impietatis exemplum" (an example of piety and of impiety).[35] Emblematic juxtaposition is fulfilled in *As You Like It* by the contrast between the brooding Jaques, cynical toward both youth and age, and the frame of an active youth loyal in the care of age.[36]

Finally, those who have both by nature and nurture lived entirely in the green world—such as the literary parodies Corin and Silvius and the realistic satires Audrey and William—are presented as sharply limited, callow, naïve, or downright fools. The primary purpose of the satellite plots is clearly the comic parody of love situations in the main line of action, not that the main line of action necessarily becomes any less serious. The green world of Arden is but one ingredient in the careful mixture designed by Shakespeare to complete and at the same time test Orlando.

The whole requires nature, nurture, fortune, and will.

Hercules in Love

We have already seen Orlando's strength of will in the repudiation of his brother's tyranny, in the wrestling match, and in the interruption of the rustic banquet. The climactic test of Orlando's "athletic" virtue is in his mock contest with Ganymede to dissuade him from his love (IV. i). This test of a lover's fidelity, so traditional a part of romance, is the ironic means by which Rosalind is herself "defeated" by love. Just as Orlando overthrew her heart as well as Charles in the wrestling match, her love for Orlando paradoxically deepens the more he defies her mock attempts to destroy his love for her. Orlando is no mean contestant; despite Rosalind's considerable learning and wit, Orlando's faithfulness proves itself stronger. He is no conventionally handsome and slightly stupid leading man, such as Bertram in *All's Well*. Orlando has earlier proved the agility of his mind in a wit combat with Jaques, in which he clearly defeated that verbally dextrous malcontent (III. ii. 337ff.).

The pattern of overthrow in the play is also presented in the negative terms of usurpation or displacement, in turn linked to the requirements of natural law. Orlando is displaced by his eldest brother from his birthright, yet he would never think of overthrowing Oliver in the way Frederick has usurped the birthright of the exiled Duke. One violation of natural law is not redeemed by another. On the contrary, it is natural law as understood by Shakespeare and his audience—the ideal bonds of family and friends—that paradoxically creates innumerable instances of good out of obstacles or evil. Orlando saves the life of a brother who had come into the forest to kill him. Celia remains true to Rosalind despite the changing attitudes of Frederick. And Orlando remains faithful to Rosalind despite separation and the feigned attempts of Ganymede to overthrow his love for her. As we see, it is Ganymede (another classical role, one strong in Neoplatonic suggestions) who is herself overthrown by love. In the "usurpation" of the forest from the deer by the exiled Duke and his men, as described by Jaques, furthermore, negatives are turned back once again into positives. The absolutes are neither victory or defeat, nor submission or usurpation, but the far more sophisticated principles of natural law. **1909633**

The famous scene in Act IV of the wit combat and love test between Rosalind and Orlando is the climax of the play's series of specifically theatrical paradoxes. Nowhere else has Shakespeare so elaborately handled the motif of Italianate disguise. His audience would have been quick to appreciate the wit of a dramatist who casts a boy actor as a girl disguised as a boy taking the part of a girl in order to "cure" the love-sick Orlando. Despite Shakespeare's delight in the theatrical possibilities offered by the boy actors and the temptation of modern directors to discover elements of the perverse, Orlando is most emphatically meant to be in love with a girl, not a boy acting the part of a girl. Recalling once again the Herculean pattern of Orlando's heroism, it might seem at first that this love is a lapse in Orlando rather than the final test of virtue. Still familiar is the comedy of Hercules in love with Omphale, emasculated as he accomplishes her household tasks. Another tradition concerning Hercules in love, however, had sprung up during the Renaissance. In his well-known book on the Herculean hero, Eugene Waith has explained the transition: "When the material of romance was introduced into the heroic. . . . the Herculean hero, who had a warrior's low regard for women, came to be portrayed as a lover also." His "love as well as his valour became an object of admiration."[37] In the *Amorum emblemata* of

Otho Vaenius (Antwerp, 1608?), one emblem shows Hercules with Cupid's arrow through his breast (pp. 32–33).[38] The themes are both defeat and triumph, for the labor shown is the slaying of the Hydra (Plate 5). The authorities for the motto, "virtutis radix amor" (love as the root of virtue), are Plato and Cicero, and the printed English version of the emblem poem goes:

> Moste great and woorthie deeds had neuer bin atchyued,
> If in respect of loue they had not bin begunne,
> Loues victorie hath made more victories bee wonne,
> From loue-bred virtue then thus were they
> > first deryued. (p. 32)

Defeated by love, Hercules is paradoxially triumphant over his enemies.

Oliver too is defeated by love. He has been shamed into repentance by Orlando's rescue of him from a lion, but he is converted to seeking the life of an Arcadian shepherd by falling in love with Celia disguised as Aliena. There has been much Victorian criticism of this detail, based on a comment by Swinburne, on the grounds that Oliver does not deserve Celia. But to a Shakespearean audience Oliver's willingness to give up the patrimony to Orlando in full contrition for his sins (a contrition Claudius never achieves in the prayer scene of *Hamlet*) would have been accepted as a clear proof or test of both his true love and his true conversion into a man worthy of Celia.

The final conversion of the play, that of Duke Frederick, is even more quickly and simply handled. An old religious man he meets in the forest on the way to the extermination of his brother's following is so persuasive that he ends by handing back the dukedom to its rightful owner, thus confirming the quality of his conversion. The event is reported by the second son of Sir Rowland, Jaques de Boys, whom the audience sees for the first time. His sudden appearance with the report of a sudden event multiplies the sense of romantic wonder.

Most wonderful of all is the lovely ornament of the masque of Hymen, with which the play concludes. One of the illustrations in Vincenzo Cartari, *Le imagini de i' dei* (Lyons, 1581), reveals how the Renaissance thought Hymen should look (Plate 6). When Richard Lynche translated Cartari into English (London, 1599), he did not include the material on Hymen, but Cartari's description of his illustration, translated below, is a record of iconographic common-places undoubtedly known at least in part by Shakespeare and informative about the possible details of Hymen's original stage appearance in *As You Like It*:[39]

> Hymen was shown by the ancients in the form of a handsome young man crowned with a diversity of flowers, in his right hand a lighted torch and in his left hand a red veil (or it could be saffron) with which new brides covered their head to face the first time they went to their husbands. And the reason for this (as I promised to tell a little earlier) is that the wives of priests among the ancient Romans almost always wore a similar veil. Because they were not allowed to divorce, as others were, the covering of the bride with the veil came to mean the desire for the marriage never to be dissolved. This does not preclude also the symbolic meaning of the chaste modesty of the bride, which is the same as Pudor, respected by the ancients so much that it was worshipped like a god. (p. 165)

The very artifice of the sudden introduction of an allegorical figure in Hymen has distressed many modern producers of the play, some of whom have substituted one of the merry band of the Duke Senior to act the role of the god of true marriage, but Shakespeare suggests no such thing. This is clearly intended to be one of Shakespeare's masquelike entrances, like those of Ceres in *The Tempest* and Time in *The Winter's Tale*. The entrance of Hymen also occurs in *The Two Noble Kinsmen* (I. i), complete with a boy in a white robe strewing flowers in his own path and nymphs with wheat in their hair. The Renaissance ideal of connubial love as married chastity is embodied in Hymen as a Neoplatonic abstrac-tion central to the romantic action of *As You Like It*. He significantly emerges at the very moment Rosalind reveals her true indentity by throwing off her disguise. Hymen is the final paradox of the play. Although it would probably never occur to Shake-speare to think consciously in such terms, the structure of this play is based upon Platonic synthesis rather than Aristotelian mean. Peter G. Phialas has argued for the compromise of opposites: "Shakespeare's comic point of view . . . qualifies both the Petrarchan hyperboles of romantic lovers like Orlando and the exclusively physical concerns of anti-romantic characters like

Touchstone. . . ."[40] Phialas is right in stressing reconciliation within the play, but Shakespeare is achieving the union of Neoplatonic worlds, such as those of soul and sense, rather than the midpoints of the Aristotelian mean. Ideal love as married chastity, for instance, is symbolized by Hymen in Spenser's "Epithalamion," and Shakespeare expands this theme in "The Phoenix and the Turtle." The belief that lovers faithful to one another unto death retain their chastity is but one of many paradoxes celebrated in Shakespeare's teasing poem:

> So they lov'd, as love in twain
> Had the essence but in one;
> Two distincts, division none:
> Number there in love was slain.
> . . . .
> It was married chastity. (ll. 25–28, 61)

The paradoxical point of union between appetite and restraint found in married chastity, between mythological abstraction and the particulars of the pastoral life, between nature and nurture found among courtiers in the green world, between innocence and sophistication in young lovers, and between the body and the soul in the athlete of virtue: this is the still point of the turning worlds in *As You Like It*. In the Forest of Arden, Orlando, both Hercules and David, is invited to the banquet of civility. The "perfect ceremony of love's rite" is not yet drowned. As for the tone in which this mythic dimension is expressed, Richard Knowles, in his important article on this aspect of the play, makes careful critical qualifications about the degree to which Shakespeare's audience might have been conscious of philosophic themes. He distinguishes William Arrowsmith's term "conversion" from "allegory," "symbolism," and "iconology." Such a "conversion" is "teasing, unanchored, suggestive of the mystery it is meant to record," only glimpsed "on the fringes of our emotional field," and occurs momentarily in *As You Like It* as a result of seriocomic classical and biblical reminiscences. "We tend to take more seriously characters who are like the gods even in half-comic ways. . . ."[41] The precise quality of Orlando as both hero and seriocomic lover is indeed impossible to translate into the limitations of scholarship. At this point "the play's the thing."

2

The Merchant of Venice: Divine Comedy

If Orlando and Hymen are far more important to *As You Like It* than is usually believed, Shylock is far less central to *The Merchant of Venice* than directors of the play and classroom discussions have traditionally made him. Teachers of Shakespeare are fully aware of the focus of student interest. They know how easily Shylock, like Falstaff, can run away with the play as a melodramatic reading or theater experience. And no wonder, for everyone knows how the last half-century in Europe has made of Shylock's religion a basis of massive injustice. Setting aside for the moment the issues created by a renewed modern sensitivity to the evils of prejudice, however, we will see that *The Merchant of Venice* has iconic stage imagery which confirms the recent critical consensus that this is one of Shakespeare's most coherent plays.[1]

Recent criticism has increasingly come to accept the play's major paradox as the reconciliation of justice and mercy.[2] *Measure for Measure,* later in Shakespeare's career, is built on the theological deep structure of a godlike Duke imposing justice upon his creation-commonwealth, but with the merciful qualifications inspired by a virgin intercessor before the throne of power, authority, and grace. Shakespeare last uses this pattern in *The Tempest,* as we will be reminded toward the end of this book. Antonio as a merchant of Venice has none of the godlike majesty shared by the Duke of Vienna and Prospero, yet the most important theological issue in these three plays is the same: mercy and justice reconciled. This issue in *Merchant* is expressed on the simplest level as the apparent opposition of the Church and the Synagogue, or as Portia opposed to Shylock. The trope was a medieval commonplace abundantly detailed in many sources, including one of the illuminations of the twelfth century *Hortus deliciarum,* an illumination attributed to Herrad of Landsberg (Plate 7). The opposition is between the Old Law of justice and the New Testament of mercy, illustrated by the Crucifixion.[3] The crucifix separates a series of parallels drawn from opposing worlds: the saved thief (on Christ's right) and the damned thief (on his left); the legendary centurion who believed in Christ the moment after piercing his side with a spear and the reputed Jew with sponge and vinegar who refused stubbornly to convert; St. Mary (who never lost her faith) and St. John (who lost his with the other disciples after the Crucifixion and before Pentecost); and, finally, the Church, with a chalice in her hand receiving the blood of Christ and seated upon a beast conflating the emblematic attributes of the four writers of the Gospels, and the Synagogue, blindfolded, holding the Old Law, and mounted upon a stubborn ass. The sun and the moon flanking the top of the cross are cosmic symbols for the New Testament and the Old, God and the devil, Christianity and Judaism, the Children of Light and the Children of Darkness, life and death, and mercy and justice. The cosmic battle momentarily eclipses the sun, but rushing winds rend the curtains in the Temple, shown at the top of the illumination.

The mode of thought here is clearly based on many contrasting parallels, stated and implied. Our first impression of *The Merchant of Venice,* however, is that most of its parallels are complementary. For instance, what begins as the main line of action, the love plot whereby several suitors address one woman, is concluded with parallel betrothals between Bassanio and Portia, and then Gratiano and Nerissa, the friend of the one marrying the maid of the other. As Gratiano remarks to Bassanio midway through the play: "My eyes, my lord, can look as swift as yours: /You saw the mistress, I beheld the maid" (III. ii. 198–99). Yet several instances of contrasting parallels can easily be seen as well. The subplot, whereby Bassanio's financial needs in wooing Portia are served by Antonio's bond to Shylock, quickly becomes an insistent line of action, with Shylock a new focus for the play. The title refers either to him or to Antonio or to both, but both of them are major only in the subplot, which Portia enters by crossing over from the main plot. The interweaving, however, is so close that we might most accurately describe the play as having two plots, which are in turn both parallel and interwoven. The interweaving has been briefly suggested; the contrasting parallelism emerges most clearly in the contrast Portia provides to Shylock, the thematic contrast of the Church and the Synagogue. Even within the flesh-bond line of action initially described above as the subplot the same contrast reoccurs. Antonio is the Church once again to Shylock as the Synagogue, with the further variation of Antonio as self-sacrificing savior complementing the intercessor lady. In the two plays where Shakespeare most emphasizes the theme of justice and mercy —*Merchant* and *Measure*—the plea of mercy is consistently stated by a young woman, Portia in the one, Isabella in the other, with the virginity of Isabella a major issue in the action of her play, although we are also meant to remember that Portia will not consummate her marriage until her husband's friend is saved from death (III. ii. 300ff.).

Antonio as a conventional redeemer within the context of medieval and Renaissance religious symbolism is borne out at many points. Perhaps least defined in these terms is his first appearance on stage as the stock character of a man melancholy without cause.[4] The play subsequently fails to develop him as a sufferer from real or feigned melancholia, such as Hamlet or Jaques, and Antonio's first appearance might remain a loose end were he not so quickly cast as a savior of Bassanio, a prodigal who hopes to marry Portia in order to pay off his many debts, including those already owed Antonio. Antonio's mysterious melancholy may thus have been intended by Shakespeare as the thematic introduction to the prophetic "man of sorrows, and acquainted with grief" (Isaiah 53:3) familiar to most of us by way of Handel's *Messiah*. Even if we include the famous speech of Antonio threatening to spit once again upon Shylock should occasion warrant, Antonio never initiates conflict with Shylock on stage. As for the spit, it provides the basis of one of the major critical arguments used to make Antonio into a hypocritical Christian. I see no such intention on Shakespeare's part. His characters (including ladies and aristocrats, as well as merchants) often spit at each other in the heat of righteous indignation.[5] Antonio's consistent behavior on stage at least, especially at the crucial trial scene, is amazingly meek and submissive. His role seems most emphatically that of self-sacrificing savior, a role he shares in a mysterious way with Portia, who says in the casket scene, "I stand for sacrifice" (III. ii. 57).

As for Shylock, his character is one of continual self-justification. He uses the story of Jacob and the sheep to justify the taking of interest, and Antonio makes the proverbial observation that the "devil can cite Scripture for his purpose." Nor is this the only equating of Shylock with the devil. The link is constantly repeated, especially in the satellite plot concerning Launcelot Gobbo. Shylock's servant is torn between taking the "devil's advice" to run away from his master (one of several details in this play from the Renaissance application of the prodigal son parable) and staying with his master, a "very devil incarnation" (II. ii. 26). Launcelot as a mistreated servant is another aspect of the stock Renaissance comic treatment of melodramatic Jews, who both starve and beat their dependents. That Launcelot is only starved is another instance of Shakespeare's characteristic softening of his subject, but Shylock is no less wicked for all that. The very name Shakespeare assigns him is possibly the English spelling of a Hebrew word meaning "cormorant." This bird, which preys on fish, was a proverbial emblem for anyone greedy and rapacious, but especially usurers.[6] Launcelot leaves his rich but miserly master for the service of a poor but generous gentleman, Bassanio, who enjoys "the grace of God" (II. ii. 137). In so doing he escapes the abode of Satan, a hellcastle described as such by even Jessica, the daughter of the house, when she says farewell to her father's escaping servant: "I am sorry thou wilt leave my father so. /Our house is hell; and thou, a merry devil, /Didst rob it of some taste of tediousness" (II. iii. 1–3). Salanio is even more direct in his identification of Shylock as the devil: "Let me say amen betimes, lest the devil cross my prayer, for here he comes in the likeness of a Jew" (III. i. 18–19). Everything this devil insistently demands is in the name of justice, simple justice. Even in the trial scene, when Portia offers to pay off the debt twenty times over, ". . . none can drive him from the envious plea /Of forfeiture, of justice, and his bond" (III. ii. 284–85). Pride and envy are his Satanic motives, and Antonio is indeed a man to envy. Shylock is enraged by the high regard his enemy has with both the governors and a host of friends.

In no other play by Shakespeare is there such a sense of multiple friendships. The play opens with one group of friends interlocking with another group of friends, for Antonio's companions are also the friends of those close to his kinsman and friend Bassanio. Nor does quantity lack quality. Antonio instantly offers himself as bond for Bassanio so his friend may pursue a romantic quest in Portia. No conflict between love and friendship exists early in the play, as it does in *Two Gentlemen of Verona* when Proteus quickly puts his love for Sylvia over his friendship for Valentine. The commitment between Bassanio and Antonio goes to the very gates of death. The emotional quality of the bond between them is so intense that Shakespeare has Salarino report the departure of Bassanio for Belmont as an offstage event. According to Salarino, Antonio's eyes filled with tears, and "turning his face, he put his hand behind him, /And with affection wondrous sensible /He wrung Bassanio's hand . . ." (II. viii. 47–49). The final test of this love is in the trial, where Antonio remains steadfast to the end, without flinching for a moment. His magnanimity first of purse and then of life stands in total opposition to Shylock's simple greed. As for Shylock's friend Tubal, almost nothing comes of the relationship beyond Shylock's use of him as a messenger. Thus, in virtually all the details of the relationship between Antonio and Shylock these men stand as contrasting parallels to each other, the humble magnanimity of the Church opposing the obdurance of the Synagogue.

The Caskets

The riddle of the three caskets is assigned the place of climax in the middle of the play, although it has always seemed minor to most directors when compared to the pound of flesh issue. Yet it was obviously to get the money to allow Bassanio to woo Portia and to enter the contest of the caskets that Antonio pledged his pound of flesh in the first place. Perhaps directors are already beginning to regard the casket scenes less as ornamental interruptions to the real focus of action in the pound of flesh and more in the context of the allegorical dumb shows assigned in the Senecan tradition to the act divisions of a play. If so, audiences will increasingly see how the two issues of caskets and pound of flesh contribute to the same pattern of largely contrasting parallels.[7]

Shakespeare has given the love test in *The Merchant of Venice* much greater symbolic complexity than it had in his probable source for the main line of action, Fiorentino's *Il Pecorone* (1558). There one lover passes three tests. In the play three suitors choose among three caskets. Portia is practicing filial piety by adhering to her father's dying wish concerning the choice of the right casket by a successful suitor. Her submission to her father's will may seem hopelessly servile to us, but she is an orphan possessed of enormous wealth and thus very vulnerable to fortune hunting. As her father is implied to have foreseen, she has a host of suitors, and these from every nation. Nerissa need only remind Portia of her father's virtue to cheer up a mistress echoing Antonio in her initial presentation to the audience as a melancholy soul:

> Your father was ever virtuous, and holy men at their death have good inspirations; therefore the lott'ry that he hath devised in these three chests, of gold, silver, and lead —whereof who chooses his meaning chooses you—will no doubt never be chosen by any rightly but one who you shall rightly love. (I. ii. 24–28)

Up to this point, even Bassanio has expressed little concern about Portia beyond the way her fortune might pay off his debts as a prodigal. His character, also, must be tested before he is dramatically acceptable as a husband who will marry Portia primarily for love rather than hope of gain. The issue centered at this point on Bassanio leads to his eventual contrast with Shylock, for whom all human values are really material values: a man is a pound of flesh, a daughter is difficult for Shylock to distinguish from ducats, and servants are to provide maximum work for minimum food. In both central issues—the caskets and the pound of flesh—one of the sustained conflicts is between love and merchandise, as recent critics of the play have been quick to see. Furthermore, the actual ritual of the choice of caskets is a symbolic comment on the action of the whole play, a kind of Senecan dumb show, as suggested above. The choice is both "lott'ry" (II. i. 15) and test of character. The game of chance as a primitive method of making decisions or determining truth is well-known to anthropologists. Making the right choice can also be a revelation of character, as Aristotle underlines in his *Poetics*. The choice works both ways: the good man illustrates his character by making the right choices in life,

and the gods inspire their favorite to make the right choice—
Morocco: "Some god direct my judgement!" (II. vii. 13). And on the
redemptive level of meaning, salvation is both the fruit of divine
grace and a reward for merit, as we will see when it finally comes
Bassanio's turn to choose.

The first choice falls to the Prince of Morocco. His complexion is
black, a color Portia does not find attractive (II. vi. 79).[8] Morocco
is very sensitive on this point, comparing his blood (his courage as
a man) with "the fairest creature northward born" (II. i. 4). The
blackness of Morocco as a trait to be overcome, along with
Shylock's religion, clearly and rightly violates modern sensitivities;
and, undoubtedly, Portia's comment about Morocco's "complexion" is often explained away as a reference to his character. Only
in *Othello,* however, does Shakespeare present a favorable character
who is also black, and even there Othello is aware that his color is
against him. Portia insists that she is not led by appearances any
more than Morocco would wish to be judged by them, and, that if
he be the worthy husband identified by the choice of the right
casket, he will be completely acceptable to her. This commonplace
theme of appearance and reality has already been established in
the immediately preceding scene, cited in the discussion above,
having to do with Shylock. We recall how after Shylock's
invocation of the story of Jacob and the sheep as justification for
lending money at interest, Antonio remarked, "The devil can cite
Scripture for his purpose." Antonio concluded his speech with, "O,
what a goodly outside falsehood hath!" Morocco begins his
presentation of himself to Portia by telling her not to be put off by
his outward appearance, but rather to judge him by his inward
worth as a man. The issue is thus reversed from the citing of
Scripture, as the deceptively good appearance of a bad motive, to
black skin, as the deceptively bad appearance of a good man. But
Shakespeare is misleading us here for the sake of yet another
reversal of issue. As it turns out, Morocco is as bad as he looks to
Portia, and his use of the warning about maintaining the
distinction between appearance and reality is comparable to
Shylock's citing of Scripture. Both cite truth, the one Scripture and
the other a moral commonplace about appearance and reality, but
both are precisely as bad as they look. Shylock is the iconic stage
image of a Jew (undoubtedly made to "look" his part) and
Morocco the iconic stage image of a black man. Recall Aaron the

Moor in *Titus Andronicus* for an extreme instance of the iconic implications to the Renaissance of blackness. Blacks were identified with the descendants of Cain (often conflated with Ham, or Cham), his mark their color.[9]

Shakespeare seems to be using both Morocco and Shylock to indicate that not only must an audience be aware of distinctions between appearance and reality, they must also learn to know when the iconic appearance is the reality, even when a character deceptively quotes the authority of the Bible or standard moral sentiments. The true character of Morocco is fully exposed by his choice of the golden casket. His defective moral values are revealed in the process of elimination which brings him to it. The leaden casket is unacceptable because its inscription demands that " 'Who chooseth me must give and hazard all he hath.'' Morocco cannot imagine risking all with the belief that nothing at all might come of it. Men who risk should be expected to hope for gain. Yet we the audience are meant to know that such calculated "risk" accepts the principle of risk not at all. And this limitation of Morocco stands in sharp contrast to the example of Antonio, who risks his life itself so that his friend may enter a "lott'ry" for the woman he wants to marry. It is true that Antonio vastly underrates the degree of risk, but it is there nonetheless and it is total. The theme of risk even introduces the play, in the speeches of Salarino and Salanio, who suggest that Antonio is sad because he has risked a great fortune at sea, itself the emblem of the extremes of profit and loss. As for the silver casket, " 'Who chooseth me shall get as much as he deserves.' " Morocco at first feels unworthy of the lady, but his arrogance quickly convinces him that his qualifications of birth, wealth, grace, and desire (which he calls "love") easily merit her. This choice is ironic in the context of a later scene in the play. The issue of what we deserve at the hands of God, justice or mercy, is crucial to the pound of flesh denouement in the fourth act. According to the assumptions of an earlier century none of us deserves all that he desires. Only the arrogantly proud would think so. Morocco would have chosen the silver, however, had his eye not been distracted by the greater glitter and value of the golden casket, which promises that " 'Who chooseth me shall gain what many men desire.' " The statement clearly fits Portia, desired by all the world (as will be mercy in the Day of Judgment); gold brings ten times the value of silver; and Portia could never be associated with anything so base as humble lead. The choice is apparent. But, of course, this time it is only apparent, not real, and the conclusion is total loss. Behind the glitter is a memento mori, a skull whose eye holds a scroll. Morocco has already called the lead casket a coffin too base for a soul like Portia's: "Is't like that lead contains her? 'Twere damnation /To think so base a thought; it were too gross /To rib her cerecloth in the obscure grave" (II. vii. 49–51). Yet the golden casket is the true coffin. The appearance of value has been taken for the reality, and the conclusion is death. Wealth may enclose spiritual rot, as gilded tombs do worms, just as usurers may pursue for a lifetime a course bringing eternal loss of that which should be of lasting worth.

When the Prince of Arragon, whose very name suggests his character and who should also look the fop, arrives at Belmont, he, like Morocco, takes three oaths: never to reveal his choice, and both to woo no other maiden and to leave promptly should he fail. The first oath and the last (recalling the plight of Penelope) are practical; the second, about wooing no other woman, underlines the moral issue. Not only is Portia being wooed, but her suitors are obviously being tested in a general sense as both men and potential husbands. Portia should not have a bad man imposed upon her as a husband, nor should any other woman. Arragon's first refusal is of the leaden casket, because, once again, its appearance is so unpromising. Then he refuses the golden casket because he arrogantly considers himself above the rude multitude, and thus would not wish what most, or even many, men desire. The silver is chosen because Arragon thinks himself worth so much more than other men: "I will assume desert" (II. ix. 51). The issues are virtually the same as they were with Morocco. The scene is an elegant variation, and Shakespeare runs more quickly over this episode. The image inside the casket—a "portrait of a blinking idiot"—is the blind reflection of a snob blinded to the truth by pride, living with the Platonic shadows of appearance rather than the substance of reality.

Bassanio's choice is, of course, the one we have been awaiting; furthermore, his choice of the right casket will be the result of both merciful grace and his strength of character. Portia has already fallen in love with him and encourages him to seek every advantage before choosing. Her love is expressed directly to him in a riddle disclaiming that love, whereby she makes it clear that she

will do everything to help him make the right choice short of
violating her father's last instructions to her. Therein lies the
merciful grace: the freely given help contained in her loving
encouragement and also possibly in the song sung to the music
Portia orders to be played to inspire Bassanio while he makes his
choice. Long famous is the observation that the first four lines of
the song end in words which rhyme with "lead," as does the
internal rhyme in the second line of the second stanza.[10] In
addition, a director might instruct Portia to hover around the
leaden casket, perhaps casting her eyes toward it, or trailing a
sleeve over it. But he might also direct Bassanio to fail to catch
these more explicit hints, for Bassanio is assigned a speech in which
he is clearly meant to make the right choice for the right reasons.
Therein lies the justice: that Bassanio deserves Portia on his own
merits. He begins his reasoning by making a distinction other
suitors have clearly failed to make in the right way, the difference
between appearance and reality, relating that in turn to the issue
of the devil citing Scripture: ". . . In religion, /What damned
error but some sober brow /Will bless it, and approve it with a
text, /Hiding the grossness with fair ornament?" (III. ii. 77–80).
The oblique parallels with Shylock are continued with the paradox
of women who most purchase their beauty by the weight (in other
words, cosmetics) being the ones with the lightest morals:
". . . Look on beauty /And you shall see 'tis purchas'd by the
weight, /Which therein works a miracle in nature, /Making them
lightest that wear most of it" (III. ii. 88–91). The implied link with
the issue of the bond is that man, like woman, or beauty, or justice,
is not truly measured by the pound. Quantity is inferior to quality,
if indeed not its opposite. Bassanio's meditation then turns to the
extremely popular memento mori topic of a skull, already introduced as an iconic stage image through its discovery by Morocco,
and perhaps to be left out for Bassanio to notice.

Gold is too often mere ornament, silver too often associated with
commerce; therefore, Bassanio chooses humble lead and wins the
lady. Humility is the primary qualification in this play for human
success, standing directly opposed to the commercial success of
Shylock, who, as we shall see, is most prideful in his conviction of
self-sufficiency. The leaden casket contains the portrait of Portia,
and Bassanio's earlier meditation on the deceptions of ornamental
beauty is finally turned into a blazon of Portia's true beauty,

paradoxically rendered in a counterfeit painted shadow. Supporting these paradoxes, however, are one-dimensional iconic facts:
Morocco and Arragon, like Shylock, "look" bad and are; Bassanio
"looks" good (certainly to Portia) and is. But then paradox
reemerges when he who looks good is the only one who can tell the
difference between what only looks good and what really is good.
Shakespeare is here using iconic means to create the same
ascending stories of ironic dramatic effect he accomplishes with the
female page disguised as a man in plays such as *As You Like It* and
Twelfth Night, and elsewhere in *The Merchant of Venice* for that
matter. Despite the far greater fame of the trial scene, Bassanio's
casket scene is possibly an even greater triumph of art. Not only
does Shakespeare create the ascending levels of irony concerning
appearance and reality described above, but what must also be
self-evident by now is the way in which he makes of this casket
scene a play within the play, reflecting the whole in microcosm.
The scene clearly has much in common with the iconic Senecan
dumb show set at the midpoint of action.

Another aspect of the reflection in miniature is the possible use
of the stage image of all three caskets to suggest coffins. A
death's-head was in Morocco's golden casket; lead, as Arragon
points out, is regarded as a suitable material for coffins; and
Bassanio's meditation on beauty is rich in the conventional tropes
of the ars moriendi. Productions can represent the form of the
caskets as miniature coffins or unmistakable jewel boxes. In the
sixteenth century *casket* was not used to describe a coffin, but the
metaphorical sense that lies behind its ultimate application to the
box holding a corpse is found in Shakespeare. In *King John,* the
Bastard describes the discovery of Arthur's body as the discovery of
an "empty casket" robbed of "the jewel of life" (V. i. 40). The
body of Arthur is the casket and his soul the jewel, but it is only
one more step to seeing a coffin as a casket or a casket as a coffin,
and we recall how Morocco calls the leaden casket a coffin too base
for a soul like Portia's. Portia's caskets do contain small objects—a
death's head, a picture of a blind fool, and her own (probably
miniature) portrait—and there is little doubt that the containers of
these objects are meant to be small, as the ending of the word *casket*
implies; but there is no reason that the probable rectilinear form of
the caskets could not have recalled coffins to an audience. If it did,
still more Renaissance motifs, especially those associated with the

ars moriendi, can be brought to mind. What better place, for instance, than a coffinlike box for the memento mori of the death's head ironically discovered by Morocco, who has rejected the leaden casket as a coffin? Skulls were the most popular Renaissance reminders of death and were household objects in either their literal form or in the form of commonly used items, such as silver watches, which made the owner know that it was indeed later than he thought (Plate 8). A beautifully executed skull watch was reputedly owned by Mary Stuart.[11] Three coffinlike caskets lined in a row confronting three socially notable men might also have been linked by the Renaissance audience with the familiar parable of the Three Living and the Three Dead. Samuel Chew, in his *Pilgrimage of Life,* devotes a section to this legend, which apparently originated in European folklore and then crossed the channel to England. Two dozen murals on the subject, some still extant, are known to have existed in fifteenth- and sixteenth-century English churches. The subject as a theme of medieval Latin drama is mentioned by both Karl Young and E. K. Chambers; it appears as the basis of miniatures in medieval illuminated manuscripts; and it is repeated in graphics printed in Renaissance books (Plate 9).[12] The story concerns three living men, often kings or those of high estate, suddenly confronting three dead skeletons, often crowned. The skeletons were frequently shown to arise from their coffins and startle the horses of the three living, who are in the midst of the chase. The even more familiar Dance of Death has the same implications: always be ready in the midst of life to die; humble your heart before the power of death. Not only does the first of Portia's caskets contain a death's-head, but the entire test was the inspiration of Portia's father on his deathbed, according to Nerissa, who encourages Portia by reminding her that "holy men at their death have good inspirations." Finally, both Morocco and Arragon fail the test because of their pride, and Bassanio passes because of his humility.

The suggestion offered here for the shape of the caskets as coffins is very tentative, but it is certainly far less conjectural than Freud's famous interpretation of them,[13] and it does at least take a very well-established Renaissance frame of reference into account. Furthermore, the parallels of mercy and justice can be subsequently linked to the issues of life and death, salvation and damnation, the New Law of love and humility and the Old Law of selfishness and pride. By this point, it should be clearly apparent that the parallels in this play operate on two complementary levels. It will be increasingly seen that mercy and justice, life and death, the Old Law and the New are not only opposites but complements. These parallels oppose each other and yet rely upon each other, with the level of opposition in turn complementing the level of union. Morocco, for instance, calls the leaden casket a coffin too base for a soul like Portia's; yet Bassanio finds in humble lead his salvation from debt and the graceful image of his lady. To live in others we must die to self. St. Paul delighted in the endless ramifications of paradox, even to the point of paradox within paradox. Shakespeare's century was a period of Platonic revival very hospitable to Paul as the first great Christian Platonist. The intellectual mode of the real unity to be found beyond apparent conflict informs the highly complex structure of *The Merchant of Venice*, as it does *As You Like It*, to a remarkable degree. As instances of parallel, conflict, complement, and union accumulate, the play's real core of unified opposites will be seen to refute its apparent dramatic surface of disjointed and anticlimactic events.

The Rings

One of the most frequently cited instances of anticlimax in Shakespeare is the fifth act of *The Merchant of Venice*. After the magnificent dramatic effect of the trial scene in Act IV, Act V strikes many audiences as trivial domestic comedy having to do with missing love tokens. Yet the episode of the rings clearly illustrates the reconciliation of apparent opposites—this time love and friendship—on which the entire paradoxical structure of the play relies. The rings given to Bassanio and Gratiano by Portia and Nerissa are also iconic stage images. The ring as a love token is familiar as the basis of countless bawdy jokes in the Renaissance. As the emblem of a sexual organ the ring has a fame second only to the sword. The source of the innuendo is obvious enough when we consider how the ring is usually given by a man to a woman with the specific instruction of never passing it along to another man. Variations on this theme of reserved chastity are also possible, as in *The Two Gentlemen of Verona*, where Proteus betrays Sylvia by sending the ring given him by her to his new love Julia. And in

Cymbeline Posthumus gives Imogen the modification of a bracelet and she gives him a diamond ring, with Iachimo stealing the bracelet from her and receiving the ring from him, as a reward for seemingly winning the wager struck over the issue of her chastity.

The symbolism in *Two Gentlemen* is very obvious and the ironies very complex in *Cymbeline*. *The Merchant of Venice* stands at a midpoint. The rings given the men by the women are a pledge of their chastity, which the men are in turn implicitly called upon to defend to the point of death. When the men give these rings to two other seeming men, no matter how great the debt, even life itself, the implied bond between husbands and wives is violated. The men are in effect rewarding other "men" for services rendered with the very chastity they agreed to defend when they accepted the rings. The symbolic breach is paramount, but luckily the seeming men are really women—indeed the very women whose chastity is being symbolically given away to satisfy a debt. The literal ring becomes a figurative circle in which chastity is returned to itself. Nevertheless, the fidelity of Bassanio and Gratiano has been tested and found wanting. The brash and irritating Gratiano does not surprise us, but to this point Bassanio has passed every test. He has not only chosen the right casket but even made a Christ-like offer to sacrifice his life to the devil could his life save Antonio's. That offer is made during the trial:

> Antonio, I am married to a wife
> Which is as dear to me as life itself;
> But life itself, my wife, and all the world,
> Are not with me esteem'd above thy life;
> I would lose all, ay, sacrifice them all
> Here to this devil, to deliver you. (IV. i. 277–82)

The disguised Portia, who earlier, in the casket scene, claimed to "stand for sacrifice," obviously does not now like the thought of Bassanio's offer to sacrifice even her, and reminds him that his wife might wish to have something to say about such a magnanimous offer. In a way, the device of the rings demanded in payment is the test of the offer made by Bassanio to "lose" Portia to the "devil." Would Bassanio truly "sacrifice" everything he has in the world (by now a huge fortune), as well as his own life, and even his wife, to fulfill his obligations to Antonio? Bassanio is never given the opportunity to prove the substance of the first two offers, but he is being tested on the third point in the ring episode of the fifth act.

The results of the test, like the principles of sacrifice, are another instance of paradox in the play. The positive result is in the gratitude it proves. Bassanio does love Portia, as he loves his life, but he also owes both Antonio and then the "doctor" more than it seems he could ever hope to repay (as all mankind similarly owe a gracious God). The conflict within Bassanio when he is asked for the ring is thus in part based on the familiar theme of love versus friendship. In the romances and plays of Lyly, the romances of Sidney, and *Two Gentlemen of Verona*, friendship is the higher virtue, as we are meant to see when Valentine offers Proteus Sylvia. Antonio has more than adequately proved his friendship to Bassanio. In giving the ring Bassanio proves the quality of his side of that relationship by in effect putting friendship before genuine love. His debt to Antonio, furthermore, is being discharged toward the "man" who saved his best friend's life, to whom he is also deeply grateful. As he tells Portia later in describing the surrender of the ring:

> What should I say, sweet lady?
> I was enforc'd to send it after him;
> I was beset with shame and courtesy;
> My honour would not let ingratitude
> So much besmear it. . . . (V. i. 215–19)

The positive results of the test are to be found in the way it confirms the quality of both Bassanio's friendship and his gratitude, two of the highest Renaissance virtues. The negative aspect of the outcome, however, is the one most apparent to the woman who has imposed the test, Portia. The putting of friendship over love can hardly be expected to please her, yet the conflict between love and friendship here, as in *Two Gentlemen*, is resolved, and by the competing friend. In *Two Gentlemen* the conflict created when Proteus puts love over friendship is resolved when he is shamed by his friend Valentine's offer of the lady into foregoing his passion for the lady. In *The Merchant* the conflict created when Bassanio puts friendship over love is fully resolved when Antonio offers no less than his immortal life as a new bond insuring the love between Bassanio and Portia:

> I once did lend my body for his wealth,
> Which, but for him that had your husband's ring,
> Had quite miscarried; I dare be bound again,
> My soul upon the forfeit, that your lord
> Will never more break faith advisedly. (V. i. 249–53)

The old bond (to the devil) allowed Bassanio to woo Portia. By means of this new bond, this New Covenant, the outstanding contraries of love and friendship are unified. The friend offers himself as bond for the love due to the lady. This, added to Bassanio's earlier plea for merciful forgiveness, brings Portia's disclosure of the iconic stage image of the ring and her true identity. The recognition scene so popular as a denouement in the romance, with establishment of identity often provided by a keepsake, is here turned into a rich reconciliation of all the highest medieval and Renaissance ideals: love, friendship, gratitude, self-sacrifice, forgiveness, and humility. Bassanio must admit a degree of guilt before he can ask Portia for forgiveness—". . . forgive me this enforced wrong" (V. i. 240)—and also quite obviously before he can be forgiven. Without a just humility and a merciful forgiveness on everyone's part the complex and difficult reconciliation of the opposites in human experience and between men is hardly possible.

Scales and a Knife

One of the most memorable of scenes in Shakespeare is surely the trial of the case of the debt owed Shylock by Antonio. The same crucial question that lies at the center of all the conflicts in the play is asked of Shylock by the Duke early in this scene: "How shalt thou hope for mercy, rend'ring none?" (IV. i. 88). Shylock immediately opposes the Old Law of justice to the New Law of mercy when he replies: "What judgment shall I dread, doing no wrong?" The opposition here established between the Church and the Synagogue is one that distinguishes all religions, a distinction which has been more than once pointed out in recent criticism of the play.[14] A very brief summary of this issue will allow us to move on to fresher material.

Historians of religion often divide its manifestations into two major categories: religions of justification (such as Islam and orthodox Judaism) and religions of salvation (such as the mystery cults and Pauline Christianity). In religions of justification the believer is saved by obeying divine laws. In religions of salvation the faithful are redeemed by a divine act. The central tenet of Pauline Christianity, therefore, is the death and resurrection of Christ. Men are saved by their faith in that event and its implications. The first of these implications is grounded in the Fall: all men, no matter how good before men, are defective before God. The first step in Christian faith, then, is the humble acceptance of this defectiveness. Portia tries to convert Shylock to the belief that without God's merciful intervention none of us would see salvation because none of us entirely merit it: ". . . in the course of justice none of us /Should see salvation; we do pray for mercy" (IV. i. 194–95). Christ's death makes salvation for all men, no matter how good or how bad, possible, however, because that death is God's just payment to Satan for the souls of men.

The death of Christ renders God's justice to the devil; but in the same event God's mercy is granted to all mankind, whose immortal life is foretold in the Resurrection.

A common trope of medieval theology surviving well into the Renaissance and its iconography was the notion of the Four Daughters of God, based on the Psalms: "Mercy and truth are met together; righteousness and peace have kissed each other" (85:10). In the allegorical medieval development of the passage, Mankind is brought before a heavenly parliament, or trial, and saved by the reconciliation of Justice (or Righteousness) and Truth with Mercy and Peace when Christ volunteers to satisfy justice by dying in payment for man's sins. Many iconographic expressions of this trope in the Renaissance can be cited.[15] Still read in classrooms today is the medieval morality play *The Castle of Perseverance* (ca. 1425), where the debate extends over more than four hundred lines. Even in the late seventeenth century a painting (dated 1681) of the entire debate was produced by Johan Lauw.[16] But when the Duke wonderingly asks Shylock how he can expect mercy, rendering none, he is asking a question totally apart from Shylock's religious frame of reference. The Duke has Christ's merciful sacrifice of himself for the sake of mankind in the back of his mind. He is asking Shylock how we can hope to benefit from man's mercy, let alone God's, if we do not ourselves render mercy to other men. Shylock as a self-respecting (and self-justifying) Jew, who obeys both God's laws and the laws of Venice, sees himself as having no need for mercy, either God's or man's, and thus no just obligation to render it to other men. *

But critics of the play have gradually seen that hidden within the issue of Christian mercy here is also the issue of God's justice. Justice and mercy do not simply stand on the opposing sides of a medieval illumination, such as the one in the *Hortus deliciarum,* but are part of a unifying paradox. Neither justice nor mercy—those seeming opposites—can be sacrificed without a diminishing of God's irreducible nature. Christ's death satisfies both the just demands of Satan and mankind's need for mercy. For humans, the further moral implications to Pauline Christianity are to be found in the justice of exchanging mercy for mercy. We partially repay God's mercy to us by our merciful deeds rendered to those God loves, other men. Justice *demands* mercy. This sequence of recognitions and responses can only begin in our humility, our sense of our own inadequacy and dependence before God. If Shylock can only be confronted with that in himself, the Duke's question, and later Portia's similar question, will have meaning for him, because we are meant to see at these points that Shylock does truly believe himself a just man and thus fully justified in demanding strict payment. Without the humble recognition of his own dependence, however, the question about rendering mercy for mercy is nonsense to him. Both his pride and the religious frame of reference assigned him by Shakespeare make it nonsense.

Yet Shakespeare also wants us to see that Shylock does not fully know the experiential meaning of justice, and he makes us literally see this fact by the articles Shylock holds at the climax of the trial. In the probable source, *Il Pecorone,* the Jew brings no more than a razor. But in the play Shylock holds in one hand balances brought to weigh Antonio's flesh and in the other a knife ready to dissect that flesh.[17] Samuel Chew has specifically related the iconographic meaning of these symbols to their iconic use in this play. In *The Virtues Reconciled* Chew points out that Shylock makes the claims of justice, but he does not hold the proper attributes of a sword and scales. Rather he parodies that image by holding a dagger, stock symbol of perfidy, and scales.[18] It has further occurred to me that the scales might even have been held unbalanced in a Renaissance production. In all representations I have seen of Justice personified, invariably as a woman, her scales are perfectly even,[19] but in an allegorical tableau of corrupted Justice (ca. 1515–20), carved in linden wood by Hans Leinberger, the scales are weighted to favor the case of a rich man opposed in law to a poor man (Plate 10).[20] This group of three wooden figures was originally displayed in the courthouse of Nuremberg.[21] The group shows the rich man dipping into his purse for a bribe, while the poor man is reduced to the meager resources of human pity for his defense. Another significant detail for our purposes is the replacement of female Justice by a male judge, also the case with Holbein's corrupt judge in the Dance of Death series of woodcuts (1538),[22] where the issue remains that of wealth versus poverty. Quite obviously literal judges were male at the time, but I sense that Shakespeare may also be playing Shylock, as a false judge, off against Portia, as true Justice grounded in Mercy. A further possible iconic variation is the way the pathetic and impoverished Antonio is set against the wealthy Shylock while the case is being argued before the Duke, a true judge properly full of pity for Antonio. The blocking of this scene so as to relate the various speeches to the shifting iconic patterns possibly intended by Shakespeare could be a tantalizing prospect for a director versed in Renaissance iconography. Such blocking might even end up working in its own right for perhaps purely dramatic reasons. The possibilities are at least worth a try.

In any event, Shylock only claims justice; he does not represent it. Its fullest representation is in the laws, human and divine, which refute him. Shylock's failure to represent justice is further revealed when he is tested by having it imposed upon him instead of being allowed merely to impose it upon others. A full believer in justice would accept its dictates in both directions, both for him and against him. Shylock fails this test when he attempts to mitigate the severe demands of justice upon himself once Portia clarifies the law to his disadvantage. Shylock's attempts to slip out as easily as he can (starting at IV. i. 313) stand in contrast to the frame of Antonio. Early in the scene Antonio is humble before fate, asking no mercy from Shylock and more willing than anyone else to get on with the presumably just sentence.

The theme of Shylock's hypocrisy has run throughout the play until it reaches this climactic point. At our first introduction to him he discusses the arranging of the bond with Bassanio (I. iii), asking how he can get the assurance of Antonio, only to be

surprised by the accidental arrival of his old enemy. Seeing
Antonio at a distance Shylock remarks in an aside to the audience:
"How like a fawning publican he looks! /I hate him for he is a
Christian" (I. iii. 36–37). Yet his first words to Antonio are
". . . Rest you fair, good signior; /Your worship was the last man
in our mouths" (54–55). This fawning welcome in the context of
the aside is a fully dramatic way of conditioning our initial and
lasting view of Shylock's hypocritical character. The word
"mouth" is also a possible serious pun pointing toward the
ultimate cannibalistic demand for Antonio's flesh, but more likely
the word recalls Bassanio's dinner invitation (28). The invitation is
initially refused in the self-righteously expressed name of dietary
laws, but subsequently accepted ". . . in hate, to feed upon /The
prodigal Christian . . ." (II. v. 14–15). In this last speech,
addressed to Jessica, Shylock steps for the moment into the double
stock roles of New Comic miser-father and hungry Roman
parasite, but the most consistent stock characterization he sustains
in the play is that of Jonsonian religious hypocrite in Jewish form.
He is not all that far away from Zeal-of-the-land Busy, in
Bartholomew Fair.

Because he is a religious hypocrite, his not truly believing in
justice becomes an essential paradoxical aspect of Shylock's
inability to believe in or render mercy. Late in the trial scene
Antonio, as foil to Shylock, pleads before the Duke mercifully to
spare Shylock's life, although he himself has received anything but
mercy from Shylock. It is Antonio's idea that part of the lightened
sentence be conversion to Christianity. This "merciful" demand is
possibly the most repugnant detail in the whole play to many
modern readers, including no doubt a good many Christians. It
reeks of coercion of conscience.

Some historians of drama have simply instructed us to accept
this detail as part of the conventional ending produced by a bad
life brought into line at the conclusion of a comedy. Oliver
converts at the end of *As You Like It,* Angelo at the end of *Measure
for Measure,* and so on. But E. M. W. Tillyard has stated a thesis
that might cause us to consider for a moment at least one other
possibility: that Shylock is genuinely converting to Christianity as
a result of Portia's careful construction of the case against him.[23]
Tillyard does not claim that Portia's pleading with Shylock is
having any effect, but he does point out that Portia holds the

THE MERCHANT OF VENICE

trump card of Antonio's salvation from the beginning, that card being the capital punishment assigned by the law to an alien plotting the death of a Venetian citizen if the Duke so decrees. Thus Antonio and his friends could have been saved a great deal of anxiety by an instant rescue effected by Portia's citing of the law, "Antonio in effect not needing any mercy at all," in Tillyard's words.[24] Why then, asks Tillyard, does Portia go on so about mercy in her famous plea to Shylock? The only justification he can see is an attempt on Portia's part to convert Shylock to a belief in Christian mercy, an attempt she abandons when she cites the laws which will save Antonio in any event.

One answer to Tillyard's line of reasoning can be found in the way any lawyer reserves his substantive arguments to the end. It is a legal commonplace that the substantive appeal to the court be saved to the last, after the failure of arguments based on procedure. In other words, if Shylock can be induced to withdraw his claim on Antonio's flesh, the case will be dismissed on the grounds of procedure alone and the substantive case based on the law need never be introduced. Furthermore, the substantive arguments in this case bring with them severe potential punishments for Shylock. If Portia is to embody the mercy she defends as a moral principle she must first allow Shylock to withdraw from the case on his own volition and without penalty.

Yet Tillyard's argument does stimulate an interesting and arguable possibility: that Portia's tactics in this scene have not one but two primary and complementary purposes, the salvation of Antonio *and* the salvation of Shylock. Nor must Portia be seen as abandoning Shylock's salvation when she relentlessly cites the hard laws that defeat his claims on Antonio's flesh. Her pleading with Shylock at the beginning of the trial is an abstract appeal to reason that has no effect on him, but if humility be the entrance to salvation, then her seemingly harsh treatment of him at the end might be regarded as intended to provide an existential experience of that same humility, one designed to let Shylock discover the helplessness and frailty he shares with all men. Yet her earlier arguments should have convinced a less stubborn, more rational man. In them Portia appeals to both the principle of justice claimed by Shylock and the mercy she herself embodies, as in those famous lines so crucial to the whole scheme of Pauline salvation:

> Therefore, Jew,
> Though justice be thy plea, consider this—
> That in the course of justice none of us
> Should see salvation; we do pray for mercy,
> And that same prayer doth teach us all to render
> The deeds of mercy . . . . (IV. i. 192–95)

It is but mere justice to render mercy to men if one expects it from God. But Shylock replies substantially the same way to Portia as he earlier did to the same plea made by the Duke: I am guiltless of crime; I need no mercy from man or God; "My deeds upon my head!" (IV. i. 201). This answer must almost inevitably recall to Shakespeare's audience the traditionally ignorant shout of the Jewish people when Pilate offered them Christ as a Passover dispensation. They demanded Barabbas instead (a figure mentioned at IV. i. 291); Pilate washed his hands of guilt; and the mob shouted for the crucifixion of Christ, saying "His blood be on us" (Matthew 27:25). This detail in the gospel story of Christ's death has been used by Christians to justify the most un-Christ-like treatment of his fellow Jews through the centuries, and it is chilling to know that reference to it has only recently been excised from Catholic liturgy. But, as we know, the absurd belief that somehow the Jews themselves are to be blamed for the killing of God in the form of a Jew was nevertheless one of the less savory beliefs of many centuries, including Shakespeare's.

The Renaissance audience's major recognition in the trial scene would be of Shylock's ignorance of his own human fallibility, and his consequent inevitable dependence on the mercy of men and God. Portia has used a wedge argument for mercy based on the assumedly shared principle of justice, but Shylock's prideful and stubborn belief in his own perfection and sufficiency defeats this valid line of reasoning. The only recourse is to prove existentially to a proud Shylock his own insufficiency. The resulting process figuratively strips Shylock naked for the sake of his own salvation, as Lear is both literally and figuratively stripped naked in the storm scene for the sake of his. In *The Merchant of Venice*, Antonio is instructed by Portia to "lay bare your bosom" (IV. i. 247), and thus he stands like Lear stripped and vulnerable, but like Christ literally stripped for execution. In the case of Shylock, figurative stripping certainly occurs, and it may even have occurred to some extent literally, as we shall see. Portia forces Shylock into a painful recognition of the weakness and the resulting dependence on others he shares with all men. He is stripped of money, the power to revenge himself against his daughter, and even the guarantee of life. Then he is told to convert. This difficult detail in the play can possibly be read in a new way if we accept the view that it is now for the first time psychologically possible for this humbled man truly to convert. Portia does ask him for his specific agreement to the alternative to death to be found in conversion and the other conditions, and he does reply, "I am content" (IV. i. 389). The tone of these words is under the control of a well-trained actor; they can be heartfelt or not depending on the interpretation of Shakespeare's intention here. In clear contrast once again is the probable source, where the defeated Jew wildly tears the bond in a rage. Most crucial is the tone of Shylock's exit speech: "I pray you, give me leave to go from hence; /I am not well; send the deed after me /And I will sign it . . ." (IV. i. 390–92). Shylock can be rendered here, as he usually is, as a broken, pathetic old man; or he can be seen as a man beginning the completion of a genuine conversion to an entirely new framework of values and beliefs, his sickness a "dark night of the soul," an essential phase of true spiritual resurrection. Shakespeare illustrates the entire pattern in *The Tempest*, when Alonso is converted after being led by Prospero through an existential process of spiritual discovery, although the issue of freedom in the tragicomedy makes for a different total effect, as I will explain in Chapter 6.

If we see a spiritual process occurring in Shylock, we will also see that his iconic stage presence shifts from false justice to true repentence. The scales and the knife could easily slip from his hands during the transition, but by what could they be replaced?

The conventional symbols of the penitent were a white gown and a candle. The most famous penitent in Shakespeare is clearly Lady Macbeth in the Act V sleepwalking scene, where she wears a white nightgown and carries a taper. Martha Hester Fleischer has explained this instance of iconic stage imagery, used earlier by Shakespeare in *2 Henry VI* (Dame Eleanor Cobham in II. iv). In Heywood's *2 Henry IV* the stage directions call for a penitent Mistress Jane Shore to enter *"in a white sheet, barefooted, with her haire about her eares, and in her hand a waxe taper."* According to Fleischer, in *Macbeth* "you should perceive at once the ironic reference to the conventional scene of penance. Lady Macbeth still will not admit to remorse; but when her conscious mind is no longer in control, when she is asleep, her burden of guilt forces her to do endless and fruitless penance."[25] Fleischer may have known, but does not mention, another clarifying instance, one from *The Merchant of Venice*. When Jessica escapes the hellcastle of her devil-father she disguises herself as a boy and passes through the streets in the role of a torchbearer to her Christian lover Lorenzo, himself disguised for a masque:

> *Lor.* Descend, for you must be my torch-bearer.
> *Jes.* What! must I hold a candle to my shames?
> They in themselves, good sooth, are too too light.
> Why, 'tis an office of discovery, love,
> And I should be obscur'd. . . . (II. vi. 40–44)

This chapter already includes its share of guesses, but if the reader will indulge a final hypothesis, we might consider the possibility that in the original production of the trial scene Shylock defined Shakespeare's intention more clearly with his appearance than with his words. He might have left the stage with a candle, perhaps one introduced by a recording clerk earlier in the trial. As for the white garment, it might have been exposed earlier in a scuffle when it seems that Shylock is the one to be executed. A richer outer cloak could have been pulled away to reveal an undergarment of white. When Portia tells Shylock that if he sheds blood or takes more than precisely one pound of flesh he will die, Gratiano exalts, "Now, infidel, I have you on the hip" (IV. i. 329). That Gratiano may be speaking literally about this hold in wrestling preparatory to the throw is suggested two lines later when Shylock pleads, "let me go." The male penitent would be a variation on the more common iconographic form of a female, standing in the tradition of the Magdalene (Luke 7:37–50). But it is Shakespeare who gives us clear iconic male instances in the penance of Claudio at the tomb of Hero (*Much Ado*, V. iii), where *"three or foure with tapers"* (Q–1600; sig. I2v) are men, addressed as "masters," who watch with Claudio through the night. As for the white garment of a male penitent, a toga is surely meant by the stage directions of *Coriolanus* in the scene (II. iii) where the protagonist must stand in the *"gowne of Humility"* (F1–"Trage-dies," p. 12).

The final act of *The Merchant of Venice* brings two possible reinforcements for what I have been suggesting. When Portia and Nerissa approach Belmont, the returning mistress comments, "That light we see is burning in my hall. /How far that little candle throws his beams! /So shines a good deed in a naughty world" (V. i. 89–91). The dramatic context does far less to justify the presence of this passage than its biblical and theological allusiveness. Much has been written recently about the doubling of Shakespeare's actors; what a delightful opportunity for the "doubling" of an iconic stage property. The same candle (of a significant and memorable color) could be used by Jessica (whose "torch" is a candle) and her father Shylock; and it could finally reappear in Portia's "hall." As for a concluding hint of a new spiritual course for Shylock, Nerissa's last words report that Lorenzo has been made his father-in-law's beneficiary, by "a special deed of gift," nor is there any suggestion at this point of coercion.

Penance and loving forgiveness are the chords in the joyful harmony of the universe symbolized in the conventional theme of the music of the spheres, so familiar to all students of the Renaissance. That music is introduced into the last act as an iconic stage image when Lorenzo concludes his lovemaking to Jessica accompanied by sweet music. Much earlier in the play Shylock expressed his irritation at the music played in the streets to accompany the masquers to their revels:

> Jessica:
> Lock up my doors, and when you hear the drum,
> And the vile squealing of the wry-neck'd fife,
> Clamber not you up to the casements then,
> Nor thrust your head into the public street
> To gaze on Christian fools with varnish'd faces;
> But stop my house's ears—I mean my casements;
> Let not the sound of shallow fopp'ry enter
> My sober house. . . . (II. v. 27–35)

Neoplatonic doctrine asserts the baseness of those who dislike music, the nobility of those who respond to its harmonies. The harmonious soul must be attracted to music, the disordered soul repelled. As Lorenzo tells Jessica in his famous aria:

> The man that hath no music in himself,
> Nor is not mov'd by concord of sweet sounds,
> Is fit for treasons, stratagems, and spoils;
> The motions of his spirit are dull as night,
> And his affections dark as Erebus.
> Let no such man be trusted. . . . (V. i. 83–88)

Were men capable of perfection they might even hear the heavenly music created by the stars and planets following the course of their proper orbits, but the flesh holds even the best men back from perfection. The Christian adaptation was to identify the music of the spheres with the supernal hymns of joy created by the seraphim and cherubim around the throne of God. The transition was in the identification of the stars and the planets with angels. Thus souls enjoying the fruits of salvation would one day hear the seraphic hymns of praise, but the enjoyment of music on earth was a prelude.[26] The harmony begins within the natural soul, as Lorenzo implies to Jessica at the beginning of his aria when he cites the effect of music upon wild animals. First established in individual souls, the harmony can then occur among men. The masquers are accompanied to their revels by musicians; Bassanio chooses the correct casket to music and after a song is sung; and Lorenzo makes love to Jessica while music plays.

All the seemingly disparate lines of action in *The Merchant of Venice* are harmonized both by the repeated union of contraries and by recurrent themes: the virtue of humility tested by the caskets and lacking in an unjust Shylock, whose unchallenged pride blinds him to his own need for mercy; the merciful forgiveness of Shylock by Antonio and Bassanio by Portia when her ring is given away; the friendship that brings Antonio to the verge of dying for Bassanio and Bassanio to the offering of the ring as a reward for saving Antonio's life; and the true justice of forgiving others in the hopeful expectation of receiving merciful forgiveness for one's own inevitable imperfections. These and many other chords in the play create a unified harmony linking heaven and earth.

In concluding his play Shakespeare returns to the heavenly music he introduced with the inspired casket, but *The Merchant of Venice* is far from the only play with iconic musical resonance.

Surely the most familiar instance of all is during the reconciliation of Cordelia and Lear; and my next chapter will attempt to show how the culmination of Richard II's spiritual maturation is in the midst of music.

3

Richard II: Second Adam

Richard II is like a medieval French tapestry or an engraved suit of Renaissance armor; its beauty stimulates connoisseurs to remark upon the exquisite finish of its details: the artful weaving together of the historical sources or the golden inlay of the verse. A vast amount of historical detail is sewn into the fabric of the play, and marvelous poetry is richly bestowed upon a poet-king. *Richard II* remains a play for all that—neither chronicle nor lyric, but an action for the stage. Behind the arras is Sir Pierce of Exton; within the armor is Richard of Bordeaux. Beneath the glitter of his verse is the durable metal of sixteenth-century devotional literature. Suffused with blood and tears, references to the Crucifixion, and the meditations of a fated king, the play renders the psychological reality of spiritual growth in the midst of physical loss and decay. Richard falls as a king, only to rise as a man, one who finally speaks the language of a tormented body releasing an emergent soul. All the verbal and stage images center on Richard. Bolingbroke, laconic and withdrawn, seems more like the foil, the shadow to Richard's substance, when viewed within the symbolic deep structure of the play.

The grammar of the play as a play, however, as dramatic irony, is quite different. There Bolingbroke is the substance of a king, politic and self-controlled, his iron will focused on a single goal—the achievement and defense of a crown. The degree to which Bolingbroke is meant to be aiming for the crown from the very beginning of the play is admittedly the subject of considerable

critical controversy. But Richard's involvement in the murder of
Woodstock is known or suspected by everyone; and the widow,
Gaunt, and York are specifically shown by Shakespeare to be in on
the open secret. This juxtaposition of early scenes can make an
audience feel that Bolingbroke is meant to be seen as perfectly
aware of the acute embarrassment his challenge to Mowbray will
cause Richard. Also remember that Bolingbroke is reported back
in England before he could have known of Richard's confiscation
of his inheritance (II. i). Shakespeare probably wants us to see
Bolingbroke as Richard's implacable rival and enemy from the
very beginning, whatever may be subsequently proclaimed to the
contrary by the oath-breaking Bolingbroke and his supporters.
Herein lies one of the primary bases of dramatic irony throughout
the play, but especially the first half.[1] Richard, on the other hand,
is on a dramatic level the mere shadow of monarchy: vain,
impulsive, and arrogant, regal only in his eloquence and his
beauty.

But when the mind's eye searches the symbolic levels reaching
beyond the dramatic ironies, it is Richard who dominates every
scene, whether we see him on stage or not, and Bolingbroke who
fades into the shadows. That this was also Shakespeare's intention
is expressed in the way he has reserved all the most emphatic
iconic images for Richard. These images are in turn anchored to a
rich deposit of religious associations drawing Shakespeare's contemporaries into a fundamental acceptance of Richard as a
god-king. Although his fall is the fall of a man, it could only occur
in a fallen world, a world capable of crucifying God himself.

In this play, especially, the stage images are closely linked to the
most recurrent verbal images. Particularly noteworthy are images
of blushing and pallor, blood and tears, and sun and water. The
events of the play are based on the circumstances leading up to the
exhausting and fratricidal Wars of the Roses. As is known to every
student of English history, the "red rose" of the House of Lancaster
was opposed to the "white rose" of the House of York in the years
that followed Richard's deposition, and thus the color symbolism
of the opposition of red and white is both especially appropriate
and especially well understood by critics. Richard blushes or turns
pale on several occasions. Gaunt's admonitions on his death bed
"Make pale" the king's "cheek, chasing the royal blood /With fury
from his native residence." When Salisbury brings news of the

defection of the Welsh (III. ii), Richard says: "But now the blood
of twenty thousand men /Did triumph in my face, and they are
fled; /And, till so much blood thither come again, /Have I not
reason to look pale and dead?" But Richard also blushes, "As doth
the blushing discontented sun," when Bolingbroke's military
return to England brings the king to the walls of Flint Castle. Even
the "pale-fac'd moon looks bloody on the earth" (II. iv. 10) to the
superstitious Welsh.[2] Whether the blushing and paleness characterizing Richard illustrate verbal or stage imagery depends on the
control an actor has over his body. Actors have been known to
control both tears and blushing. Even so, in instances such as these
an audience will see largely what it is told to see. And thus we
might consider the possibility of psychological stage imagery: the
stage "presence" of an imagined iconic reality, such as the love
garden of the Capulets or the chaotic storm raised by Prospero.
Despite fake trees, or the thunder produced by a cannonball
rolling down a trough, the audience will invariably imagine most
of what it "sees."

Perhaps the roses of York and Lancaster also help to explain
why Shakespeare returns so often to blood and tears in establishing
a religious atmosphere of spiritual growth for Richard. Richard
was the last Plantagenet fully invested with hereditary credibility,
the last king before the civil wars to combine the blood of the two
subsequent houses. It was not until the marriage of Henry VII
with Elizabeth of York that those two streams of blood were
theoretically combined once again in the birth of Henry VIII.

Blood goes through a wide range of meanings in the play, like
"nature" in *Lear*. It can be hot with anger (as in I. i. 51),
significantly royal (as in I. i. 71), or even literal (as in I. i. 157). It is
most memorable, however, when it is associated with sacrifice and
the family. In the speech of Woodstock's widow to John of Gaunt
in Act I, scene ii, Edward's seven sons are seen by her as vials of
sacred blood. The church kept the blood of saints and martyrs in
crystal vials for the veneration of the faithful; the sons are then
both saints and reliquaries, as well as "seven fair branches
springing from one root." One of these, Woodstock, has been cut
by "murder's bloody axe."

The implied parallel is the Tree of Jesse, a standard subject for
stained glass windows in English churches and cathedrals, with
extant examples at Wells Cathedral and in Dorchester Abbey, near

Oxford. The root was Jesse, the trunk David, the final bloom Christ, the authority Isaiah and the first chapter of the Gospel according to Saint Matthew. Based on the prophecy in Isaiah 11:1–3 ("And there shall come forth a rod out of the stem of Jesse, and a branch shall grow out of his roots . . ."), the descent of Christ from Jesse was traced through his royal son David in order to accommodate the first chapter of Matthew. Christ was born of the House of David, the most distinguished family among God's Chosen People. Not only is he the son of God, but his genealogy puts him foremost among the sons of men. The sanction for his kingship comes from both God and man. Most of the medieval and Renaissance stained glass windows showing the popular Jesse Tree stressed the imposing array of kings who stood between Jesse and Christ.[3] The image of Christ as a carpenter's son did not become popular until the nineteenth century. Nor was Christ's descent from kings confined to stained-glass windows. The title page of *A Booke of Christian Prayers* (London, 1578), attributed to Richard Day, expresses one of the popular commonplaces of the day when it shows Christ descended from twelve kings, including Solomon, Ahaz, and Manasses. These kings are arrayed on two branches springing from Jesse, with a culminating Virgin and Child, supported by a rose, at the top. Joseph, the parent to whom Christ owed his descent from Jesse according to Matthew, is excluded from this illustrious family (Plate 11).

The widowed Duchess of Gloucester applies the submerged Tree of Jesse metaphor to her slain husband Woodstock. In this way she imbues his death with the infamy shared not only by the fratricide of Abel but by the crucifixion of Christ. The blood of Woodstock lives in his brother Gaunt; therefore, he has all the more reason to avenge so foul a crime. But Gaunt replies to his sister-in-law in a way that puts the implied metaphor back into its proper frame of reference. Like Christ, the king relies on human and divine sanctions, human in his royal ancestry and divine in his consecration. That consecration was effected by anointing with oil in the manner of Old Testament prophets anointing kings, as Samuel anointed David to the future kingship. The revenge of Woodstock's murder is impossible because its proper object is the king, divinely appointed chief magistrate of the realm. Killing him would suggest the sin shared by the murderers of Christ.

Gaunt, of course, does not need to explain everything that I have just explained. The concepts have already been introduced in the ironic framework of the Duchess of Gloucester's call to revenge by stressing the obligations within a family tree, stated in terms bringing to mind the royal and sanctified Tree of Jesse. Gaunt's few words answer her arguments by metaphor and analogy with the directness of aphorism:

> God's is the quarrel; for God's substitute,
> His deputy anointed in His sight,
> Hath caus'd his death; the which if wrongfully,
> Let heaven revenge; for I may never lift
> An angry arm against His minister. (I. ii. 37–41)

No matter how bad the king might be as a man, divinity shrouds him from harm, as it would a priest. Both retain the power for the performance of divine offices, the priest of the mass, the king of rule.

As the Reformation in England developed during the sixteenth century, however, priests were becoming far more accountable to the king and to the people, and kings far less accountable to the lords. The concept of sacred inviolability did not disappear; it simply went somewhere else. The anachronism in the Jesse parallel is the first strong hint of Shakespeare's intention to make of Richard a sanctified monarch springing from the tree of the Plantagenets. Regarding the royal family as blooms on a Jesse Tree originated not in Richard's time but in the time of the Tudors. After its invention, however, this Tudor iconography was to be found everywhere. Easily the most popular motif in the intricate designs sewn on Elizabethan clothing was the tree with flowers, or fruit, or both. The most popular flower in these designs was, of course, the red and white Tudor rose. The influences seem to be both the Tree of Jesse and the Indian Tree of Life.[4]

On his second visit to England, in the 1530s, Holbein the Younger joined the forces employed by the lethal enemy of his former patron, Sir Thomas More. These forces were the intellectuals employed by Henry VIII to develop what is now commonly known as the "Tudor myth." Among other artistic services, Holbein designed a title page for Edward Halle's later editions of his chronicles, occasionally cited as a minor source for *Richard II* and certainly known to Shakespeare. The title page is modeled on the Jesse Tree. Two branches support the leading historical figures of the Wars of the Roses. The title of the third edition (London, 1550) describes the figure at the top of the tree as "the high and prudent Prince Kyng Henry the eyght, the indubstate flower and very heire of both" lineages of York and Lancaster (Plate 12.) As we know, Henry VIII's mother was Elizabeth of York; his father, Henry VII, descended (in a rather tortuous way) from John of Gaunt, Duke of Lancaster, and his third wife, Catherine Swynford. Bolingbroke was the offspring of Gaunt's first marriage, to Blanche of Lancaster. Because the Tudors were descended from Gaunt's third marriage and Bolingbroke from the first, Shakespeare was not in danger of stepping on any toes in depicting Bolingbroke as a usurper who drove full legitimacy from the English throne until it was restored by Henry VII in his marriage to Elizabeth. At this point in English history a Jesse Tree parallelism was made to work for the Tudors. Just as Christ was more king than carpenter, the king came to share the authority of Christ, as we have seen from the title page of Halle's chronicles, where two branches rise to a single culmination in Henry VIII, at the top. Nor did this myth disappear in the succeeding reigns. In the year of Elizabeth's coronation (1559), a Jesse Tree designed to symbolize the uniting of the houses of Lancaster and York was erected in Gracious Street to honor the new queen.[5]

The artful assimilation of older religious orthodoxy into the Tudor's new religion of the state is fundamental to the sources of the double tetralogy, from *Richard II* to *Richard III*.[6] These eight plays thus became as much a tapestry of praise to the Tudors as were the hangings in the vastly enlarged palace of Whitehall. This royal residence was once York Place, the London residence of the Archbishop of York, but in Henry VIII's reign it was the new cathedral of state. The coronation of the English monarch had become revitalized as a quasi sacrament, helping to fill the vacuum created by Reformation opposition to the five traditional sacraments not sanctioned by the Bible.[7] According to the Ten Articles (1536), the first articles of faith issued by the Church of England during the Reformation period, only baptism, penance, and the eucharist are upheld as sacraments. Some restoration of Catholic doctrine occurred in the Six Articles (1539) and the King's Book (1543), but in the Thirty-nine Articles (1563), Article 25 defines only baptism and the eucharist as sacraments "ordained of God." The other five are carefully left in limbo.[8] Among those five, marriage retained its power still, although it had not quite the same status it was given at the Council of Trent. Shakespeare uses its traditional power to augment the sanctity of coronation when Richard answers Northumberland's insistence that the king and his queen part, he to Pomfret and she to France: ". . . you violate /A twofold marriage—'twixt my crown and me, /And then betwixt me and my married wife" (V. i. 71–73). As for the two biblical sacraments, baptism and communion, Richard invokes his baptism, the sacramental confirmation of his ancestry (he seems to be saying), when he rhetorically denies his name and title to Northumberland in the deposition scene:

> No lord of thine, thou haught insulting man,
> Nor no man's lord; I have no name, no title—
> No, not that name was given me at the font—
> But 'tis usurp'd. Alack the heavy day,
> That I have worn so many winters out,
> And know not now what name to call myself!
> O that I were a mockery king of snow,
> Standing before the sun of Bolingbroke
> To melt myself away in water drops! (IV. i. 254–62)

This passage is but one of many in which several patterns of imagery coalesce. The name of king and the water of baptism melt into a man of snow melted in turn by the risen sun of the usurper whose presence melts Richard into tears.

Gaunt's sentiments about Richard's divine right of kingship, as mentioned already, are largely anachronistic to the fourteenth century, just as the Gaunt of history is almost totally different from the Gaunt of *Richard II*. The sentiments of Shakespeare's Gaunt are those created by the new theology of sixteenth-century England, when the king replaced the pope as the final authority in discipline and doctrine, and the throne of William the Conqueror rather than the throne of Peter was the source of ultimate power, both temporal and spiritual. Thomas Starkey, the chaplain to Henry VIII, laid the foundations of the new doctrine of royal supremacy. In his *Exhortation to Unity and Obedience* (1536), he followed the lead of Melanchthon (1497–1560), the successor to Luther as apologist for the new Protestant nations of northern Europe. According to Starkey, things good are defined by God's word in scripture, things bad by God's prohibition in scripture, and things indifferent by their absence from scripture. Papal authority is not explicitly expressed in the Bible; therefore, it is subject to time and place, "sometymes good, sometymes yll." As for sixteenth-century England, it is "yll," and the king must provide the authority once held by the pope.[9] Whitehall was the new cathedral, the Privy Chamber the place of ex cathedra pronouncements—still literally "from the chair," but now a chair of state, the throne of England. Above the throne in the Privy Chamber Holbein painted a family portrait of Henry VII, Elizabeth of York, Henry VIII, and Jane Seymour, third wife of Henry VIII and mother of Edward VI. The union of the two houses was the new Donation of Constantine, this time in reverse, with the church giving itself to the empire, instead of the empire giving itself to the church.[10] With the weight of the Tudor myth shaping the play, no wonder J. Dover Wilson feels a powerful undertow of ritual throughout *Richard II:* it "ought to be played throughout as ritual. As a work of art it stands far closer to the Catholic service of the Mass than to Ibsen's *Brand* or Bernard Shaw's *Saint Joan.* "[11]

It is well known that Shakespeare did not compose *Richard II* first among his double tetralogy, but this play is nevertheless first, in a sense, both in its delineation of first historical causes and in its stated and implied political theology. *Richard II* is consistent with the assumptions on which the other histories, no matter what their order of composition, are based. The first assumption is that the Tudors are the saviors of England, the second that all power concludes in the crown they wear, and the third that the rituals surrounding the person of the king have the sacred authority of rituals occurring within a cathedral.

Eden and the Place of Skulls

Richard is the dominant iconic stage image in the play, the real presence, the incarnation of divine kingship, as central to the limited context of English history as Christ is to the broader context of sacred history. With all his imperfections, he is authority made flesh and dwelling among his subjects. The Second Coming, nevertheless, was to occur with Henry VII, the truly Christ-like Richmond of *Richard III,* perfect as man and king. From this second point of view, Richmond is to be a Second Adam, restoring the losses of Richard II as a First Adam. In the course of the play Shakespeare emphatically casts Richard II as both Adam and Christ, and thus as both First and Second Adams. That a quasi-divine monarch is to be viewed paradoxically as an Adam falling from grace and corrupting his garden is well established in the play. Gaunt's famous praise of England (II. i), memorized by English schoolboys to this day, describes the ". . . precious stone set in the silver sea, /Which serves it in the office of a wall," as an "other Eden, demi-paradise." "As is the sepulchre in stubborn Jewry /Of the world's ransom, blessed Mary's Son," it "Is now leas'd out . . . /. . . /. . . now bound in with shame." Shakespeare returns to the metaphor of England as Eden, fallen into ruin because of an inattentive gardener, in the iconic verbal and stage imagery of the garden scene at Langley. This famous scene immediately follows the climax of the play, Richard's tragic fall to the condition of Bolingbroke's virtual prisoner, occurring at Flint Castle. The queen has been awaiting news of her husband's fate. She seeks distraction in the garden only to overhear the gardener describe Richard's capture by Bolingbroke. Springing from hiding, she berates the gardener:

> Thou, old Adam's likeness, set to dress this garden,
> How dares thy harsh rude tongue sound this unpleasing news?
> What Eve, what serpent, hath suggested thee
> To make a second fall of cursed man?
> Why dost thou say King Richard is depos'd? (III. iv. 73–77)

The gardener and Richard are thus concentrated into a single Adam. Richard fell, according to the gardener, when he neglected "our sea-walled garden." The sense of the hortus conclusus, the enclosed gardens of Eden and England, is echoed from Gaunt's earlier speech.[12] Richard was warned in Gaunt's subsequent advice to him, as Adam was clearly warned by God; both fell. As the gardener says of Richard, ". . . O, what a pity is it /That he had not so trimm'd and dress'd his land /As we this garden! . . ." The queen describes his ruin as "a second fall of cursed man." Paul was the authority for the concept of Christ as a Second Adam.[13] The connections are more associational than logical, more paradoxical than discursive, but Shakespeare clearly wants us to see in Richard both Adam and Christ. Furthermore, as

Christ, he is meant both to be sent by God and to be the offspring of man, somehow both divine and human.

Overarching the entire fundamental religious symbolism of this play is the medieval iconographic commonplace of the three trees of Eden, Jesse, and Calvary.[14] Richard is fallen Adam, sanctified king, and ultimately crucified Christ.

The parallel between Richard and Christ is strengthened at several points, especially in Act IV, so that it carries, as a whole, far more weight than it does in those dramatic instances where Richard claims a Messianic authority for himself. Critics are right to see that Richard proclaiming himself a Christ is usually expressing self-dramatization, self-pity, or self-righteous indignation. But Shakespeare also intends the multiple levels of symbolism to include an anagogical level taken seriously. The truly religious implications of the parallel are confirmed by the attitudes and language of John of Gaunt and then the Bishop of Carlisle. Before Richard's deposition, the Bishop of Carlisle warns that England shall be called "The field of Golgotha and dead men's skulls" as the result of the civil wars sure to come. Richard's words upon his subsequent entry, guarded by his former courtiers, should be heard as a dramatic echo to Carlisle:

> Yet I well remember
> The favours of these men. Were they not mine?
> Did they not sometime cry, 'All hail!' to me?
> So Judas did to Christ; but he, in twelve,
> Found truth in all but one; I, in twelve thousand, none.
> God save the King! Will no man say amen?
> Am I both priest and clerk? Well then, amen.
> God save the King! (IV. i. 167–74)

The union of the sacred and the human is expressed here in the familiar prayer, "God save the King!" Within the context of Richard's comparison of his former subjects to Judas is Richard's own need for salvation. He no longer hears his traitorous subjects cry "God save the King," but in saying it for himself he confesses his own need for God's salvation. His double nature is further underlined by his need to enact the roles of both ordained priest and appointed clerk, "both priest and clerk." The nature of the king parallels the nature of Christ, both God and man; the nature of Richard parallels the nature of Adam, both God-appointed to tend his garden and fallen to the state of sinful man in need of God's salvation. In this speech Shakespeare has probed Richard's double nature as deeply as he ever will, but he brings the parallel between the king and Christ back to the mind of the audience on at least two subsequent occasions.

The first of these is very obvious. In the deposition scene, Richard compares his persecutors to Pilate: "Though some of you, with Pilate, wash your hands, /Showing an outward pity—yet you Pilates /Have here deliver'd me to my sour cross, /And water cannot wash away your sin" (IV. i. 239–42). The second occasion is very understated. When Northumberland tries to part Richard and the queen in order to convey the guarded and perhaps bound Richard to Pomfret Castle, Richard attacks Northumberland by warning him that he will never be trusted by Bolingbroke. The principle of precedence, so important an issue in the play, applies here. Having helped to destroy one king, Northumberland will always be feared by the new one. The reply is terse: "My guilt be on my head, and there an end. /Take leave, and part; for you must part forthwith" (V. i. 69–70). With the words, "My guilt be on my head," Shakespeare's audience was probably being instructed to think of the ecce homo episode in the life of Christ, a popular subject of devotion.[15] Once again, as in *The Merchant of Venice,* the persecutor of a Christ figure welcomes the responsibility. As for the sequence of events surrounding this episode in Christ's Passion —the flagellation, presentation before the mob a first and second time, and crowning with thorns—the Gospel accounts do not agree. Our concern, however, is the visual conventions of the ecce homo, which emerge in the late Middle Ages as one result of the mystical interpretation of Christ's Passion as a series of psychological stages. The earliest example of the ecce homo subject dates from the tenth century, but it is not fully popularized until the cheapness of graphic art in the sixteenth century makes wide distribution of the image possible in Northern Europe. A Dürer ecce homo, from the *Engraved Passion* (published 1513), is still famous (Plate 13). In the usual renderings Christ is nearly naked but for the mockery of a purple robe and a crown of thorns, his body is scarred by flagellation, his head is bloody, and his sorrowful face is wet with tears. He stands with head bowed and hands tied or clasped before him.[16] The scourged Christ is offered freedom by Pilate if the people will choose him as a Passover dispensation. Christ is brought before the people to behold, but (as we recall) they want Barabbas instead, whose name suggests a robber, although Luke describes him as a revolutionist. Pilate washes his hands of guilt in the fate of Christ, and the people shout, "His blood be on us." The devotional image of a suffering Christ before the mob, the ecce homo, implies the question, "Which do *you*, the beholder, choose?" Northumberland's terse reply, like Shylock's self-justification in the trial scene ("My deeds upon my head"), probably sent a shudder through Shakespeare's English audience.[17] In his few words Northumberland joins Judas and the mob as betrayer and crucifier, and he accepts his roles with the full consciousness of the implications for himself: "My guilt be on my head, and there an end." As for Richard, if he assumes the conventional posture of Christ in the innumerable versions of the ecce homo, head bowed and hands tied or clasped before him, the iconic stage image would reinforce its probable iconic verbal context.

Another aspect of the ecce homo is the image it portrays of a suffering Christ. Second only to the image of the Crucifixion itself in this regard, the figure of the beheld Christ is rendered in Renaissance art to express a full range of psychological and physical pain. Richard undergoes his noblest mental suffering thus far in the trial of the deposition scene, just as Christ suffers similar preparatory anguish in the Garden of Gethsemane and the trial before Pilate. In both instances trusted followers betray their lord. Other events add physical suffering. Christ is scourged and Richard is heaped with dust and rubbish. For Christ, the ecce homo episode epitomizes both kinds of suffering. His face in the Dürer is grief-stricken by the betrayal of those he has loved and trusted, here overwhelmingly recalled in the mob's rejection of him. He wears a mock crown of thorns, causing his flesh to bleed. Christ's body, partially clothed by the purple robe of a king, is covered with the scars of the whip, imposed during his flagellation, another popular meditational subject. Tears, expressing his full range of suffering, stand in his eyes. He is truly the "man of sorrows, and acquainted with grief" foretold by Isaiah. Tears, both literal and figurative, are highly recurrent in *Richard II*. In another recollection of the circumstances of the ecce homo, York weepingly describes to his duchess the arrival of Bolingbroke and Richard in London after the deposition of the king at Westminster. The duke is overcome by emotion when he comes to the detail of the mob throwing "dust and rubbish on King Richard's head" (V. ii. 6). The fickle crowd is clearly for the hero of the moment. All cry, "God save thee, Bolingbroke," none "God save" Richard. Rather, ". . . dust was thrown upon his sacred head; /Which with such gentle sorrow he shook off, /His face still combating with tears and smiles, /The badges of his grief and patience" (V. ii. 30–33). Shakespeare underlines the natural associations between the tear-stained face of Richard, described by York, and Christ as the Man of Sorrows when he has York imagine the walls of the houses along the street covered with "painted imagery" declaring "Jesu preserve thee! Welcome Bolingbroke!" (V. ii. 17). A similar irony would have occurred had the mob shouted, "Jesu preserve thee, good Barabbas," when he was offered as Passover alternative to Christ.

Darkness was falling over the face of England, as if Paradise were suffering a second fall and the Place of Skulls a new crucifixion. The sun would not fully shine again until England was redeemed by a new Christ, the Earl of Richmond, whose Tudor blood and flesh made the red and white of Lancaster and York incarnate. So went the well-known "Tudor myth." Yet Shakespeare is also enlarging and refining the assumptions of this "myth" in the course of his histories and, to some extent, his tragedies. A crucial difference between the civil wars led by Bolingbroke and Richmond, for instance, is that Hereford is violating the sacred oath of allegiance he took at Richard's coronation, an event whose sacramental and irrevocable nature was attested in part by that very oath. Both Richmond and Macduff, on the other hand, flee the nation rather than be among those pledging fealty at Westminster and Scone. These truly good men refuse to witness the anointing of illicit kings. The clear refusal of an oath and the willingness to bear the sacrifices of self-imposed exile give Henry Tudor and the Thane of Fife the moral cause which permits successful opposition to an established ruler in battle without calling down the wrath of divine providence upon the historical consequences. Bolingbroke breaks not only his coronation oath but other oaths as well, as we are reminded more than once in the *Henry* plays, and these violations of one's word to God seem to make the essential difference between right and wrong in Shakespeare's understanding of British history.

Another way in which we can be confused by Shakespeare's attitudes toward Richard's kingship and Bolingbroke's usurpation is the blurred view modern Christians have toward the divine authority Christ held in earlier centuries. For Christians today the Son's divinity is largely based on his ideal teaching and behavior, if believers incline one direction, and on his Miracles and Resurrection if they incline another. It is not that Richard the King is primarily *like* Christ in either personality or power—quite the opposite in both cases—but that he has the *authority* of Christ. As a man, however, Richard is meant to be seen by the audience as suffering like Christ, and thus undergoing human maturation, as I will develop more fully toward the end of this chapter. Christ suffered indignation inappropriate to a man, let alone someone with the authority that comes from God. The anointed Richard, whose coronation was accepted by all, shares that authority for a number of reasons unrelated to his all-too-human fallibility. His sanctions are quite simply his Plantagenet blood, his nomination by Edward III, his coronation, and the oaths of his nobility. For these reasons, not because of his merits, his divinely ordained place is upon the throne of majesty; and woe to England when he falls.

Fall of the Sun

Other paradigms, derived from pre-Christian mythology, are fundamental to *Richard II* as well. The Renaissance was familiar with the four standard classical falls of Ixion, Tantalus, Icarus, and Phaeton. Richard is presented to the audience as a type ,of Christ, an Adam, and finally a classical sun-king. As sun-king he is linked to the familiar myth of Phaeton. In the third scene of Act III the *"trumpets sound"* and the king *"appeareth on the walls"* of Flint Castle (Q1–1597; sig. F4v). Richard hesitates to abandon the only protection he has left, the castle walls represented by the upper stage of the public playhouse in which the play was first performed. He is thus "above," awaiting the arrival of Bolingbroke "below." Fortune has caused the defection of everyone Richard had trusted—the superstitious Welsh, the fickle common people, an overtaxed Parliament, and the vacillating vice-regent, York. Yet Richard still appears at least to retain Fortune's Castle. As I recalled in my preface, Dame Fortune is most often associated by

students of the Renaissance with a wheel carrying her favorites up
to the heights and her victims down to the depths. Less familiar is
her association with a castle, with worldly aspirants climbing its
walls and the defeated falling from its battlements. For example,
an anonymous sixteenth-century Italian woodblock shows a castle
much like that of Sant' Angelo in Rome, surmounted by Fortune,
with aspirants climbing the walls (Plate 14).[18] Even though no
mere physical stronghold is sufficient to defend a crown, Richard
seems to retain the proper position of a king, at the top of the
castle. York is immediately impressed with the first glimpse of the
man he once served: ". . . looks he like a king. Behold, his eye,
/As bright as is the eagle's, lightens forth /Controlling majesty . . ." (III. iii. 68–70). The king still has the magic of his
position, figurative and literal. Bolingbroke must destroy even that
if he is to gain total power, and he sends Northumberland to
request Richard to "come down." Richard knows that the seeming
request will quickly become physical force if he resists. He thinks it
better to put off that indignity for the moment, and thus he
complies, but not without full awareness of what compliance of
king to "traitor's call" really means. We all know his famous lines:

> Down, down I come, like glist'ring Phaethon,
> Wanting the manage of unruly jades.
> In the base court? Base court, where kings grow base,
> To come at traitors' calls, and do them grace.
> In the base court? Come down? Down, court! down, king!
> For night-owls shriek where mounting larks should sing.
>   (III. iii. 178–83)

Within this passage coalesce the most important rise and fall
patterns of imagery in the play: the many iconic stage images of
literal rise and fall, in this case from the heights of Fortune's Castle
to its base court, from the upper stage to the lower stage; the
passage from day to night, verbally recalled at several key points in
the play; and the closely related association of Richard with the
sun, a sun-king glorious in appearance, who nevertheless falls
through folly, like Phaeton, the impetuous son of Apollo.[19]
Phaeton insisted on driving his father's sun-chariot through the sky
before he had the skill to manage its fiery steeds. The car plunged,
the sun burned the Sahara dry and the Africans black, and
Phaeton fell to earth. Phaeton's fall was second only to the fall of

Icarus as a popular subject of didactic Renaissance paintings and graphics. The fall of Phaeton is one of four classical falls engraved by Henrik Goltzius, the Dutch painter, probably in 1588 (Plate 15).[20] The greater popularity of Icarus perhaps resulted from his wings, which suggest a direct parallel with the fall of Satan, a winged angel. For the Renaissance, Icarus illustrated how the sun (God) will melt the waxen wings (Pride) when the proud aspirant flies too high. The moral was the same as the one drawn by Boccaccio in his famous de casibus series of tragedies: if you do not aspire to the heights you will not fall to the depths. Phaeton's fall, however, was probably much more terrifying to the Renaissance than the fall of Icarus, because it was cosmic. The sun itself fell with Phaeton, an event even greater than the world falling with man in *Paradise Lost.* And, as we know, the sun is frequently associated throughout the history of mankind with God's power and authority at the center of his creation. When Richard falls, the kingdom falls, for Richard is both man and divinely appointed authority. There can be no question of aspiration before destruction, for Richard is never any higher than he ought to be, by birth and by coronation. Shakespeare uses the Phaeton image to stress the parallel destruction of political and cosmic orders in Bolingbroke's usurpation of sovereignty. The climax of *Richard II* prefigures the climax of *King Lear,* where the heavens, the state, the family, and Lear's mind all fall to ruin in a single cataclysm.

Much critical interpretation stresses Richard's tendencies toward self-dramatization and self-pity. He is surely meant by Shakespeare to be a man who brings his fall upon himself, a fall all the greater because he is a human being who happens to be king. Richard is the rewarder of flattery rather than merit, disrespectful of age and hereditary rights, arbitrary in the gathering of taxes, weak in war, and apparently the direct cause of his own uncle's murder; all these crimes and follies spring from defects of vanity, love of luxury, and youth. He relies too much on divine protection and hardly at all on strength of character. From the moralist's point of view Richard deserves what he gets. But that is not precisely Shakespeare's point of view. Shakespeare is much closer to suggesting that he causes what he gets. In this sense the play is a "mirror for magistrates." Kings can cause their ruin; God has obviously allowed it to happen over and over again in history. Only a fool believes otherwise. Carlisle's speech on the coast of

Wales about God not allowing the king's downfall makes the
bishop sound both naïve and pompous, even though he goes on to
imply that "God helps those who help themselves." Richard's
response returns to the earlier point, despite Aumerle's translation
of the later one, and the king arrogantly predicts Bolingbroke's
instant defeat when confronted by the "deputy elected by the
Lord" (III. ii. 57).

A danger, nevertheless, exists in regarding too much of what
Richard says about his own position from too great an ironic
distance. That distance is tempting because we all want to make
one of Shakespeare's less obviously dramatic plays as dramatic as
we can. From the older emphasis on poetic justice we have moved
to the New Critical emphasis on dramatic irony. Both positions,
taken to excess, miss a fine point of symbolic balance achieved by
Shakespeare in his rendering of Richard. Richard is vain; he
certainly does indulge in self-dramatization; and he fondles
self-pity. He is probably least attractive when he whines, as in the
speech immediately after he hears of the execution of Bushy,
Green, and the Earl of Wiltshire:

> Let's talk of graves, of worms, and epitaphs;
> Make dust our paper, and with rainy eyes
> Write sorrow on the bosom of the earth.
> Let's choose executors and talk of wills;
> And yet not so—for what can we bequeath
> Save our deposed bodies to the ground?
>
> . . . .
>
> For God's sake let us sit upon the ground
> And tell sad stories of the death of kings. (III. ii. 145–56)

Most of the death speeches and poems in the Renaissance seem
morbid to moderns, who feel that the healthy attitude is to think
about the subject not at all, but this speech would be regarded as
morbid by even Shakespeare's audience. Richard is embracing
death as a way of giving up in life, literally sitting upon the ground
as he speaks the next twenty-one lines, and losing all dignity, both
as king and as man. As Carlisle finally points out, he is wailing.
But the audience already knows what to think of this speech
because it is prefaced by the phrase, ". . . of comfort no man
speak," and it comes at the end of a rhetorical series of speeches

PLATE 1   Francesco da Sant' Agata: *Hercules and Antaeus* (ca. 1525). Bronze.
National Gallery of Art, Washington, D.C. Widener Collection. *Photo: Courtesy of
National Gallery of Art.*

PLATE 2 "Wrestlers," from Raphael Holinshed, *Chronicles,* 2 vols. (London, 1577), 1, "The Historie of Englande," p. 15. *Photo: By permission of the Folger Shakespeare Library, Washington, D.C.*

PLATE 3 Donatello: *David* (ca. 1450). Bronze. National Museum (Bargello), Florence. *Photo: By permission of Alinari-Art Reference Bureau, Ancram, N.Y.*

Aₑ ₙ ₑ ₐ s beares his father, out of Troye,
When that the Greekes, the same did spoile, and sacke:
His father might of suche a sonne haue ioye,
Who throughe his foes, did beare him on his backe:
    No fier, nor sworde, his valiaunt harte coulde feare,
    To flee awaye, without his father deare.

Which showes, that sonnes must carefull bee, and kinde,
For to releeue their parentes in distresse:
And duringe life, that dutie shoulde them binde,
To reuerence them, that God their daies maie blesse:
    And reprehendes tenne thowsande to their shame,
    Who ofte difpise the stocke whereof they came.

PLATE 4 "Aeneas and Anchises," from Geffrey Whitney, *A Choice of Emblemes* (Leyden, 1586), p. 163. *Photo: By permission of the Folger Shakespeare Library, Washington, D.C.*

PLATE 5 "Hercules as Lover," from Otho Vaenius, *Amorum emblemata* (Antwerp, 1608), p. 32. *Photo: By permission of the Folger Shakespeare Library, Washington, D.C.*

PLATE 6 "Hymen," from Vincenzo Cartari, *Le imagini de i' dei* (Lyons, 1581), p. 164. *Photo: Courtesy of Arizona State University Library, Tempe. Special Collections.*

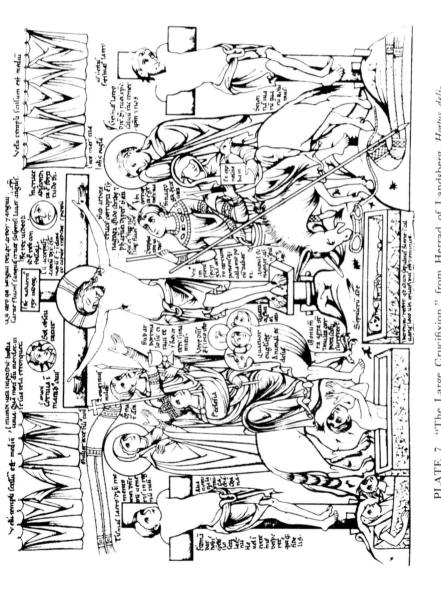

PLATE 7 "The Large Crucifixion," from Herrad of Landsberg, *Hortus deliciarum* (last half of 12th century), fol. 150r. MS tracing by Bastard. Bibliothèque Nationale, Paris. *Photo:* Hortus (Strasbourg: Trübner, 1879–99).

PLATE 8 Isaac Penard: Skull watch (ca. 1650). Silver. The Metropolitan Museum of Art, N.Y. Gift of J. Pierpont Morgan, 1917. *Photo: Courtesy of The Metropolitan Museum of Art.*

For Wednesdaye.

PLATE 9 "The Three Living and the Three Dead," from Richard Fox, *The Contemplation of Sinners* (Westminster, 1499), sig. F2v. *Photo: By permission of the Newberry Library, Chicago.*

PLATE 10 Hans Leinberger: *Corrupt Justice* (ca. 1515–20). Linden wood. German Museum, Nuremberg. *Photo: By permission of Marburg-Art Reference Bureau, Ancram, N.Y.*

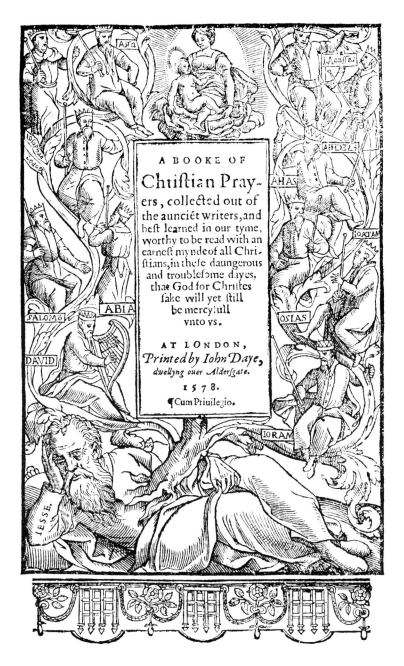

A BOOKE OF
Chriſtian Pray-
ers, collected out of
the ancíet writers, and
beſt learned in our tyme,
worthy to be read with an
earneſt mynde of all Chri-
ſtians, in theſe daungerous
and troubleſome dayes,
that God for Chriſtes
ſake will yet ſtill
be mercyfull
vnto vs.

AT LONDON,
Printed by Iohn Daye,
dwellyng ouer Alderſgate.
1 5 7 8.
¶ Cum Priuilegio.

PLATE 11   "Jesse Tree," from *A Booke of Christian Prayers* (London, 1578), title page. *Photo: By permission of the Folger Shakespeare Library, Washington, D.C.*

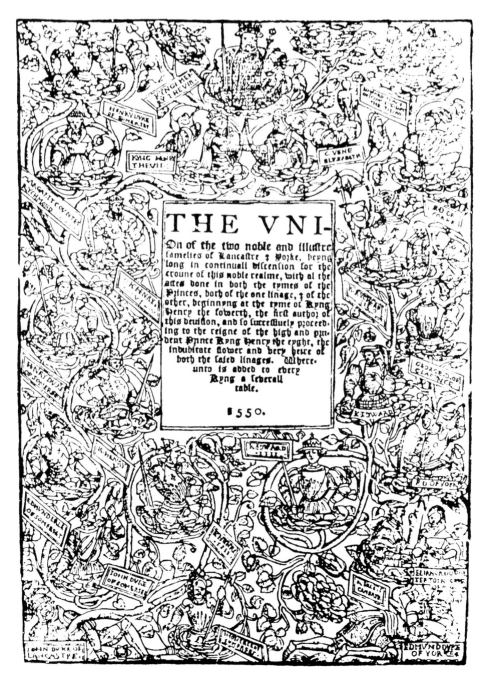

PLATE 12 "Tudor Tree," from Edward Halle, *The Vnion of . . . York and Lancaster*, 3d ed. (London, 1550), title page. *Photo: By permission of the Folger Shakespeare Library, Washington, D.C.*

PLATE 13   Dürer: "Ecce homo," from the *Engraved Passion* (1513). University
Art Collections. Arizona State University, Tempe. Gift of Mr. and Mrs. Read
Mullan. *Photo: Courtesy of University Art Collections.*

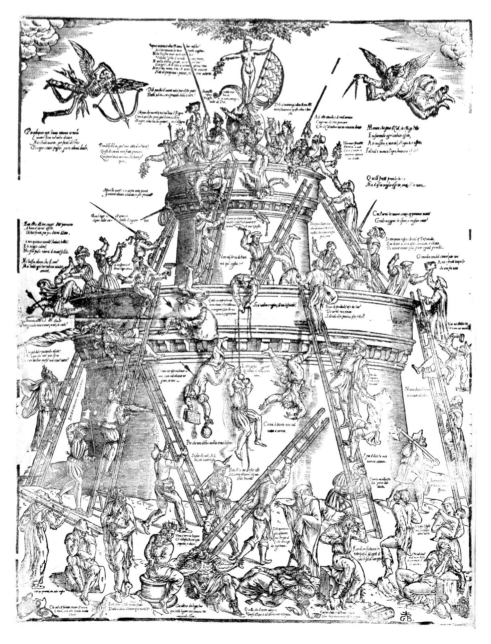

PLATE 14 "Fortune's Castle" (16th century). Italian woodcut. *Photo: By permission of the Warburg Institute, London.*

PLATE 15   Henrik Goltzius: "The Fall of Phaeton" (ca. 1588). Engraving.
Photo: By permission of the Warburg Institute, London.

PLATE 16 "Temptation to Despair," from *Ars moriendi,* 4th ed. (Augsburg, 1465), p. 7. *Photo: Courtesy of The Pierpont Morgan Library, N.Y.*

PLATE 17 Master of Flémalle: *Mérode Altarpiece* triptych (ca. 1428). Right panel, "St. Joseph in His Carpentry Shop." The Metropolitan Museum of Art, N.Y. The Cloisters Collection. Purchase. *Photo: By permission of The Metropolitan Museum of Art.*

PLATE 18 Master of Flémalle: *Mérode Altarpiece* triptych (ca. 1428). Center panel, "The Annunciation." The Metropolitan Museum of Art, N.Y. The Cloisters Collection. Purchase. *Photo: By permission of The Metropolitan Museum of Art.*

While Hercules laye ſleeping (as I reade)
  Two wayes he ſawe full of difficultie,
The one of pleaſure, at ende geuing no mede,
The other of vertue auaunſing eche degree,
But of both theſe two wayes when that he
Had ſought the ſtate, the ende, and the ſtraightnes,
The way he entred of vertue and goodnes.

Therfore O reader that haſte will to encline
To ſoueraine vertue that is incomparable,
Thy minde applying ſtedfaſt to her doctrine,
Ouer reade this ballade, for it is profitable,
And though thou thinke it but a fayned fable,
Yet reade it gladly, but if thou be to haut,
Flee from it faſt and finde in it no faut.

We pardon require where as we do offende,
Graunting the ſame to other bſing to write,
None doeth ſo well but ſome may it amende,
But namely if it be done without reſpite,
None without lepſure can borde of fault endite;
And mans wit as dayly doth appere,
Sometime is dull, ſometime perfect and clere.

With

PLATE 19 "Dream of Hercules," from Sebastian Brant, *The Ship of Fooles,* trans. Alexander Barclay, 2d ed. (London, 1570?), fol. 239v. *Photo: By permission of the Folger Shakespeare Library, Washington, D.C.*

T H E moufe, that longe did feede on daintie crommes,
  And fafelie fearch'd the cupborde and the fhelfe :
At lengthe for chaunge, vnto an Oyfter commes,

Felo de fe. Where of his deathe, he guiltie was him felfe :
  The Oyfter gap'd, the Moufe put in his head,
  Where he was catch'd, and crufh'd till he was dead.

Ifidoruslib. 1.de   The Gluttons fatte, that daintie fare deuoure,
fummo bono.   And feeke about, to fatisfie theire tafte :
Gulæ faturitas
nimia acié men- And what they like, into theire bellies poure,
tis obtundit in- This iuftlie blames, for furfettes come in hafte :
geniumque euer-
tere facit.   And biddes them feare, their fweete, and dulcet meates,
  For oftentimes, the fame are deadlie baites.

PLATE 20 "Mouse and Oyster," from Geffrey Whitney, *A Choice of Emblemes*
(Leyden, 1586), p. 128. *Photo: By permission of the Folger Shakespeare Library,
Washington, D.C.*

PLATE 21 Inigo Jones: "A Crier of Mousetraps" (1638). Pen and brown ink washed with sepia. Chatsworth, Derbyshire. Devonshire Collections. *Photo: Courtesy of the Trustees of the Chatsworth Settlement.*

PLATE 22 "The Jesuits Taken in Their Own Net," from *The Rat-trap* (London, 1641), title page. *Photo: By permission of the Folger Shakespeare Library, Washington, D.C.*

THE
RAT--TRAP:
O R,
The IESVITES taken
in their owne Net, &c.

Difcovered in this yeare of Jubilee, or Delive-
rance from the Romifh faction ; 1641.

Imprinted 1641.

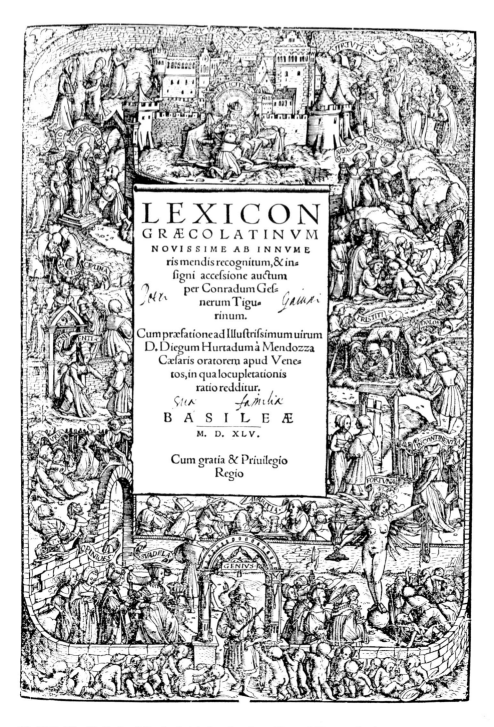

LEXICON
GRÆCOLATINVM
NOVISSIME AB INNVME
ris mendis recognitum, & in=
signi accessione auctum
per Conradum Ges=
nerum Tigu=
rinum.

Cum præfatione ad Illuftrifsimum uirum
D. Diegum Hurtadum à Mendozza
Cæfaris oratorem apud Vene=
tos, in qua locupletationis
ratio redditur.

BASILEÆ
M. D. XLV.

Cum gratia & Priuilegio
Regio

PLATE 23 Holbein: "Genius" title-border, from Conrad Gesner, *Lexicon graeco-latinum* (Basel, 1545), title page. *Photo: By permission of the Beinecke Rare Book and Manuscript Library. Yale University.*

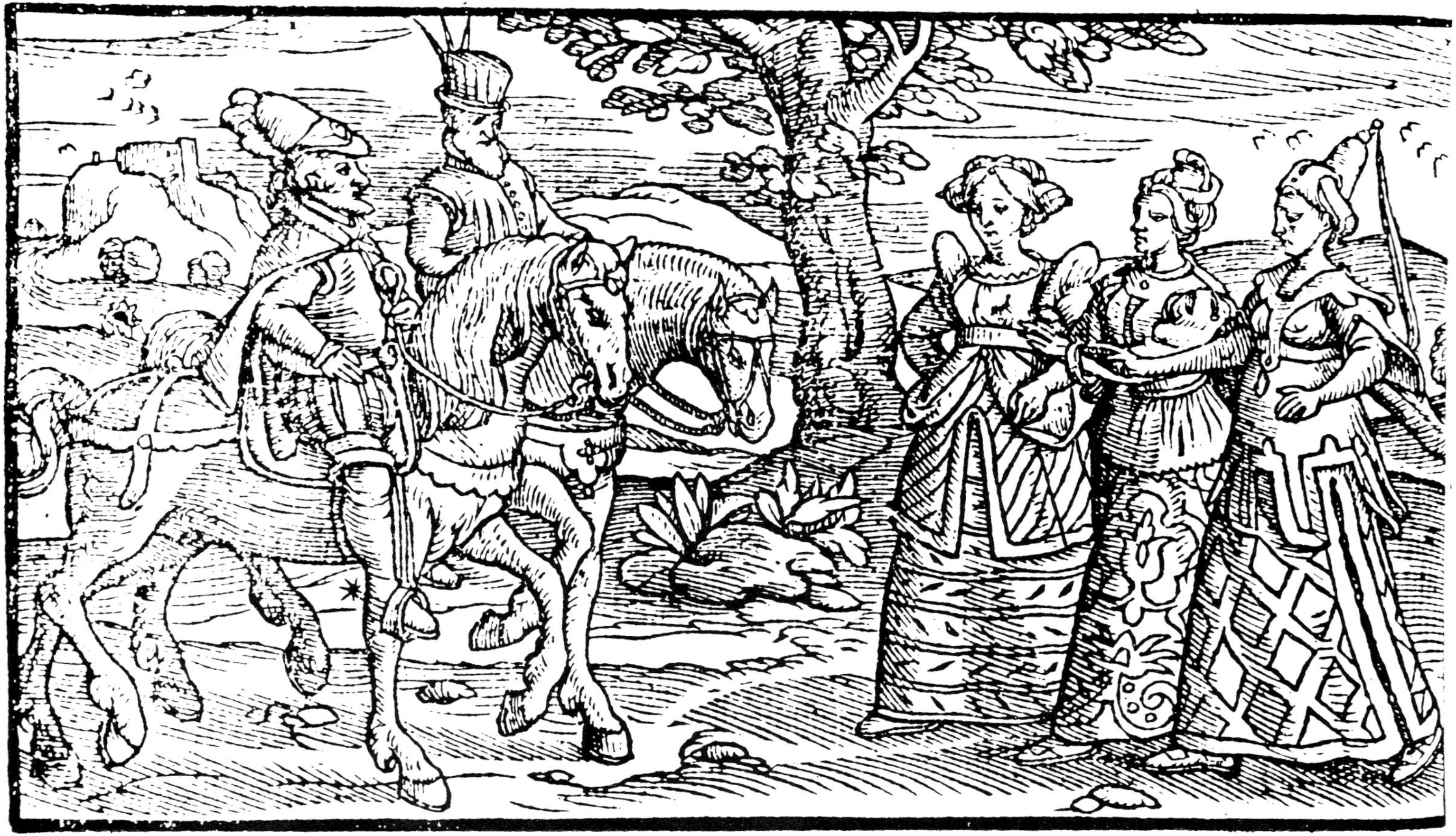

PLATE 24 "The Three Women," from Raphael Holinshed, *Chronicles*, 2 vols. (London, 1577), 1, "The Historie of Scotlande," p. 243. *Photo: By permission of the*

PLATE 25 "The Three Fates," from Vincenzo Cartari, *Le imagini de i' dei* (Lyons, 1581), p. 251. *Photo: Courtesy of Arizona State University Library, Tempe. Special Collections.*

PLATE 26 "Dolphin and Anchor," from Priscian, *Grammatici libri omnes* (Venice, 1527), Aldine colophon on title page. *Photo: Courtesy of Arizona State University Library, Tempe. Alfred Knight Collection.*

PLATE 27 "Hell Cauldron," from *The Kalender of Shepardes*, trans. R. Copland, 7th ed. (London, 1570?), sig. F1r. *Photo: By permission of the Folger Shakespeare Library, Washington, D.C.*

PLATE 28 "Hellcastle," from *The Book of Hours of Catherine of Cleves* (ca. 1435). Illuminated MS. The Pierpont Morgan Library, N.Y. *Photo: Courtesy of The Pierpont Morgan Library.*

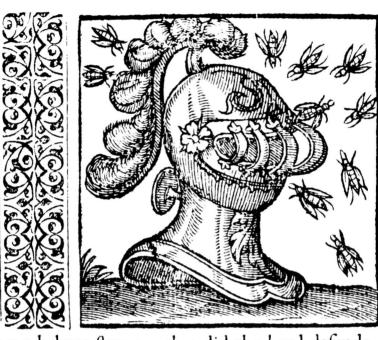

THE helmet ſtronge, that did the head defende,
Beholde, for hyue, the bees in quiet ſeru'd:
And when that warres, with bloodie bloes, had ende.
They, hony wroughte, where ſouldiour was preſeru'd:
   Which doth declare, the bleſſed fruites of peace,
   How ſweete ſhee is, when mortall warres doe ceaſe.

PLATE 29 "Helmet," from Geffrey Whitney, *A Choice of Emblemes* (Leyden, 1586), p. 138. *Photo: By permission of the Folger Shakespeare Library, Washington, D.C.*

PLATE 30 Giorgione: *La tempesta* (ca. 1507). The Academy, Venice. *Photo: By permission of Alinari-Art Reference Bureau, Ancram, N.Y.*

PLATE 31 Wenceslaus Hollar: "Fortune" (1625). Drawing. Victoria and Albert Museum, London. *Photo: By permission of the Victoria and Albert Museum.*

PLATE 32   Dürer: "The Great Fortune" (1501–2). Engraving. *Photo: By permission of the Warburg Institute, London.*

PLATE 33 "Harpies," from Jacob de Zetter, trans., *Speculum vertutum* (Frankfurt, 1644), no. 69. *Photo: By permission of the Beinecke Rare Book and Manuscript Library, Yale University*

PLATE 34   Bellini: "Nemesis" (ca. 1498). One of five allegorical paintings. The
Academy, Venice. *Photo: By permission of Alinari-Art Reference Bureau, Ancram, N.Y.*

EMBLEMA I.

Principium in tereti quæris quicunque figura,
Principium inuenies hîc vbi finis erit.
Sic Christum vero quisquis reuereris amore;
Quæ vitam hora tibi finiet, incipiet.

PLATE 35 "Circle," from Theodore Beza, *Icones, id est verae imagines virorum doctrina simul et pietate illustrium* (Geneva, 1580), sig. Kk3v. *Photo: Courtesy of Arizona State University Library, Tempe. Alfred Knight Collection.*

whereby Richard alternates between "comfort" and "despair," in a manner recalling the highly conventional ars moriendi. Aumerle is the comforting angel and Richard enacts the role of his own bad angel when he counsels himself to despair with each piece of bad news about the defection of his supporters. He is both literally and figuratively giving up in the stage image of finally collapsing in an undignified heap upon the ground. The speech is morbid because it accepts both political and spiritual destruction. The important thing for Richard's soul, of course, is not what happens to him in this world but how he meets it, and here he is meeting it very badly. But he has also come to the bottom; like Lear, if he is to survive at all he must work his way out of a spiritual pit reached midway through the play. And work his way out of it he does, with only brief and infrequent relapses.

In virtually all of his speeches after the despairing midpoint of the play, Richard constantly recalls to Shakespeare's audience the most fundamental principles of Tudor kingship. The burden of enunciating these principles was considerably increased the moment John of Gaunt died, leaving York to state them in the midst of his own vacillation. But from the midpoint in Act III onward Richard assumes the bulk of the responsibility for defending the principles on which the whole divine order.of the English state rested in the sixteenth century. The choric speech by the Bishop of Carlisle in the deposition scene, in which he predicts the Wars of the Roses, is also extremely important, but the sustained task is Richard's. Shakespeare's skill as a dramatist is in the way he uses Gaunt to start the audience off on the right foot, moves into an extremely complex handling of Richard as a defective man but increasingly able advocate of his own divine right as king, and concludes with Carlisle underlining the terrible mistake committed by England in supporting Bolingbroke against Richard.

As for the source of Shakespeare's Tudor myth, it has often been assigned to Edward Halle or to Holinshed. Shakespeare undoubtedly read books based on the myth, but he did considerably more than read during his lifetime, as we well know. The myth was everywhere: in the pulpit in a time when pulpits were outside because no church could accommodate the crowd; in the streets when civic pageants welcomed the monarchs or foreign dignitaries; and in a thousand visual sources, from tapestries to title pages. The myth had a single message: the Tudors had restored the divine authority of kingship lost in the time of Richard II. When Richard fell, England fell.

It may seem to a modern audience that when Richard compares himself to Phaeton at Flint Castle he is indulging in a character-istic hyperbole. After all, it is only a slight physical descent Bolingbroke requests through Northumberland, not the descent of the sun from the sky. Yet the hyperbole here is consistent with the attitude toward England expressed by Gaunt in his speech to York before Richard's arrival at the deathbed. England is a garden, a demi-Paradise, and Shakespeare makes us come to see Richard as a sun at the center of what could be a microcosm of perfection. His eclipse brings darkness to the land.

The sun did, in fact, literally fall at the play's early perform-ances. The title page of the authoritative First Quarto (1597) describes "THE/Tragedie of King Ri-/chard the se-/cond./ *As it hath beene publickely acted/by the right Honourable the/Lorde Chamberlaine his Ser-/uants.*" *Tragedy* meant the fall of great and powerful men, and *public performance* usually meant performance in an open-air theater. We know that these performances took place in the afternoon, probably from two to four, when the sun was in all likelihood declining over the exposed roof line of the public playhouse. We might at least entertain the idea that Shakespeare built that moment into his play, with the climactic line, "From Richard's night to Bolingbroke's fair day" (III. ii. 218). This line comes at the very center of the play. It indicates the completion of Richard's loss of physical support. From this point on Bolingbroke steadily rises to the throne and Richard steadily loses all opportu-nity for maintaining or recovering it. The outcome of the action was uncertain to this point; the rest of the play is a kind of foregone conclusion, with the dramatic interest shifted to the way Richard responds to the fait accompli of his defeat. Something very similar, having to do with the literal descent of the sun during the contemporary open-air performance of a Shakespeare play, may be happening in *Julius Caesar.* After Cassius commits suicide, Titanius returns, too late, and remarks: ". . . Cassius is no more. O setting sun, /As in thy red rays thou dost sink to night, /So in his red blood Cassius' day is set! /The sun of Rome is set. Our day is gone" (V. iii. 60–63). These lines, toward the very end of the play, are appropriate to the reddening of the sky in the late afternoon of an English winter sunset.

If we admit the sun itself to be an unusual iconic stage image in these instances (and there may be more in Shakespeare), the line in *Richard II* about Richard's night and Bolingbroke's fair day becomes richly ironic and paradoxical. Richard's night is England's night; even Bolingbroke's day is England's night. The very sun, as in the myth of Phaeton, falls from the sky. The divinely ordained universe may not send angels into the field against Bolingbroke, but we have a Miltonic sense of man falling and nature feeling the wound. The cosmic order here, as in *Lear*, responds to the fall of kings. The later descent of Richard from the walls of Flint Castle is possibly meant to be an echo of this earlier climax. Richard becomes a figurative sun falling from the upper stage to the lower. His descent to the forestage is microcosmic, but the hyperbolic allusion to Phaeton restores the scale. Richard's lines at this point should probably be spoken not in a self-dramatizing crescendo, as is usually the case, but with a grim awareness of the real defeat that occurs when a king obeys the demands of a subject. Richard's undignified response to his agonizing situation has already been concluded with "I talk but idly," at the end of a self-pitying speech several lines above the Phaeton speech.

What the king does is always meant by Shakespeare to be far more than the thing itself. We have already seen that in Richard's confiscation of the lands of Lancaster; by this action he sets a precedent whereby his own hereditary rights are called in question, as he is reminded by the Duke of York (II. i. 186ff.). The Duchess of Gloucester introduces the theme of precedence into the play when she warns Gaunt that in tolerating the death of his brother and her husband he shows the "naked pathway" (I. ii. 31) to his own life. The same theme is recalled toward the end of the play in Richard's warning to Northumberland that the new king will never trust a man who has helped him get rid of the old king.

The scene at Flint Castle is also based on the principle of precedence. When Richard obeys the insistence of Bolingbroke that he "come down" to meet an exile, the king loses the last authentic vestige of his authority, no matter how Bolingbroke may for the moment try to disguise the fact. And try he does; at

Richard's arrival *"he kneeles downe"* (Q1—1597; sig. G2r). The audience is informed on several occasions of Bolingbroke's skill at creating a public image of humility. In a long speech to Aumerle, after Bolingbroke's exile, Richard reveals the suspicions aroused by his cousin's humble courtesy to the common people, "Wooing poor craftsmen with the craft of smiles," and providing a "brace of draymen" with the "tribute of his supple knee" (I. iv. 28–33). Bolingbroke seems to have the same idea in mind at Flint Castle, later expressed just before the deposition scene: "Fetch hither Richard, that in common view /He may surrender; so we shall proceed /Without suspicion . . ." (IV. i. 155–57). But Richard is very alert to these attempts at public relations and the making of a corporate image. When he confronts a kneeling Bolingbroke in the base court, he insists he stand: "Up, cousin, up; your heart is up, I know, /Thus high at least, although your knee be low" (III. iii. 194–95). At the phrase "Thus high," Richard should touch the crown he still wears in show. Later, that crown will become the basis for a literal tug of war in the deposition scene, but for the moment it still rests upon its proper head. The only thing left to Richard at this point is the prestige of his coronation and his crown. Were England populated by virtuous men such as John of Gaunt, these would be sufficient to sustain his authority. But the untended garden is invaded. The audience is destined to hear of ashes thrown on the anointed head and to see the crown resting on a usurper's brows. For Shakespeare's audience the real battle might have been seen as just beginning at Flint Castle. King and exile are face to face at last; who will outface the other? But an even larger spiritual question emerges as well. Can Richard inherit the kingdom of light and wear the eternal crown? As for the political framework of England, can even the strongest of immoral men sustain a usurped authority? These related issues are keyed into the imagery of the sun, of rise and fall, and of night and day. And this iconic imagery is in turn powerfully linked to the theme of shadow and substance.

The Mirror

Surely the most famous episode in this play is that of the shattered mirror in the deposition scene. Bolingbroke and Northumberland are staging a scene (much as Richard had staged the combat scenes at the beginning) to serve the political necessity of public opinion. Richard must seem to relinquish the crown voluntarily and he must do so in public. According to York, the king has agreed to abdicate, but it is soon apparent that Richard has no intention of allowing Bolingbroke to get both the crown and everyone's good opinion as well. Richard has agreed to come to Westminster Hall only because he too wants an audience, one he can bring to see Bolingbroke as a ruthless usurper. Thus the deposition scene is one of the most dramatic scenes in Shakespeare. Two stage directors struggle over the content and interpretation of the script, as they do with similarly brilliant theatrical effect in Pirandello's *Six Characters in Search of an Author.* And as in another play by Pirandello, *Right You Are, If You Think You Are,* a mirror is used by the playwright as an emphatic symbol of the most complex ambiguities. The Platonic theme of appearance and reality, so pervasive throughout both Shakespeare and Pirandello, is in turn rendered by them both from every point of view. What is only apparent one moment becomes real the next, and what was seemingly real becomes illusion.

Mirrors have long been associated with magical effects, the philosophical point of most magic being the ambiguity of reality, an idea well understood by Lewis Carroll in writing *Through the Looking Glass.* When Richard uses one of his last prerogatives as king to request a looking glass, Bolingbroke decides to humor him, but the audience should feel that Bolingbroke is making a serious mistake. The mirror will magically restore some of the king's almost totally eroded power, and it will do so by exposing the reality behind Bolingbroke's carefully contrived script. Shakespeare had used the mirror as a verbal image in *Richard III* (I. ii. 262–63). There it was given a highly conventional association with vanity, a meaning still entirely familiar to us. When the mirror reappears as an iconic stage image in *Richard II* it also has that commonplace meaning: "O flatt'ring glass, /Like to my followers in prosperity" (IV. i. 279–80). But it obviously stands for much more this time. While the servants are going for the mirror, Northumberland tries to conserve time by having Richard himself read aloud a list of the charges against him. This attempt at humiliating self-accusation does not occur in Holinshed, 2d ed. (1587), who merely lists some thirty-three charges against the king (charges whose publication was deferred), after quoting Richard's written resignation. The resignation as quoted in Shakespeare's source makes no mention of wrongdoing. In the play, however, Richard understandably compares Northumberland to the devil who holds up a list of the sins of a dying man in order to tempt him to despair: "Fiend, thou torments me ere I come to hell" (V. i. 270). This was one of the conventional episodes in the ars moriendi sequence of alternating comforts and temptations. The third in a popular series of woodcuts illustrating this sequence shows a dying man accused by devils of perjury, murder, avarice, and fornication (Plate 16). Holding a parchment listing yet other sins is a devil saying, "ecce peccata tua" (behold thy sins).[21] We may be meant to feel that when Bolingbroke tells Northumberland to be quiet he must see how just ahead lies a parallel between himself and Satan, who sends out the devils to the bedsides of dying men. Northumberland insists that the Commons will not be satisfied with the deposition unless Richard confesses his failure as a king, and Richard quickly gives an answer which effectively changes the subject back to where he wants it—the mirror. The mirror will be the book, like the record kept in heaven, in which he can read himself with all his imperfections, from wrinkles to sins. In this way the mirror becomes a microcosm of his entire life, his "weaved up folly."

The shape of an ordinary Renaissance mirror is possibly related to Richard's idea that he will find in it all his sins. Only unusual and very costly Elizabethan mirrors were flat; most of them were convex, blown into the round bull's-eye shape so popular later in the early nineteenth century, during the Regency period of furniture design.[22] Those who have ever looked into such mirrors know that what is reflected is rendered in comprehensive miniature. An entire drawing room is reduced to the scale of a doll's house. Richard finds the truth in miniature when he suddenly confronts his entire life as he gazes at the wrinkles etched by the suffering he has caused himself by his own folly. The iconic stage image is the Renaissance emblem of both vanity and truth. The seeming contradiction has been sorted out by Samuel Chew:

> When the King held the looking glass in his hand there may have been those in the audience who were reminded of a complex of contradictory associations, for on the one hand the

mirror is an oft-occurring attribute of Pride and Vainglory, and on the other hand it is often an attribute of Wisdom, who knows herself, and of Prudence, who looks before and after. For the spectator in whose memory these meanings flashed Richard would become the embodiment of Pride and Vain-glory and also a travesty of Wisdom and Prudence, as indeed he is. Furthermore, when the King dashes the mirror to the ground and comments upon the brittleness of glory, we remember the figures of *Fortuna Vitrea* and those representations of the goddess where, as in Bellini's painting, she holds in her hand a brittle globe of glass.[23]

The convex shape of the standard Renaissance mirror would also serve the association Richard's mirror might be thought to have with a globe. And thus we have arrived at a third meaning for Richard's mirror: the power of Fortune, with everything that goddess implies about the tragic rise and fall of powerful men. When Richard dashes the brittle glass to the ground he adds yet another stage image of fall to a long list, from the many gages thrown to the ground in challenge throughout the play to possibly the sun itself falling in the sky. At the same moment Shakespeare keys a stage image of tragic fall into the theme of shadow and substance.

This theme, familiar to students of Shakespeare in Sonnet 53, is first introduced into *Richard II* by Bushy's attempts to "comfort" the Queen after she has bidden farewell to her husband, gone to put down an Irish rebellion. Bushy moralizes the image of her tears:

Each substance of a grief hath twenty shadows,
Which shows like grief itself, but is not so;
For sorrow's eye, glazed with blinding tears,
Divides one thing entire to many objects,
Like perspectives which, rightly gaz'd upon,
Show nothing but confusion—ey'd awry,
Distinguish form. So your sweet Majesty,
Looking awry upon your lord's departure,
Find shapes of grief more than himself to wail;
Which, look'd on as it is, is nought but shadows
Of what it is not. Then, thrice-gracious Queen,

More than your lord's departure weep not—more is not seen;
Or if it be, 'tis with false shadow's eye,
Which for things true weep things imaginary. (II. ii. 14–27)

Bushy's sophistry (expressed in courtly conceits seriously parodying religious meditation on a holy image) is cold comfort to the Queen, whose "inward soul / Persuades" her that her grief is caused not by what she outwardly sees but by what she inwardly feels. Therein lies the real distinction between Platonic shadow and substance, appearance and reality. In this instance the theme is linked to the stage image of a tear-stained eye, in turn compared to a trick painting, or "perspective."[24] In the deposition scene the theme is related to the stage image of a literal mirror. The vainglory, so much a part of Richard in prosperity, is thrown to the ground by a sorrowful king, now fully aware of its cost. Broken into a hundred pieces is the reflection of a face etched into a hundred surfaces by sorrow. Adversity has quickly destroyed the earlier appearance of kingly sway. The painful realities of power have overcome the illusions of the past. When Richard sees his face reflected he recognizes in that shadow the substance of what he has become, as well as the folly of what has brought him to it—the folly of living in dreams of absolute security. But the paradoxes to be drawn are endless.

Richard had begun this inner journey of self-discovery from the midpoint in the play, as I have already suggested, much as Lear is to begin his journey with the storm scene. The moment in Act III is one in which Richard, like Lear, is tempted to give up entirely the struggle to survive. Richard has just heard of the desertion or defeat of one group of supporters after another. He is so despondent that he foolishly discharges the troops he has brought back with him from Ireland: ". . . let them go / To ear the land that hath some hope to grow" (III. ii. 211–12). The fortitudinous Aumerle is about to urge restraint, but Richard interrupts with: ". . . He does me double wrong / That wounds me with the flatteries of his tongue" (III. ii. 215–16), Richard is now seeing flattery where it is not, just as earlier he saw it not where it was, but his new determination to face the cold facts of his existence is nevertheless the beginning of a sustained spiritual growth. From this point onward Richard moves from the Christ-like authority he knows he ought to have but fails to inspire in the responses of his subjects, to the Christ-like fortitude that brings meaning out of suffering. His changing personality gradually alters from paper Christ to the imitation of Christ. In counterpoint, his defective Adamic self is slowly deepened into true humanity the more fully he is expelled from his rightful garden.[25]

In the deposition scene the broken mirror suggests a particular spiritual plateau, a state of mind once called "a broken and contrite heart." In the passage cited above, Chew forces Richard into a one-dimensional mold by calling him at this point "the embodiment of Pride and Vainglory and also a travesty of Wisdom and Prudence." The ritual act of breaking the mirror should also make the audience feel that Richard is reaching true wisdom by breaking the spirit of pride within himself. We should feel that Bolingbroke is not speaking the truth but only desperately trying to toss off Richard's dramatic gesture as mere playacting, little more than just another plea for sympathy, by the caustic: "The shadow of your sorrow hath destroy'd /The shadow of your face . . ." (IV. i. 292–93). Bolingbroke is a man of few words, but that does not mean everything he says is the straight and honest truth: too often he has impressed critics as an Elizabethan John Wayne. Iago in the presence of Othello has far less to say than Othello. It is possible to stand too close to Bolingbroke and too far from Richard. We should be very close to Richard indeed in the deposition scene, not simply because he is an anointed king, but because he is becoming the true master of the situation, as a king ought to be. His reply to Bolingbroke's sneer about the "shadow" of his sorrow is a wedge argument whereby Richard accepts the outward and visible act as a shadow, but retains his inward and spiritual grief as the substance:

> Say that again.
> The shadow of my sorrow? Ha! let's see.
> 'Tis very true: my grief lies all within;
> And these external manner of laments
> Are merely shadows to the unseen grief
> That swells with silence in the tortur'd soul.
> There lies the substance; . . . . (IV. i. 293–99)

We are inevitably reminded of the Queen's reply to Bushy early in the play. The grief is genuine. But the "broken and contrite heart" neither pities itself, as Richard had done earlier, nor does it ask pity from others, as Bolingbroke has accused Richard of doing now. In the deposition scene Richard is making the public confession Northumberland so ardently wanted, but it is not the confession Northumberland and Bolingbroke had in mind. It is a confession *before* men, not *to* men. The confession is to God.

As for his relationship with men, Richard as a man has more fiber and self-respect than ever before, a self-respect that should not be confused with his earlier vainglory. We know a change has been completed because Richard, true king at last, inspires heroic action in other men. Shakespeare devotes the rest of this crucial scene to Richard's perfectly dignified withdrawal, Bolingbroke's prudent attempts to say as little as possible, and the dramatic revelation that the total effect on those who oppose Bolingbroke is to firm their resolve to the point of what is to be the Oxford conspiracy. As the former King Richard is conveyed to the Tower of London under guard and Bolingbroke hurries off to prepare his own coronation, the Abbot of Westminster turns to the discontented Aumerle and the Bishop of Carlisle to declare: "A woeful pageant have we here beheld." Counterrevolution has begun among those who have remained behind on stage. The abbot chose the word "pageant" advisedly. The previous action has indeed been a pageant—a formal presentation of great themes, often in emblematic form, with each gesture, movement, or object weighty in implication. The major themes are the personal one of honor, the political one of kingship, and the dramatic one of tragic fall. The objects are Aumerle's gage, the contested crown, and Richard's mirror. Partly because of the potency of these iconic stage images, Richard has in some mysterious way managed to win his deposition, for it is not until this point that counterrevolution begins. Richard's political victory is a by-product of his essential victory over himself. I do not envy the actor who must play the deposition scene. The temptation to the actor must be strong to simplify Richard into what the politician Bolingbroke tells us he is: a mere posturing actor.

Some very distinguished critics of *Richard II* have seen the last act as very unsatisfactory. A. P. Rossiter has called it "half-revised Old Play. . . . a ragged, muddled end."[26] Whatever its defects, it does carry through and complete the patterns of thought, iconic imagery, and action already established earlier in the play. In his characteristic way, Shakespeare prepares the audience for his protagonist's tragic fate by a brief, intimate scene with a servant. In *Julius Caesar* the scene is between Brutus and the lute-playing servant Lucius, in *Othello* between Desdemona and Emilia. In the last act of *Richard II* the former king and a groom recall happier days. Earlier in this penultimate scene Richard has prepared himself unwittingly for death by means of a meditation comparing his prison to the world. If setting is an aspect of stage imagery, then this is one of the most sustained stage images in the play. The audience is told, as in the case of the blushes, what it is seeing, and in this instance it is seeing a prison cell. That it must imagine the reality presented is very much a part of what Richard is saying to himself. Richard's meditation is a private preparation for death, just as his earlier confession and psychological victory over Bolingbroke in the deposition scene were public preparations for life. Very early in *Richard II* the audience was led by John of Gaunt to regard England as a little world of perfection, a microcosm. Now Richard sees the prison cell as the emblem of his mind, in turn containing the little world of his own thoughts, engendered by his female brain and his male soul. Though alone, therefore, he does not lack for company, especially when he has the thought that many have shared his fate. From this he passes to the many roles he can play in thought, the many lives he can mentally enact. Here the audience is suddenly reminded that the little world of the prison cell imaginatively before them is contained in the little world of the public playhouse, "where all the world's a stage." And if plays are life in miniature, if theaters, with their heaven, earth, and hell, are the universe in small, then life itself may be no more than a microcosm, and an imperfect one, of the cosmos, with its heaven, earth, and hell. Life thus seen becomes a fitful passage, where all men share displeasure until death. "Being nothing" is the only cure for never being enough. Richard suddenly notices the "still music" that has been playing for several lines. The iconic stage image of the music recalls the familiar Platonic doctrine of the music of the spheres, already recalled at the end of my chapter on *The Merchant of Venice*. In *Richard II*, *Julius Caesar* (IV. iii) and *King Lear* (IV. vii), the audience is meant to feel that the soul of the tragic hero is at peace in music, strengthened before fate, made "absolute for death."

Richard briefly meditates on the music, but suddenly realizes that as he stands meditating Bolingbroke is rushing toward greater and greater success. The spell is broken. Richard reverts to an earlier instability, just as Hamlet is to do when he leaps into the grave of Ophelia after a long, stabilizing meditation on life and death with the skull of Yorick in his hand. Having reached spiritual ripeness does not insure abandonment of the struggle to remain in either case. No matter how mature the soul, it is always endangered, always in need of renewal and support.

Horatio apparently helps Hamlet to restore his equilibrium offstage between the first two scenes of Act V, or at least so the first line of scene ii suggests. In *Richard II,* a compassionate stable boy who once cared for Richard's favorite horse—Barbary, now the spoil of Bolingbroke—helps a supplanted king to restore his new and creative self. In all of England at least one person still cares about his former king and with great difficulty has come to comfort him in prison, a corporal act of mercy due any man, let alone a king. This moment of support from another human being helps Richard to meet his violent end courageously, taking more than one assailant along with him to the Last Judgment. When Richard's stricken body falls to the prison floor, he instructs his soul to "mount . . . up on high." We see his misfortunate body fall, the last iconic stage image of the play. Perhaps the original audience of the play also "saw" the last thing it was told to see in the play: not blushes nor a prison cell, but Richard's soul, mounting "on high." Fortune's wheel has finally melted into the paradoxes of falling to rise and dying to live.

In the following chapter, on *Hamlet,* we will be concerned with another spiritual journey. This one will be less focused, however, on iconic stage imagery and more dependent on hints provided by brief verbal pointers, although once again the combination is of both Christian and classical iconography: a patristic mousetrap set for the devil and a Greek philosopher's pilgrimage of life.

4

Hamlet: Sane Madness

One of the most attractive metaphors in all of Shakespeare is Hamlet's title for his play within the play: "The Mouse-trap." For with this tragedy of Duke Gonzago, the slightly transposed reenactment of the poisoning of the late king by his brother Claudius, Hamlet's finely wrought and skeptical mind has planned a device designed to "catch the conscience of the King." Thereafter, and for the first time, Hamlet knows for sure and Claudius knows that he knows. The uncle, in terrified recognition, rushes from the hall as Polonius demands, "Lights, lights, lights!" and Hamlet seeks final intellectual confirmation from his Stoical friend Horatio for what has already been confirmed by his senses—the obvious guilt of Claudius. This pivotal event in Act III was a trap set by one who would cleanse a diseased kingdom, and Hamlet names his device accordingly.

When asked earlier by Claudius what he called his courtly entertainment, Hamlet replied, " 'The Mouse-trap.' Marry, how? Tropically." Innumerable editors have pointed out the pun on "tropically," a word pronounced in Shakespeare's day like "trapically," the spelling in the First Quarto (1603; sig. F4r), a text probably based on a memory of the spoken lines. Thus the title indicates both a figure of speech, or trope, and a trap. So arresting is this metaphor that many critics have sustained it in their discussion of this decisive portion of the play, but perhaps none more fully than J. Dover Wilson in his vastly influential study, *What Happens in Hamlet.* In his fifth chapter, "The Multiple

Mouse-trap," he uses the metaphor in virtually every conceivable
sense, speaking of "uncle-mouse" and "cheese for his majesty the
mouse." In the following passage Wilson asks one of the key critical
questions posed by the play within the play:

> The play is a Mousetrap, the jaws of which must snap upon
> the imprisoned victim suddenly, unexpectedly, overwhelm-
> ingly. . . . [The King] must be lured gradually and
> unconsciously; . . . the audience must feel satisfied that he
> knows nothing of what awaits him, until the jaws snap; if
> they do not feel this, the sport of the great Claudius-drive will
> be spoilt.
>   He must know nothing, but they must know everything.
> How, then, was Shakespeare to make this parallelism plain to
> the spectators?[1]

An obvious part of the answer to this question is in what Hamlet
tells Horatio just before the performance of the play within the
play: "There is a play to-night before the King; /One scene of it
comes near the circumstance /Which I have told thee of my
father's death" (III. ii. 73–75).

If, however, we consider the rich iconographic associations the
mousetrap had for the medieval and Renaissance mind, it is
possible to see the brief mention of the play's title itself as a
symbolic microcosm communicating to the audience much of the
elaborate irony on which the whole dramatic action of *Hamlet*
pivots.

Mousetrap for the Devil

The mousetrap was a commonplace Renaissance symbol. In the
twentieth century its conventional Renaissance meaning was first
pointed out by Meyer Shapiro, in his article on the meaning of the
Mérode Altarpiece.[2] In this early fifteenth-century Annunciation by
the Master of Flémalle, the right-hand panel of the triptych shows
St. Joseph in his carpentry shop, manufacturing a mousetrap
(Plate 17). The allusion is ultimately to a passage in St. Augustine's Sermon CCLXIII, "On the Ascension of God," where we
learn:

The devil exulted when Christ died, but by this very death of Christ the devil is vanquished, as if he had swallowed the bait in the mousetrap. He rejoiced in Christ's death, like a bailiff of death. What he rejoiced in was then his own undoing. The cross of the Lord was the devil's mousetrap ["muscipula diaboli, crux domini"]; the bait by which he was caught was the Lord's death.[3]

The theological concept stresses an ironic reversal that could not fail to appeal to a dramatist, just as it appealed to an artist caught up in the drama of Christianity. The *Mérode Altarpiece* shows the donors venerating the Virgin in the left panel, the Annunciation in the center panel, and the manufacture of a mousetrap in the right panel, as mentioned above. The center panel (Plate 18) establishes four parallel events: the Old Testament prophecies of Christ, the Incarnation, the Crucifixion, and the defeat of the devil. Just as Christ enters the womb, symbolized by the room in which the Virgin reads the prophecies of his coming, the trap is being prepared for the devil's entry, as shown in the right panel. Just as the prophecies foretold the coming of the victorious Christ, the appearance of Christ foretells the defeat of the devil. Just as Christ takes on the garment of flesh, to become the embodiment of eternal life, he does so to die, as we are reminded by the cross the foetal Christ carries over his shoulder. His death, however, is to be the defeat of death, his imprisonment in the flesh the means by which all men are to be released from the captivity of hell. The most delicate paradox of all is the Virgin Birth symbolized by the rays of light which pass through the window high in the wall. Just as light passes through a pane of glass without shattering it, the Holy Ghost, traditionally associated with the life-giving rays of the sun, quickens the Virgin's womb without a violation of her maidenhood.

To return more specifically to the thinking of St. Augustine, the outwitting of the devil was the primary reason for God's Incarnation of himself in Christ. Thus, in the words of Shapiro, the "human flesh of Christ is a bait for the devil, who, in seizing it, brings about his own ruin."[4] Supplementing this ironic reversal, by which the devil is defeated at the very moment when he thinks himself most secure, is a further dramatic irony. We, to whom the mysteries are visually revealed, are aware; the devil is unaware.

As we see in the *Mérode Altarpiece* triptych the emphasis in medieval pictorial representation is more upon paradox and parallel than upon ironic reversal and dramatic irony, the characteristic emphases of drama, with its greater stress upon a continuous sequence of events rather than the isolation of a few central events. In the art of the neoclassical Renaissance, with its tendency to concentrate upon a single event, the symbolism of the mousetrap is correspondingly simplified. This point may be illustrated by two or three versions of a ubiquitous Renaissance subject, one already touched upon in my earlier chapter about *As You Like It.* The subject is Hercules at the Crossroads. The story was the most popular of the many added to the body of classical legends about him. In the famous Annibale Carracci painting based on the theme (1595–97), the youthful Hercules sits at the crossroads, propped up by his identifying emblem, the knotted club. He must make a difficult choice between the primrose path of dalliance bearing off into lush, tropical vegetation on his right (a downward path indicated by an alluring Venus) and the steep and stony way ascending on his left (a path instructed by Virtue). Those who have seen the painting are easily reminded of Ophelia's words to the rakish Laertes, when her brother warns her against involvement with Hamlet:

> But, good my brother,
> Do not, as some ungracious pastors do,
> Show me the steep and thorny way to heaven,
> Whiles, like a puff'd and reckless libertine,
> Himself the primrose path of dalliance treads
> And recks not his own rede. . . . (I. iii. 46–51)

An early woodcut, which originated in the late fifteenth century although it was reprinted later as well, shows with perfect clarity the thorns and primroses stressed by Shakespeare in Ophelia's lines (Plate 19). This woodcut appears in Alexander Barclay's popular English translation of Sebastian Brant's *The Ship of Fooles,* 2d ed. (London, 1570?),[5] on the page with a moralizing poem, part of which reads: "While *Hercules* laye sleeping (as I reade) / Two wayes he sawe full of difficultie" (fol. 239v). The several references to Hercules or to his labors in *Hamlet* reaffirm the importance of Hercules as a standard of heroic Christian humanism.

A final example of the theme of Hercules at the Crossroads is a work of art much closer in time to *Hamlet,* a late sixteenth- or early seventeenth-century engraving after Jan Saenredam.[6] Hercules, a type of Christ in his role as Everyman, pauses at the crossroads, trying to make up his mind. Should he take the path of virtue? It is represented by Minerva, goddess of wisdom, with her vertically held picture of figures struggling up a steep cliff. Or should he go the way of vice? Its obvious appeal is represented by a nearly naked Voluptas beneath a tree supporting a horizontally placed picture showing nude gluttons at a banquet table, where they swill wine. But most compelling for us is the object in the cavernlike hollow at the base of the tree of Vice—a boxlike mousetrap, open and waiting.[7] The consequences of vice are, of course, less appealing than its appearance, just as a trap holds more than cheese for a mouse, but the Augustinian sense of irony, of surprise, is fading into a conventional symbol for the perfectly predictable consequence of vice.

Despite Shakespeare's dramatic emphasis on ironic surprise, we cannot be sure that he knew or intended precisely the Augustinian convention of thought.[8] We can be reasonably certain, however, that he and his audience were familiar with closely related concepts. Augustine was one of the most frequently quoted authorities in the sermons appointed by Elizabeth to be read in pulpits, and in other sermons as well. But even if Englishmen with an average education and exposure to sermons did not know precisely the Augustinian mousetrap for the devil illustrated by the *Mérode Altarpiece,* they almost certainly did carry in their minds a great many symbolic associations with mice, traps, and mousetraps. The Bible is always an obvious source of commonplaces.[9] In Leviticus we learn that the mouse, along with the weasel and the tortoise, is among the "unclean . . . creeping things that creep upon the earth" (11:29). In I Samuel mice are among the plagues that infect the land (6:4).

As for traps, several passages emphasize their tendency to provide an ironic reversal to hopeful expectations. In Psalms the enemies of the servant of God have given him a prophetic combination of vinegar and gall for his hunger and thirst. He calls down God's wrath upon them: "Let their table become a snare before them, and that which should have been for their welfare, let it become a trap" (69:22). The idea of a religious trap has been a recurrent notion in the mind of the West. The fourteenth-century

English Dominican scholar Robert Holcot (d.1349), in his *Super librum sapientiae* (1586), emphasizes the specifically bawdy implications of the mousetrap:

> "Give not the power of thy soul to a woman, lest she enter upon thy strength, and thou be confounded. . . . Turn away thy face from a woman dressed up, and gaze not upon another's beauty." These women are creatures of whom the letter says . . . , "because the creatures of God turned to an abomination," that is, to God Himself, "and a temptation to the souls of men, and a snare to the feet of the unwise." For in this mousetrap David was caught. . . .[10]

Two delightful uses of a trap emblem are found in the margins of illuminations done for *The Book of Hours of Catherine of Cleves* (ca. 1435).[11] Below the "Release of Souls from the Mouth of Hell," a rustic, apparently meant to stand for the devil, is shown snaring and caging birds, traditional emblems for the soul. One cannot help but recall Claudius's lines in the prayer scene: "O limed soul, that, struggling to be free, /Art more engag'd! . . ." (III. iii. 68–69). In the "Visitation," Elizabeth, pregnant with John the Baptist, greets the Virgin, still carrying Jesus. Below the courteous encounter, John the Baptist waits to spring a trap in which the Infant Christ is set as bait for souls. As this second marginal illumination shows, a positive as well as a negative tradition exists for the trap, here a joyful hope. A similar dual tradition exists for most medieval symbols (the garden, the woman, the bed, the city, and so forth). This way the medieval allegorist could sweep all biblical or other authoritative references to anything into one of two categories.

There is virtually no possibility that Shakespeare ever knew Holcot or saw *The Book of Hours of Catherine of Cleves;* but Henry Green[12] has argued Shakespeare's familiarity with the first emblem book in English, Geffrey Whitney's widely read *A Choice of Emblemes* (Leyden, 1586).[13] Three emblems of mice, or animals associated with mice, appear in this collection of allegorical pictures and explanatory poems. One, which does not concern us, shows mice dancing around cats caught in traps set for the mice (p. 222). Another, with the motto "captivus, ob gulam" (captive by gluttony), presents a mouse on a beach, caught with its head in an oyster shell (Plate 20). The second stanza of the accompanying poem points the moral:

> The Gluttons fatte, that daintie fare deuoure,
> And seeke about, to satisfie theire taste:
> And what they like, into theire bellies poure,
> This iustlie blames, for surfettes come in haste:
> And biddes them feare, their sweete, and dulcet meates,
> For oftentimes, the same are deadlie baites. (p. 128)

Thus, as we learned from the first stanza, the mouse was "crush'd till he was dead," trapped by his own gluttony. The association of the mouse with the varieties of gluttony is, of course, older than Shakespeare's time. In the "Prologue to the Wife of Bath's Tale," Dame Alison accuses her rich husband of coming "hoom as dronken as a Mous." And in a letter of Richard Beerly to Thomas Cromwell written in 1536, it is said that "Monckes . . . cum to mattens as dronck as myss."[14] The phrase was clearly proverbial. Also proverbial was the identification as emblems of folly of the moth in the candle flame, the bird in the snare, and the mouse in the trap. In one of the parodies of Petrarchan love poems to be found in George Gascoigne's *The Adventures of Master F. J.* (1573), the three images are presented in rapid succession:

> Of thee deare Dame, three lessons would I learne:
> What reason first persuades the foolish Fly
> (As soone as shee a candle can discerne)
> To play with flame, till shee bee burnt thereby?
> Or what may move the Mouse to byte the bayte
> Which strikes the trappe, that stops hir hungry breth?
> What calles the bird, where snares of deepe deceit
> Are closely coucht to draw hir to hir death?
> . . . .
> Fooles play so long till they be caught in deede.[15]

The third Whitney emblem, with the motto "saepius in auro bibitur venenum" (poison usually drunk in a golden vessel), shows a luxuriously dressed woman flanked by two muskcats, and wearing a third as a fur piece around her shoulders. The first three lines of the accompanying poem read, "Heare Lais fine, doth braue it on the stage, /With muskecattes sweete, and all she coulde desire: /Her beauties beames, did make the youthe to rage" (p.

79). This would seem to have nothing to do with mice, but we know that the Renaissance, either deliberately or through error, was capable of conflating the musk-bearing animals and the mouse. This emblem, like the one of the mouse and the oyster and most of Whitney's other emblems, originally appeared in the vastly popular books of the sixteenth-century Italian emblemist Andrea Alciati. Whitney's picture of the muskcats first occurred as Emblem 79 of Alciati's *Omnia emblemata* (Antwerp, 1577). Alciati's Latin poem (p. 293), however, is quite different from Whitney's English one. The Alciati starts: "Delicias & mollitiem mus creditur albus" (the white mouse is believed to mean softness and delight). As for the distinctive colors of mice, not only is the white mouse more lascivious, but it is also often paired with a black mouse in the medieval commonplace of two mice, one black, the other white, standing for night and day and associated with the Triumph of Time, following Petrarch. These mice are regarded as an image of the brevity of pleasure and the fragility of the things of this world.[16]

The Latin word *mus* can be translated to mean "mouse," "rat," or any of several other rodents or even small animals. It is also very close to *muscus,* the Latin word for "musk" and a generic term for all musk-bearing animals. And *muscus* appears in the last line of Alciati's poem: ". . . the scent of the unguent of the Arabian musk ['muscus'] is celebrated." This is not to say that Shakespeare, with his "small Latine and lesse Greeke," was necessarily familiar with all these linguistic ambiguities. What we do know, however, is that English writers conflated *mouse, mus,* and *muscus.* Edward Topsell, for instance, in his article on the mouse in his encyclopedic bestiary, *The Historie of Foure-Footid Beastes* (London, 1607), affirms:

> . . . the white Mouse is aboue all other most laciuious and leacherous, and therefore it came into a prouerbe, *Myss Leucos, Myss Cacos,* the white Mouse is an ill Mouse, of whose lust *Alciatus* made this emblem;
> *Delittas* [sic] *& mollitiem, Mus creditur albus,* (p. 505)

With the exception of its last line, the rest of Alciati's poem about the "mouse," or more specifically the muskcat, follows in Topsell. Mice had come to stand, in the popular imagination, for all that was gluttonous, lascivious, corrupt, and defiling. Indeed, even as late as 1638, a drawing by Inigo Jones for the costume of an actor in one of Sir William D'Avenant's masques shows "a crier of mousetraps" holding a boxlike trap high in the air (Plate 21).[17] The crier is one of the figures in the third entry of the antimasque, who is described as emerging from "a horrid hell, the further part terminating in a flaming precipice."[18] And on an entirely popular level a few years later an anonymous diatribe against the Jesuits is called *The Rat-trap: or, The Iesvites Taken in their own Net, &c* (London, 1641). The title page shows two Jesuits bemoaning the fate of a third caught behind the bars of an enormous trap (Plate 22). As Topsell's bestiary goes on to state, "Mice do defile, corrupt, and make vnprofitable whatsoeuer they tast, and therefore the Egyptians, when they would describe corruption, do picture a Mouse" (p. 509).

What better image for the corrupter of Denmark, the polluter of the royal marriage bed, the one who banqueted in a time proper to mourning? After the audience is shown what lies within his character Claudius is consistently presented by Shakespeare as being both diabolical and erotic, but never more emphatically than in the two scenes immediately following the enactment of "The Mouse-trap." In the prayer scene Claudius tries to beg divine forgiveness: "O, my offence is rank, it smells to heaven; /It hath the primal eldest curse upon't— /A brother's murder! . . ." Hamlet discovers him in prayer, but thinks him in a state of grace and thus refuses to kill him for fear that his revenge might be less than complete. Better to wait, ". . . that his soul may be as damn'd and black /As hell, whereto it goes. . . ." The famous irony is that Claudius was not in a state of grace; he was unable to feel true contrition because unwilling to give up the rewards of sin: his throne and his queen. In Hamlet's subsequent interview with his mother (III. iv), he comes down hard on the connubial relationship between king and queen: ". . . to live /In the rank sweat of an enseamed bed, /Stew'd in corruption, honeying and making love /Over the nasty sty! . . ." A few lines later Hamlet warns Gertrude not to let ". . . the bloat King tempt you again to bed; /Pinch wanton on your cheek; call you his mouse."

Critics of the play may have insufficiently considered the possibility of a unifying amplitude in Hamlet's title for his trap, and thus they have possibly mistaken both its dramatic tone and its dramatic meaning.[19] Levin Shücking has commented: "The farcical title, less suited to the tragic events of the play than to the reason for its presentation, clearly shows the impress of Hamlet's sarcastic humour."[20] And Professor Harry Levin has stated:

> Claudius, with mounting suspicion, has asked for the name of the play; and Hamlet has answered, 'The Mousetrap.' This is his private joke, since he has devised the stratagem in order to catch the conscience of the King. But the young scholar, instead of explaining, taunts and tantalizes the royal spectator: 'Marry, how? Tropically.' A listener who heard no more than Claudius would comprehend no more than a tautological pun, which is spelled out by the Quarto reading, 'Trapically.'[21]

The title is probably neither "farcical" nor a mere "tautological pun." More likely, it is based upon a serious attempt to relate theological or moral or psychological truth to the commonplace experiences of everyday; in that sense it is a "metaphysical" image consistent with the poetic practice of the school of John Donne. If so, it is analogous to the most famous of metaphysical images: the compass emblem in Donne's "A Valediction: forbidding mourning." We recall how the commonplace architect's compass is there used to symbolize the constancy of true love. Nor would the mousetrap have been understood by most Elizabethans as the basis of no more than a tautological pun. By Shakespeare's day, mice, traps, and probably even St. Augustine's mousetrap set by God for the devil, had a host of conventional symbolic associations for ordinary Englishmen.[22] By the time Shakespeare's audience has reached the play within the play, it has already come to see Claudius as the gluttonous, erotic devil who infects the whole body politic, the kingdom of mankind, with poison.

Finally, the play within the play, "The Mouse-trap," could conveniently have been acted in an inner recess of Shakespeare's Globe Playhouse. Even if the "inner stage" so long assumed, or anything like it, never existed, the expedient of a temporary curtained booth could serve virtually the same effect, perhaps even better.[23] The courtly audience for whom Hamlet has prepared the play would still probably witness it from the extensive forestage. And if the handful of strolling players who act out the tragedy of Duke Gonzago play their parts within a boxlike stage of whatever sort, the iconographic implications of the boxlike Renaissance mousetrap will be all the more apparent to the audience in the gallery and the pit.[24] Then the iconic stage image would not be so much the dumb show itself (as it was in the choice of the right "virtue" by Bassanio), but the actual stage set of a trap, in turn baited by the dramatic action of the mime. The devil snaps at the bait; the mouse is caught; but he is caught by one who must himself die in the process of full defeat.[25]

Pilgrimage of Life

That process of fully defeating the evil corrupting the state of man is both objective and subjective. The objective phase of the battle is in the outwitting of Hamlet's "mighty opposite," Claudius, partially by means of the "muscipula diaboli." The subjective phase of the battle, given dominance by Romantic interpreters, is Hamlet's own struggle with himself. His sustained struggle is not with the problem of making up his mind, however, but with working his way out of suicidal despair into fortitude. Hamlet is not too weak to effect a speedy revenge nor is he incapacitated for action by refined sensitivity and persistent ratiocination. If anything, we should fear that he will act impulsively and injure those as harmless as Ophelia. Even the supernatural goad of his revenge warns him away from striking out against Gertrude, whatever her guilt; and it is ironic that Hamlet hastily kills the irritating but harmless Polonius only moments after the infallible discovery of his true enemy. The struggle within Hamlet throughout the first half of the play is to restrain his capacity and his impulses, not to rouse himself into action, however he may castigate himself as the result of aggression turned inward. Many psychiatrists have commented on how often the scrupulous repression of hostility toward others redirects that hostility toward the self. This modern self-destructiveness, illustrated in Hamlet, would have been seen by the Renaissance as a variation on the spiritual dangers of despair.

Several books published at Continental centers of learning such as Basle and Cracow bore what came to be the famous "Genius" title-border of Hans Holbein the Younger (Plate 23).[26] This woodblock, cut in 1521, was popular enough to stimulate imitations later in the century. My discussion, however, will be based on the Holbein, not only because it is itself an artistic prototype, but also because it embodies all the most commonplace assumptions of Renaissance humanism about the dangers and joys awaiting mankind on his spiritual journey through life.[27] My purpose is twofold. First, it is still important to correct the Romantic overemphasis on Hamlet as a unique, or at least highly unusual, individual. Secondly, Hamlet as a tragic hero who sets himself as bait in the trap for the devil must be seen to achieve spiritual maturity in the course of the play if his sacrifice is to sustain the Augustinian reverberations. Finally, the discussion will be pointed toward the crucial differences between the received body of commonplaces illustrated in the title-border and Shakespeare's own handling of Hamlet's development.

Holbein's "Genius" title-border is also often called the "Table of Cebes" because its design is based on the *Table* of the so-called Cebes, a philosophical work written by a supposed Theban friend and disciple of Socrates. The "table," or picture, described in the treatise is shown to a seeker after truth in the Temple of Chronos and it is meant to reveal how the soul requires time in its struggle for perfection. Holbein's woodcut follows its authority closely, but we need only touch upon the points relevant to *Hamlet*. Some of the personifications are labeled, others easily recognizable. At the base of the design, after souls are admitted into life by Genius, early education combines different points of view ("Opinioes") with Persuasion ("Suedela"); Hamlet, we remember, has just returned from Wittenberg, where he received his education. The sins in Holbein are arranged into two categories: those of the world and the flesh, and those of the spirit. The Deadly Sins are Lust ("Luxurice"), Sloth, Gluttony, Greed ("Avarita"), and Excess ("Incontinentia"). In one of his bursts of self-castigation Hamlet claims a similar list for himself:

> I am very proud, revengeful, ambitious; with more offenses at my beck than I have thoughts to put them in, imagination to give them shape, or time to act them in. What should such fellows as I do crawling between earth and heaven? (III. i. 124–28)

The rhetorical question concluding this quotation underscores the sense of pilgrimage conveyed by Holbein's woodcut. But far more central to the development of Hamlet's character are the sins of the spirit: Excessive Grief ("Dolor") and Melancholy ("Tristitia"). Hamlet's grief drives him into suicidal despair, regarded then as a sin rather than a fashionable life style. In the woodcut, Penance spreads out her arms of welcome, as she does at least three times in *Hamlet*: to Claudius in the prayer scene, to Hamlet in the last scene when he promises repentance for responding as he did to Laertes over the grave of Ophelia, and finally to the dying Laertes when he offers to exchange forgiveness with Hamlet. The soul must always face new temptations, in False Doctrine ("Falsa disciplina") and the arts and sciences as the idolatrous ends of life, before it can conclude its final journey upward. Hamlet has spiritual relapses on several occasions. The sustainers are Fortitude ("Fortitudo"), Avidity ("Avadacia"), True Doctrine ("Veradisciplina"), Truth ("Veritas"), and Persuasion ("Persuasio"). The virtues, temporal and spiritual, are Temperance, Prudence, Justice, and Mercy; and Pauline Hope, Faith, and Charity. The ultimate reward is Felicity, or joy ("Felicitas"), within the Stronghold of True Felicity ("Arx verae felicitatis"). As the dying Hamlet tells Horatio, "Absent thee from felicity awhile."

Now *Hamlet* is infinitely more than a *Pilgrim's Progress*. Even *Pilgrim's Progress* is light-years away from this title-border by Holbein, whatever its graphic distinction as. a woodcut. But the play and the border do have in some ways a general similarity of shape. Quite obviously, Hamlet is meant to be seen as a young man tested by time and circumstance before reaching maturity. His maturity, furthermore, is cast in the form of overcoming spiritual temptations, although absolute moral values in the play are often, one feels, deliberately ambiguous. Recall that Hamlet listed himself as revengeful when cataloging his sins in the passage cited just above. And yet throughout the play Hamlet blames himself as a coward for not seeking a more speedy revenge. Laertes is even more explicit about the supernatural consequences for those seeking revenge:

> I dare damnation. To this point I stand,
> That both the worlds I give to negligence,
> Let come what comes; only I'll be reveng'd
> Most thoroughly for my father. (IV. v. 130–33)

Yet when Hamlet completes his revenge, Horatio's last words to his prince are "flights of angels sing thee to thy rest!" Revenge as absolutely good or bad, like madness as real or imaginary, or suicide as damnable or pathetic, is simply another one of the tantalizing and unresolved mysteries in this most famous of murder mysteries.[28]

But one pattern does emerge clearly. Hamlet must chart a course of action, remain confident in it, and effect it before he can justify his existence to himself and convince the audience of his maturity. Without the feeling that he both meets death as a man and is also completed as a man in the manner of his death, we would not fully sense the scale of tragic loss that audiences have always felt with this play.[29]

The conventions of religious meditation were probably especially important to the way in which Shakespeare's audience perceived Hamlet's spiritual growth from callow despair to mature fortitude. In the fishmonger scene (II. ii), Hamlet presents himself to Polonius as an intellectual gone mad from the reading of satire. Yet the satire is also closely linked to the traditional themes of meditational prose, as we perceive with the line, "For if the sun breed maggots in a dead dog, being a good kissing carrion——." The commonplace memento mori of worms crawling over a cadaver is echoed much later in the play with Hamlet's tormenting of Claudius about the location of the dead Polonius:

> At supper. . . . Not where he eats, but where 'a is eaten; a certain convocation of politic worms are e'en at him. Your worm is your only emperor for diet: we fat all creatures else to fat us, and we fat ourselves for maggots; your fat king and your lean beggar is but variable service—two dishes, but to one table. That's the end. (IV. iii. 18–25)

The pun on "end" as both anus and death, death in turn being one of the Four Last Things—Heaven, Hell, Death, and the Last Judgment—brings a sorrowful cry from Claudius. Hamlet drives home the point by proving how "a king may go a progress through the guts of a beggar." The buried trope is the Dance of Death, still familiar in the history of art through the famous series of Holbein.[30] The body, no matter how young, or powerful, or beautiful, is no defense against maggots and the grave. Death choses the participants for his dance without regard for when he is expected or the social positions of his guests. Here in the play the dance becomes a royal progress, the king and the beggar are both food for worms, and death can invite us to the slaughter when we think ourselves most fatted for life.

As in the earlier case of Polonius, Hamlet uses the conventions of meditation to attack an enemy, this time Claudius. But in these instances Shakespeare is also preparing for the occasions when Hamlet turns his meditations upon his own fate. The most famous instance is obviously the "To be or not to be" soliloquy in the nunnery scene (III. i). Hamlet's soliloquy-meditation is spoken while Ophelia is herself seemingly meditating on what the audience is led to believe is a religious book ("devotion's visage," "orisons," etc.). We know that the book is a mere prop used to justify her presence; but Hamlet does not know this, according to a straightforward reading of the text, which gives no indication that Hamlet overhears anything by eavesdropping. The ironies in this scene are rich enough without the modern convention of motivating Hamlet's "ungentlemanly" treatment of Ophelia by a knowledge of her weak acquiescence in the scheme of Polonious and Claudius to spy unseen. If anything, the dramatic richness of the play is increased by the effect of two similarly ironic prayer scenes framing the pivotal scene of the mousetrap. In the nunnery scene I believe it is Shakespeare's intention that Hamlet be totally unaware of both the spies who "withdraw" behind the probable arras and the playacting of the praying girl. In the so-called prayer scene itself Hamlet is again deceived by prayer, this time with ultimately fatal consequences for both himself and a good many others, when he mistakes the appearance of a contrite Claudius for the reality of true repentance. Hamlet's belief that revenge under the presumed circumstances would be inadequate becomes the basis of one of the most powerful ironies in the play when Claudius reveals to the audience in his famous concluding couplet that his soul has not been able to achieve a state of repentant grace. The power of this irony is in the completeness of Hamlet's ignorance. And the more we sense the parallels between the two framing scenes the stronger the play's pivotal mousetrap scene becomes. In each framing scene Hamlet misreads the spiritual reality of prolonged stage images: kneeling figures apparently in true prayer. In both these wings of the triptych of the three central scenes Hamlet hovers over the tableau figure, thinking or knowing himself to be unperceived, thus making his literal physical descent to Ophelia's "lap" in the central panel of the play scene an iconic nadir in Fortune's Wheel. This nadir presages in Hamlet's moment of triumph his own ultimate tragic fall. The three central scenes are further linked because Hamlet lies in the lap of the first praying figure at the moment of his long-awaited triumph of confirming the crime of the second. A famous soliloquy, furthermore, occurs in each of these three scenes.

"To be or not to be," the most famous soliloquy in all of Shakespeare, is probably intended, therefore, to be a meditation specifically aroused by the stage image of a young woman in prayer. If so, not only is the mousetrap climax given greater emphasis for having a clearer frame, but the soliloquy itself is more fully integrated into its own scene than it is in productions where Hamlet operatically addresses the air while Ophelia prays unnoticed. Hamlet should see Ophelia, "devotion's visage," immediately. The importance of an object or an image as the basis of Renaissance devotion and meditation has been fully developed by Louis Martz in *The Poetry of Meditation*.[31] Indeed, it can almost be assumed that Ophelia's book of "orisons" is in turn meant to convey the impression of a volume filled with devotional images, such as those of the Passion, combined with exposition. Seen thus, Hamlet develops his own debate with suicidal despair while studying what he takes to be the living image of an uncorrupted girl sunk in the contemplation of printed images conducive to hopeful expectation of eternal salvation. No wonder he at first speaks gently to her, and then, when aroused by her obedient and tactless insistence upon returning his tokens of a lover's devotion, flies into a rage of satirical attack upon court life, warning Ophelia to escape taint by retreat to a convent. Hamlet's emotions have been momentarily stabilized by her "devout" presence, only to be thrown into turmoil once again when the touching visual image of devotion opens its mouth to grating speech. The profound dramatic unity of the scene easily escapes notice in the reading because so much relies upon the juxtaposition on stage of the soliloquy and the observation of Ophelia in prayer.

A similar pattern of psychological stability and relapse occurs in the gravediggers' scene of Act V. An earlier theme recapitulated is the Dance of Death. The Second Clown comments on the social injustice of giving Ophelia sanctified burial when a suicide among the lower classes would be buried with dishonor. The First Clown agrees that the right to commit suicide should be shared by all, and we know that Shakespeare is comically turning the Dance of Death upside down. Instead of Death disregarding social station, social station should not stand in the way of seeking Death. Instead of no one being able to escape Death, all should have the same privilege of pursuing him. Following the reductio ad absurdum of their conclusions about the correct equality of all men in the face of death, the gravediggers are quickly engaged in a medieval debate about superiority of vocation, one recalling the medieval theme that is the central action of John Heywood's *The Four PP.* The answer to the riddle gives the profession of the gravedigger ascendancy, as we might expect; the common man's theories about his equality to the aristocracy do not keep him from thinking himself superior to his fellow laborers. The audience's awareness of this irony creates aesthetic distance from the characters.

Hamlet and Horatio enter unseen, creating another dramatic irony, but still another, and counter, dramatic irony occurs when Hamlet comments on the inappropriateness of singing while digging a grave. The very thing the audience should discern is the appropriateness of lyrics about the Dance of Death snatching another body for the grave:

> But age, with his stealing steps,
>   Hath clawed me in his clutch,
> And hath shipped me intil the land,
>   As if I had never been such. (V. i. 71–74)

The way in which Hamlet and Horatio talk about the activity of the gravediggers without making their presence known to them gives these socially superior men added dramatic ascendency. But the failure of Hamlet to recognize the appropriateness of the song puts him in the same relationship to the audience as the gravediggers are to him and we are to the gravediggers. It might even be said that the threefold structure of dramatic irony equalizes Hamlet and the gravediggers. Even though he knows something they do not know, we know something he does not know.

The theme of equality, the equality of death, is varied in yet other ways. As skulls are thrown up to make way for a new body, Hamlet moralizes these literal memento mori. All the great and the small, all the good and the bad, all the beautiful and the ugly in the history of the world are now identical skulls. The notion that nothing else remains becomes the subject of another conventional meditation, the ubi sunt, the "where are" questions first applied to a skull imagined to be that of a lawyer: "Where be his quiddites now, his quillets, his cases, his tenures, and his tricks? (V. i. 96–97). When Hamlet finally addresses the First Clown, asking, "Whose grave's this, sirrah?" the doubly equivocal answer provides another variation on the consistent theme of all men confronting death together: "Mine, sir." Even gravediggers die. The gravedigger is literally in the grave, probably standing in the theater on the steps or ladder beneath the trap. This mimetic stage image combines with the earlier iconic stage image of skulls thrown up only to fall and become the subject of Hamlet's meditation, a combination of Fortune's Wheel with memento mori. The fundamental transition has occurred, from death as something happening to everyone else, no matter how great or small, to death as happening to oneself. Hamlet's age is soon the related topic of discussion, the impersonality of anonymous skulls becomes the deeply felt memory of Yorick, and then Hamlet is unexpectedly and suddenly confronted with the dead body of his beloved. Iconic meditation has passed from anonymous skulls, through the skull of Yorick, to the mimetic reality of Ophelia's dead body. Meditation was regarded in the Renaissance as a preparation for life on earth by a turning of one's thoughts to the life to come. Hamlet has returned to Denmark with a new clarity of purpose hardened by the discovery on shipboard of the letter which would have meant his death in England. The dramatic purpose of the first scene of Act V is to provide Hamlet with spiritual preparation for the dangers and discoveries still to come. But the preparation is inadequate. Hamlet once more reverts to his old instability. Even though we admire the strength of his love for Ophelia, we know that he is making a fool of himself when he jumps into the grave. This stage image of the leap into the grave also creates iconic foreboding by repeating the pattern of tragic fall into death.

Horatio apparently takes his instructions from Claudius seriously, however, and waits upon Hamlet well, for by the next scene Hamlet is a new man. By the last scene of the play he is illustrating all the courage, fortitude, self-control, and steadfastness of purpose that the meditational literature of Christian Stoicism hoped to inspire. If anything, Hamlet now begins to illustrate these virtues even better than Horatio, who had always been their Stoic but agnostic spokesman in the past. Perhaps the meditations of the gravediggers' scene had prepared the ground that had only briefly and lightly been broken when Hamlet had leapt into the grave. Hamlet's conversation with Horatio in the beginning of Act V, scene ii asserts belief in "a divinity that shapes our ends," confidence that "the interim is mine," and contrite repentance for his behaviour to Laertes at the burial. When Osric the fop delivers the challenge, Horatio is cautious, but his caution is strangely visceral. He tells Hamlet to trust his foreboding, but Hamlet replies with one of the great fortitude speeches we expect somewhere in the course of a Shakespearean tragedy:

> . . . we defy augury: there is a special providence in the fall of a sparrow. If it be now, 'tis not to come; if it be not to come, it will be now; if it be not now, yet it will come—the readiness is all. Since no man owes of aught he leaves, what is't to leave betimes? Let be. (V. ii. 211–15)

Hamlet is now fully prepared for death in his ability to confront life. When the challenge from Laertes brings duplicity and death, he takes Claudius along to the Last Judgment. As for Gertrude, whatever her degree of sexual transgression, it is surely expiated by the poisoned cup. The contribution by Claudius of a pearl ("union") may even have iconic implications. The pearl, emblem of chastity, combines with the Renaissance jewel as a conventional means of conveying secreted poison to food or drink. Gertrude, innocent without but somehow tainted within, insists upon joining the fatal conclusion of the action. Hamlet's own inevitable fate also springs from his vital will. Horatio, whose earlier example of insistent fortitude is now better exemplified by Hamlet, is dissuaded from even a Stoic suicide by one who had toyed with suicide throughout the first half of the play.

Despite all the mysteries, resolved and unresolved, despite the centuries of debate, the play has always been an enormous stage success. It requires none of the pure love of Shakespeare behind any production of *Troilus and Cressida. Hamlet* has stark dramatic clarity. Perhaps in this play Shakespeare has trapped the audience into confronting that clarity instead of focusing on the unresolvable problems of both the read text and life. Radiantly clear is the felicity of courage, loyalty, patience, and hope. To the Renaissance these would be virtues; even in the psychological vocabulary of the twentieth century these responses to the flux and mystery of human experience have their potency still.

5

Macbeth: The Life to Come

Like *Hamlet, Macbeth* is a drama of the unexpected: much is not as it seems, few find what they seek, nearly everyone misreads the future. Woven into the pervasive pattern of clothing imagery are "strange garments" which "cleave not to their mould," and "nothing is but what is not." With the obvious exceptions of the witches and the gore, most of the stage images should glitter, allure, fascinate. Shakespeare is very careful to present the castles of Macbeth, and the charming hosts, as anything but the gothic horrors they have been in many productions since the nineteenth century. In her sleepwalking scene Lady Macbeth does say that "Hell is murky," but we find no mention of clanging chains, dripping walls, and weed-grown battlements. All of that grew in the overheated imagination of romantics like Orson Welles. Much of it undoubtedly arose from the night settings of nearly all of the scenes, so stressed by A. C. Bradley.[1] G. Wilson Knight would even drape the entire set for the play in black.[2] Yet although Duncan and his entourage arrive before Macbeth's castle at Inverness for the first time at night, the king is charmed by his arrival: "This castle hath a pleasant seat; the air /Nimbly and sweetly recommends itself /Unto our gentle senses." Banquo's reply is famous enough:

> This guest of summer,
> The temple-haunting martlet, does approve
> By his lov'd mansionry that heaven's breath

> Smells wooingly here; no jutty, frieze,
> Buttress, nor coign of vantage, but this bird
> Hath made her pendent bed and procreant cradle.
> Where they most breed and haunt, I have observ'd
> The air is delicate. (I. vi. 3–10)

Shakespeare's expression of evil here is like that of Milton and Spenser—the serpent is truly beautiful, the bower is tempting indeed.

It is a supreme irony that Duncan's gift to his hostess, delivered by trustworthy Banquo, is a diamond, whose clarity and hardness are emblems of purity and constancy. Renaissance impresas made the diamond equivalent to good faith, integrity, and lack of fraud.[3] The diamond as an iconic stage image underscores for the audience the innocence of a man who never stops trusting appearances. The gift is a forthright symbol of the giver and an ironic comment on the receiver. The precious stone ultimately resonates with Macbeth's "eternal jewel" given to the "common enemy of man," in Act III.

A contrasting iconic gift occurs in *Richard III* when the demonic Duke of Gloucester confirms his seduction of the Lady Anne by his love token of a ring. Although she mourns two men whom he gradually admits having murdered, her flattered female pride allows the faithless acceptance of a pledge of endless devotion "With all" her heart. The ring here, as in *The Merchant of Venice,* is an implied symbol of faithfulness "for ever," its circular form the emblem of eternity. Richard shares with the audience the clear ironies of his gift the moment Anne leaves the stage. "I'll have her; but I will not keep her long," he announces, thus drawing the ring into its contrasting association with mere lust. Nor does Anne's ready disloyalty toward former king and prince deserve much better.

The dramatic ironies of *Macbeth,* however, are characteristically understated. The recipient of Duncan's diamond should be played by an actress with all the reassuring charm of an Ingrid Bergman, not by one famous for her Medea, such as Dame Judith Anderson, as is often the case. The apparent goodness of an actress like Bergman can make the apparent guilt of the bloody grooms seem true—even, perhaps, for a moment of enchantment, to the audience. The personal magnetism of the actress should be great enough to make even us feel from time to time that her ambitions are appropriate and fitting. After all, we too are part of that world described by Lady Macduff just before the mass murder, ". . . where to do harm /Is often laudable, to do good sometime /Accounted dangerous folly." The practical effect of Duncan's murder is to convince the clear majority of the Scottish nobility to elect Macbeth their king at Scone and to be ignorant of the truth until the banquet scene midway through the play. In contrast to the blackness within, the visible effect of the Macbeths is allurement and reassurance. They are in the same category of Satanists as Iago, who boasts, "When devils will their blackest sins put on /They do suggest at first with heavenly shows." "Angels are bright still, though the brightest fell," according to Malcolm later in *Macbeth,* when he interviews the fled Macduff. In like manner, in contrast to the dour Scottish landscape, Inverness Castle, insofar as it is made to exist on stage, should be light and airy, inviting, hospitable, everything the blasted heath is not.

The Witches

On the heath the witches lie in wait. Unlike the castle, they must appear evil, for the audience must be fully convinced of Macbeth's responsibility for his crimes. But even the witches are not entirely what they seem, despite their hideous appearances. As symbolic presences, like the diamond, they are an example of ambiguity in iconic stagecraft. The witches are introduced amid a disordered world of thunder and lightning recalling the heath scene in *Lear,* where a mad king is reduced to the essentials of his animal nature. The witches are also linked to the base world of animals, as they prepare to fly off through the "fog and filthy air" in response to the calls of their supernatural masters, who have assumed animal forms associated with devils. Yet to the agents of evil "Fair is foul and foul is fair." The diabolical union of contraries is unconsciously expressed by Macbeth in another form when he first meets the witches: "So foul and fair a day I have not seen." The day will seem to bring good fortune to Macbeth, though that good fortune is prophesied by the agents of harm and danger; the total and real effects of the day, however, will be death and destruction, despite the most hopeful of expectations. Even

Banquo's initial response to the skinny-lipped and bearded witches is one of disorientation: ". . . What are these /So wither'd, and so wild in their attire, /That look not like th' inhabitants o' th' earth, /And yet are on't? . . ." Satanic creatures, "in the world but not of it," the witches are not entirely where they belong.

Much scholarly and critical discussion has centered on the identity of these prophetic servants of Satan. Shakespeare's well-known source for them is in the second volume of Holinshed's unillustrated second edition of the *Chronicles* (London, 1587).[4] Holinshed presents them in several roles, but seems to stress the concept of the Three Fates:

> . . . the common opinion was, that these women were either the weird sisters, that is (as ye would say) the goddesses of distinie, or else some nymphs or feiries, indewed with knowledge of prophesie by their necromantical science, bicause euerie thing came to passe as they had spoken. (p. 171)

Holinshed is presumably recording a difference of opinion existing in the legends behind his historical account. He never refers to these women as old, ugly, or witches; quite the contrary—the only thing "strange and wild" about them is their "apparell" (Holinshed, p. 170). Shakespeare himself called Cleopatra a "fairy," and nymphs are traditionally young and beautiful. It has been suggested that Shakespeare may have made the change in his play as the result of two factors: the conflation of the story of Macbeth's murder of Duncan and an account, earlier in Holinshed, of Donwald's murder of King Duff, who was made sick by witches subsequently burned at the stake; and a desire to serve the personal and scholarly interests of James I, who was a published authority on witches, as well as the theater-company patron for whom the play may have been commissioned. Recall that James had begun as a skeptic on the subject of witchcraft, but he eventually published *Daemonologie* (Edinburgh, 1597), a book cast as a dialogue between a cool and rational Epistemon trying to convince a rigidly skeptical Philomanthes that witchcraft is indeed abroad. James had been converted by what he regarded as grim personal experience, especially by an assassination plot on his life involving witches.[5] At least some people then, as increasingly now, behaved as if witchcraft were a reality and they the masters of it.

There were also those who believed witchcraft to be on the rise.[6] Serious efforts to control witchcraft were not fully legalized in England until the reign of Elizabeth, when laws were enacted making magical murder and the invocation of evil spirits capital offenses. Under James a further act provided the death penalty for necromancy, laming, wasting men's bodies or goods, and harboring familiar spirits. The English laws against witchcraft were finally repealed in 1736, after about one thousand witches had been executed since 1542. The total in Europe for the same period may have been as high as nine million.[7] English practice was thus comparatively mild, but the executions that did occur were probably very widely considered justifiable. Shakespeare, in any event, could not have gone too far wrong in gaining the interest of his audience when he specified Holinshed's vague description of the "nymphs or feiries" as that of witches.

A seemingly contradictory interpretation of them as Fates (or Parcae) also exists. In the first scene of Act II Macbeth learns from Banquo that he "dreamt last night of the three Weird Sisters," or rather the three witches. It has often been easier for the classically minded to regard them as "goddesses of destinie" than as witches. *Weird* had in Shakespeare's day, as we all know, the sense of the Old English *wyrd*, meaning fateful. It has long been observed that throughout the spoken lines of the play these fatal tempters are referred to as "Weird Sisters" more frequently than as "witches." (The usual First Folio spelling of *weird* as "weyard" probably reflects the pronunciation of the word at the time.) The prophetic greeting to Macbeth at his first encounter with the old women is cast according to the three dimensions of time—past, present, and future—and the famous woodcut illustrating the earlier edition of Holinshed's *Chronicles* (London, 1577) shows these three women as old, middle-aged, and young (Plate 24). Macbeth was thane of Glamis, he is thane of Cawdor, and he will be king of Scotland. Only a year before the probable composition date of *Macbeth*, James was welcomed to Oxford in 1605 by a ceremonial pageant. Matthew Gwinne, the author, provided three youths, "attired like nymphs or sybils" to "hail" the king and remind him that they had in the past prophesied power to him as a descendant of Banquo's issue.[8] In *Macbeth* Banquo says that the Weird Sisters look not like the inhabitants of the earth and yet are on it, a statement suggesting that they look more like inhabitants of the underworld, the traditional location not only of evil spirits but of the Three Fates. Later, in Act III, in one of the interpolated witch scenes, which was at least written by someone much closer in time to Shakespeare than we are, Hecate arranges a rendezvous " . . . at the pit of Acheron," one of the lowest pits of the classical hell.[9] Holinshed himself seems to lean toward a model for his "Weird Sisters" in classical antiquity, for he describes them as "three women in strange and wild apparell, resembling creatures of elder worlde [sic]" (1587 ed., p. 170), "elder" then meaning "ancient." And Shakespeare constantly emphasizes the pattern of three in their activities and speech. The most elaborate instance of the pattern of three-dimensional time is the raising of three apparitions in the first scene of Act IV. An armed head foretells Macbeth's conquest by Macduff, a bloody child recalls Macduff ripped from his mother's womb, and a crowned child stands for Malcolm as the true king of Scotland. The bloody child announces that ". . . none of woman born /Shall harm Macbeth," and he replies, "Then live, Macduff; what need I fear of thee? /But yet I'll make assurance double sure /And take a bond of fate. . . ." The term "fate" itself thus emerges in the dialogue to stimulate the interpretation of these sisters as Parcae.

We know that the Three Fates are among the most common allusions to classical mythology in Renaissance English compendiums.[10] In Richard Lynche's partial English translation of Vincenzo Cartari's *Le imagini de i' dei* (1580), entitled *The Fountaine of Ancient Fiction* (London, 1599), the Fates are described in their most commonplace form: as Parcae, the three attend on Pluto in the underworld and spin out the birth, life, and death of mankind (sig. P4v). Unlike his translator, Cartari illustrates his subjects. In an edition of *Le imagini* published in France (Lyons, 1581), the Fates are shown huddled together (Plate 25). The descriptive text in Cartari (pp. 250–55) includes many details about the Parcae also eliminated by Lynche in the English translation, but Shakespeare could have found all the essentials in the Lynche version and many other places as well. Earlier in the century a rendering of the Fates by the graphic artist Pierre Milan not only shows them with the emblems of their activities but also dressed in a manner markedly similar to the three women illustrated by Holinshed. Once again the women are young, middle-aged, and old. Milan was an engraver of the School of Fontainebleau and produced his

work there in the 1540s.[11] Thus Shakespeare's major concession to
the iconic convention of witchcraft is in the consistently advanced
age of his Fates.

In defining these sisters, philosophically minded critics have
long wrestled with a choice between demonic tempters and fatal
predestinators. According to most commentators, Shakespeare
intended his audience to interpret these women in the light of only
one of several possibilities: (1) the symbolic embodiment of
Macbeth's hopes and Banquo's wildest expectations; (2) the
Furies, come from the underworld to introduce a neoclassical
tragedy of ambition and revenge; (3) the Fates, inhabitants of hell
who predetermine the whole subsequent action of the play in
ritual acts of proclamation; or (4) flesh and blood witches, worldly
servants of the devil and tempters addressing themselves to man's
original sin.[12] Shakespeare probably intended his witches to fulfill
all of these dramatic possibilities at one point or another. Not only
is Shakespeare characteristically writing by scenes, but in his
Weird Sisters we also confront another Shakespearean union of
contraries, the mode of thought so very popular in the Renaissance
and so pervasive in Shakespeare.[13]

The witches are iconic stage images uniting the opposites of
destiny and freely tempted evil.

Renaissance art, both visual and dramatic, is filled with images
designed to unify apparent opposites. As I have suggested in my
introduction, the visual image was regarded as uniquely suited to
this purpose. An example seemingly remote from the witches in
Macbeth is the still popular printer's device of the dolphin entwined
about an anchor, but it beautifully illustrates a Renaissance use of
imagery that can help us to understand Shakespeare's seemingly
inconsistent witches as well. The motto usually associated with the
dolphin and anchor is "festina lente" (make haste slowly).[14] The
theological parallel is hope in the Resurrection, paradoxical
because men find it difficult truly to hope for what they have never
experienced. Both the motto and the doctrine are symbolized by a
dolphin entwined about an anchor, made famous in the Renaissance as the emblem of the Venetian printer Aldus Pius Manutius
and his descendants (Plate 26). The dolphin rapidly and repeatedly leaps above the surface of life into immortality, while the
stabilizing anchor is the emblem of Pauline hope. The image thus
provides a bridge closed to logic, a bridge between a moral precept

and a theological doctrine. Yet another popular Renaissance interpretation of this emblem equates the dolphin with inspired genius (nature) and the anchor with diligence and training (art). This last paradox is fundamental to the Renaissance concept of aesthetic creativity.[15] Such emblems were often deliberately open-ended, meant to stimulate endless interpretations in all areas of experience. In this way the printer's impresa of the dolphin illustrates a concentrated universal language instantly unifying all time and space with the Neoplatonic world of transcendent cognition.

As for the seeming opposites of fate and free will, the Middle Ages and the Renaissance found in them no necessary contradiction. Had not Boethius reconciled (and Chaucer translated) God's foreknowledge and man's free will? Still familiar to graduate students today is the fifth book of *De consolatione philosophiae,* where Boethius (in the sixth century A.D.) bears down on the reconciliation of divine omniscience and human freedom: God foresees, but does not cause. It is in the nature of man's humanity and his freedom that he is apart from God and thus will inevitably fall in a way God foresees, but man is nonetheless responsible for his sin and God nonetheless capable of redeeming it if man will accept God's invitation to atonement. Macbeth quite obviously does not accept the invitation. Dante would have placed him in the ninth, and lowest, circle of hell, where four categories of sinners are encased in ice. These cold-blooded criminals are guilty of one of the four worst sins against man: murder of kindred, treason to party or country, murder of guests, and treason to lord or benefactor. In one monstrous act Macbeth is fully responsible for all four. He breaks the most fundamental of natural bonds by murdering his kinsman, his king, his guest, and, even beyond these, his ideal of humanity, a benefactor he fully respected as a virtuous man. Furthermore, he is keenly conscious of all these implications of his crime (I. vii. 1ff.), and he never thinks of blaming the Weird Sisters for tempting him into anything but a false sense of security. Yet it was an act anyone in the audience, let alone God, could have predicted, given Macbeth's willful ambition, his wife, and his opportunity.

Shakespeare himself has provided in the dramatic structure of the play his own added integration of the forces of fate and free will. One of the most widely recognized patterns in the play is the constant reference to time described above. Macbeth defies time's rhythm by his tyrannous acts, and the audience feels a great sense of relief at the end when Macduff appears with the head of Macbeth, declaring "The time is free"—free, that is, from the contraint of a tyrant. The correct humility in the face of time is expressed by Banquo early in the play when he invokes the Weird Sisters: "If you can look into the seeds of time /And say which grain will grow and which will not, /Speak then to me, who neither beg nor fear /Your favours nor your hate" (I. iii. 58–61). This speech is one of Shakespeare's clearest definitions of the virtue of fortitude so emphasized by Renaissance Christian Stoicism. In other plays Shakespeare has characters express this virtue in more succinct forms and in more emphatic contexts—"Ripeness is all"; "the readiness is all." The central importance of the virtue of fortitude to the moral order idealized in most of the great tragedies is well understood by critics. The unusually long definition of fortitude in *Macbeth,* unusually early in the play as well, expresses Banquo's willingness to accept the consequences of time in their due order and pace and to respond with equal Renaissance Stoicism to fortune and misfortune. Banquo seems to assume that most of the circumstances of his existence are out of his control —that they are fatal, to be left in the hands of a providential God—but that man is free to sustain his own humanity by responding to invincible and mysterious change with courage, humility, and fortitude. Macbeth's career stands in clear contrast to the attitude toward time expressed in Banquo's speech. He coerces time by hastening the death of Duncan and trying to prevent the succession of Banquo's issue. In the first instance, the regicide is an accelerating of time's pace. In the second instance, the attack on Banquo and Fleance is an attempt to stop time and remain, in a sense, king forever, without passing that power on to the descendants of Banquo. Only a man enslaved to ambition would thus try to wrench himself from the rhythm of time by bending it to his will. True freedom is in the paradoxical service of time, and time is the providential ordering of events. In God's "seruice is perfect freedome," according to "The second Collect for peace" in *The Booke of Common Prayer* (London, 1596). The Collect (sig. A7r) was appointed for Morning Prayer and it has been reprinted endlessly. The commonplaces of *The Booke of Common Prayer* were, of course, put into substantially modern form in 1549, by order of Edward VI and Parliament. The natural order of time in *Macbeth* is quite obviously the death of Duncan from natural causes and the election of a new king before the coming of Macbeth to the throne. Macbeth's first dramatic opportunity for true freedom of will is to be found in the freely chosen restraint of his personal ambition in the "seruice" of God and king until the death of an aging Duncan allows the fulfillment of Macbeth's own providential fate as future king of Scotland. When his wife "reasons" and goads him into abandoning this willful restraint, he loses both freedom and will. He becomes enslaved to irrational sin, falls prey to the evil forces who use him in his attempt to bend time to the apparent service of his enslaved will, and meets his fate at the hands of those who would free time and themselves from his enslaved and enslaving tyranny.

The Cauldron

The witches, then, are iconic stage images of great complexity, and the contrasting forces they represent—both fate and free will—are equally essential to the artistry of the play. Yet both their roles come to a single demonic end, symbolized in the cauldron they circle at the beginning of Act IV. The ingredients of their hellish broth are a catalog of evil forces and events appropriate to the iconographic cauldron as one of the stock symbols for the mouth of hell. This is the familiar scene in which Macbeth demands to know the future from the witches. The answer is the procession of apparitions who emerge from the cauldron. After they state their cryptic answers to his questions, each *"Descends,"* according to the stage directions (F1–"Tragedies," p. 144). The apparitions undoubtedly returned the way they had come: through a trapdoor in the stage. As in the entrance of Hamlet's ghost, the trapdoor was the traditional way to and from the Senecan underworld. *Macbeth* contains a succession of characters—Malcolm, Fleance, and Macduff—specifically seeking revenge against Macbeth for murdering members of their families, and it is well known that Senecan conventions such as omens, apparitions, ghosts, and the imagery of hell are entirely appropriate to the revenge theme of the play.

What has seldom, if ever, been considered is the added iconic effect of the Weird Sisters themselves emerging on stage from an empty-bottomed cauldron set over the trapdoor. We know that the apparitions emerge this way. Arthur Colby Sprague records how in the early nineteenth century Macready had the witches in Act IV discovered onstage, scattered at different points in a cavern, each lost in her own thoughts.[16] Most productions, however, have revealed them to the audience already gathered around the cauldron. Yet they might emerge from it initially, an action appropriate to their role within the entire iconic framework of the play. The apparitions should negotiate their emergence with grace, although the boiling liquid in the cauldron would present a challenge to them and to the set designer (as in the case of the First Folio directions calling for the witches to *"vanish"* toward the end of the scene). Yet the designer would have been eager to cope with the problem, especially if the play were designed for the court stage, where special effects were increasingly the rage.[17] The staging problems here are as nothing compared to those in *The Tempest,* soon to be discussed. The cauldron follows the apparitions to the cellarage. According to a line assigned to Macbeth, the cauldron "sinks" (IV. i. 106), something it could not do unless it were indeed placed over a trapdoor.

The appropriateness of the apparitions arising from within the cauldron is based on the popular notion of a boiling cauldron set amid flames as an emblem of hellmouth. Very familiar to the Middle Ages and the Renaissance were the jaws of the serpent of Genesis, the whale of Jonah, and the lion of Revelation; but the cauldron was only slightly less popular as a standard image of hell, and many instances in medieval and later iconography can be cited. A woodcut of a cauldron used as an example of hellmouth by G. K. Hunter (Plate 27) is drawn from a "newly augmented" edition of *The Kalender of Shepardes* (London, 1570?). Hunter has explained the meaning of the cauldron as hellmouth in relationship to the fate of the villainous Barabbas in Marlowe's *The Jew of Malta* (ca. 1589). At the end of the play Christians and Turks are reconciled when Barabbas is dropped into the very boiling cauldron that he has duplicitously prepared for his dinner guests. Hunter explains the origin of the symbolism:

> The standard iconography of Hell in the Middle Ages was derived from the final chapters of Job, where Behemoth and

Leviathan (images of the devil) are described in graphic
detail. From these, of course, was derived the image of
hell-mouth as the mouth of a fearful monster, familiar to
many moderns from the revived Mystery Plays. But among
the descriptions of Leviathan are features that are not so
familiar: "Out of his nostrils cometh out smoke, as out of a
boyling pot or cauldron. He maketh the depth to boyle like a
pot" (xli, 11, 22). Émile Mâle has remarked the effect of these
verses on the iconography of hell: "The thirteenth-century
artist put a literal construction on these passages, and carried
his scruples so far as to represent a boiling cauldron in the
open jaws of the monster."[18]

By the eighteenth century the hell symbolism of *Macbeth* was so
misunderstood or so unacceptable to the Age of Reason that not
only the spurious Hecate but the witches were made to exit by
shooting upwards on wires, like marionettes. Macbeth's casual
comment, "Infected be the air" whereon the witches "ride" (IV. i.
138), apparently confirmed the idea that they belonged on Mount
Olympus with Homer's gods, even if they had to get there on
broomsticks.[19] The late eighteenth-century revival of the older
practice of the witches vanishing before our eyes sent them
downward. Yet Waldron, in a note to his 1789 edition of *Roscius
Anglicanus,* complained bitterly: "In the modern representations of
Macbeth, Hecate is the only character which ascends; the three
Witches . . . are improperly made to sink thro' a trap-door in the
stage, instead of being rais'd by a machine into the clouds."[20] A
modern theatergoer can only laugh at such a quaint notion, but he
is probably just as unprepared to accept their entrance through the
cauldron. Their exit through a trap outraged Waldron, and it is
true that the First Folio stage directions have them merely *"vanish"*
at the end of all of the authentic witch scenes. But their late
eighteenth-century exit downward is very close to the original
symbolic effect of the cauldron scene in Shakespeare's day. Both as
witches and as Fates their psychological and physical lodging is
in hell, and the cauldron is the stage presence of the very
hellmouth that provides passage. J. C. Adams explains in detail
how the cauldron was set up above the trapdoor so that the
apparitions could arise from it,[21] and the witches could just as
easily arise from it as well.

A Midsummer Night's Dream and *The Tempest* are clearly informed by the court masque, but *Macbeth*, which probably had its first performance in 1606, was the only one of Shakespeare's plays to begin with an antimasque in the style of the Jonsonian innovations made in *The Masque of Queens*. First presented in 1609, this entertainment marks the first time witches appear in an English court masque. The grotesque dance they perform is a foil to the idealized action that follows.[22] Shakespeare's witches also introduce an action they affect, and they too sing and dance grotesquely. The addition of Hecate by a later hand and the absurd lengthening of the dancing in the eighteenth-century productions of the play should not make us forget how close the style of the first and third scenes of Act I and the witch scene of Act IV is to the iconic style of court masques.[23] *Macbeth*, possibly also commissioned by the Master of the Revels, may even have given Jonson some of his ideas for *The Masque of Queens*, despite his public dislike of Shakespeare's dramatic improbabilities. In both cases the antimasque is designed as a foil to the subsequent action. In Shakespeare the first brief scene stands in eventual ironic contrast to the alluring presence of Macbeth, his wife, and their castles. As antimasque, the more symbolic the staging of the witch scenes, the more the artistic effect is being fulfilled and the more the reality rendered transcends the world of sense that is nevertheless meant to embody it. Formality, symbolism, and ritual have been the traditional bridges provided for entrance into that other world perceived by the mind and inhabitated by the spirit.

The Dagger

The events in *Macbeth* take place not only in the mind but in all the other dimensions of reality as well. The "actual" existence of the dagger, Banquo's ghost, and even the witches has often been debated, and every director must choose a stance before offering a production of the play. If the witches are really meant to exist, for instance, it would be rationally unacceptable, I imagine, to have them appear on stage in Act IV by emerging from a boiling cauldron. Surely the director already has his hands full with those apparitions. But if they and Banquo's ghost are expressionistic embodiments of psychology—guilty dread symbolized by the ghost and sinful ambition symbolized by the witches—then the Weird Sisters should probably appear on stage in the most symbolic way possible, perhaps even *"Enter from the cauldron."* Once again, as in the case of freedom and destiny, a one-dimensional philosophical choice is unnecessary. The witches and the dagger and the ghost all exist on every level. The Renaissance did not necessarily recognize the exclusive divisions within creation that we do, and even when the period was aware of contradictions, the paradoxical reconciliation of opposites was often invoked.

The well-worn dagger soliloquy is a case in point:

> Is this a dagger which I see before me,
> The handle toward my hand? Come, let me clutch thee.
> I have thee not, and yet I see thee still.
> Art thou not, fatal vision, sensible
> To feeling as to sight? or art thou but
> A dagger of the mind, a false creation,
> Proceeding from the heat-oppressed brain?
> I see thee yet, in form as palpable
> As this which now I draw.
> Thou marshall'st me the way that I was going;
> And such an instrument I was to use.
> Mine eyes are made the fools o' th' other senses,
> Or else worth all the rest. I see thee still;
> And on thy blade and dudgeon gouts of blood,
> Which was not so before. There's no such thing:
> It is the bloody business which informs
> Thus to mine eyes. . . . (II. i. 33–49)

The dagger is clearly meant to be a dream reality symbolizing Macbeth's temptation to kill Duncan and gain the throne. Macbeth's vacillating thoughts make it obvious that he is finding it difficult to "screw" his "courage to the sticking point." But Macbeth also addresses the dagger: ". . . Come, let me clutch thee. /I have thee not. . . ." The psychological reality is fully visible, apparent to the sense of sight. Macbeth wonders if it will appeal as strongly to his sense of touch. If it can be touched it is real, if not it is ". . . but /A dagger of the mind. . . ." Yet the illusion that spiritual reality is an illusion is here presented by Shakespeare as the symptom of a mind asked to betray its most fundamental values. Lady Macbeth carries this theme even further in her lines, ". . . The sleeping and the dead / Are but as pictures; 'tis the eye of childhood / That fears a painted devil . . ." (II. ii. 53–55). The total effect of the play is to make the audience feel that daggers "of the mind" are far more real than mere objects of metal. This is the one fundamental truth that both Lady Macbeth and her husband learn: not all the water in the world of Pilate can wash their hands clean of Duncan's blood. Thus Macbeth's "There's no such thing" is ultimately to be seen from a vast ironic distance. The "false creation" of the dagger is the most "palpable" event in Macbeth's career. Furthermore, the audience is not meant to touch the dagger any more than Macbeth is. Even if it is a stage property, it must remain an object that is but seen. It should, therefore, be a stage property, as it probably was in Shakespeare's day.[24] Cécile de Banke has used the "air-drawn dagger" to comment on the Renaissance love of literal symbolism: "A suspended dagger that moved and oozed with blood was, no doubt, a prideful property. . . . With a literal-minded audience this could not remain a dagger of the mind."[25]

But the issue here is anything but primitive Elizabethan literal-mindedness as opposed to our own enlightened capacity for imagination. The problem is, instead, the modern inability to accept sense-perceived and mind-perceived realities as compatible. The "dissociation of sensibility," although by now another worn concept, still helps to account for the modern disappearance of the dagger as a stage property, consigned to the same scientific dustheap as Joan of Arc's visions and voices. As a conventional iconic stage image the dagger is the consistent Shakespearean symbol of deceit and treachery, of assassination and ambition, standing in contrast to the nobility and justice of the sword, used earlier by Macbeth when he freely fought to serve his king by overcoming the treacherous Cawdor. The dagger also embodies the Deadly Sins of Wrath and Envy. Wrath is obvious enough, and it is illustrated in the Renaissance by Philip Galle's conventional treatment of the Seven Deadly Sins in a set of engravings executed around 1600;[26] but the dagger's less obvious iconographic association with Envy is based on this weapon being the one traditionally used by Cain to kill his brother, Abel, because he was more highly favored by God. Cain became the prototype of the crucifiers of Christ and all murderers.[27] Macbeth envies his king's power, and he is also the kinsman of the saintly Duncan. If iconic stage images provide emphasis and resonate meaning in dramatic events, Macbeth's dagger embodies the core of hidden sin that lies at the heart of alluring hellcastle.

Banquo's Ghost

As for Banquo's ghost, the stage directions read: *"Enter the Ghost of Banquo, and sits in Macbeth's place"* (F1—"Tragedies," p. 141). The ghost is seen by Macbeth alone and is thus often assumed by directors to be yet another expressionistic device rendering psychology rather than supernatural reality.[28] Lady Macbeth herself says to her terrified husband, "This is the very painting of your fear; /This is the air-drawn dagger which you said /Led you to Duncan . . ." (III. iv. 61–63). Charles Kemble, who acted Macbeth for the first time in 1782, was the first actor to dispense with the apparition of Banquo, in 1794.[29] In earlier productions the custom had been for Banquo actually to walk on stage; according to Simon Forman's diary he saw the ghost played by an actor in a performance given on April 20, 1611, although the reliability of both the report and the authorship of the diary is still clouded.[30] Edwin Forrest, who played the role of Macbeth for a short season in London in 1845, restored the ghost as a flesh-and-blood actor. Despite Lady Macbeth's description of the ghost as only another "air-drawn dagger," directors have felt free to have a ghost or not, whereas the dagger is invariably imaginary.

Banquo is not seen by the assembled guests for the simple reason that they are not guilty of his murder, nor do they yet know who is. The same principle applies to Queen Gertrude in the closet scene; she is both innocent of the knowledge of her husband's murder (at least in that scene she is) and unable to see the ghost seen by Hamlet and the audience.[31] Consider Alonzo, another Jacobean ghost, who haunts the stage in Middleton and Rowley's *The Changeling* (written ca. 1622). When he makes his second appearance (V. i), DeFlores, his murderer, exclaims: " 'Twas but a mist of conscience; all's clear again." DeFlores is clearly meant to be haunted by at least three totally compatible realities: the spirit of Alonzo, the fear of discovery, and his conscience. DeFlores and the audience see the ghost, whereas Beatrice-Joanna (partially guilty of the murder) only feels its presence. Earlier sixteenth-century ghosts, like the one in *The Spanish Tragedy,* were simply ghosts eager to witness their revenge. Those in the seventeenth century are inclined to be both visitors from another world and known inhabitants of this one as well. They are both spirits in their own right and psychological realities of the spiritual life within their murderers. This world and the next, the world within and the world without: all are one, none should be sacrificed. The Shakespearean irony in *Macbeth* is that the guests do not see the ghost, but they do for the first time see Macbeth's guilt. We, the audience, unlike the guests and unlike even Lady Macbeth, do know his guilt already, and thus should see the ghost. The stage image of the ghost is the embodiment of two fundamental ironies in the scene: the initial knowledge of guilt that is shared alone by Macbeth and the audience, and the fact that Macbeth is now beginning to operate on his own, without the knowledge, advice, or support of his wife. As Macbeth had told her earlier, "Be innocent of the knowledge, dearest chuck, /Till thou applaud the deed . . ." (III. ii. 45–46). To sacrifice all of these dramatic effects for the sake of rendering Shakespeare on stage in the style of modern psychological realism is to diminish Shakespeare.

Macbeth is at that precise point of Jacobean transition where the world of mind and spirit is given incarnate being. When Macbeth broods over Banquo's life and issue as a threat to his own, he tries to share the intensity of his anguish with his wife:

> But let the frame of things disjoint, both the worlds suffer,
> Ere we will eat our meal in fear and sleep
> In the affliction of these terrible dreams
> That shake us nightly. Better be with the dead,
> Whom we, to gain our peace, have sent to peace,
> Than on the torture of the mind to lie
> In restless ecstasy. . . . (III. ii. 16–22)

In the first line of the quotation he invites the cleavage of the two "worlds" of matter and spirit, resulting in oblivious death, rather than suffer the anxieties of guilt and dread. In life, however, "both the worlds" are one, for the body inhabited by such a mind springs awake nightly in restless anguish. Sleep, the counterfeit of death, is worse than death itself for a man like Macbeth. The passage quoted above makes of the body and soul one entity, though existing in "both worlds." Macbeth's words to his wife are spoken from the very center of the paradox of incarnation. The most dramatic events in the play are real in all dimensions: physical, psychological, and spiritual. This is not to say that the most emphatic iconic stage images—the witches, the dagger accepted by the assassin, the ghost—are necessarily physical in the usual sense, but simply that they ought to have iconic stage presence. In the case of the witches, for instance, ". . . what seem'd corporal melted /As breath into the wind . . ." (I. iii. 81–82). And yet I know of no director who eliminates actors to play the witches, preferring voices broadcast over a loud speaker, although I am sure this will occur in a production sooner or later, if it has not done so already. The true contradiction in many productions of *Macbeth* is that the very interpreters who want the witches to be pathetic and crazy old women do not want to see the dagger or the ghost of Banquo. In other words, they want the witches to be no more than bizarre physical realities, the dagger and the ghost to be purely psychological, and nothing to be supernatural. But the ritual aspects of *Macbeth* draw it so close to the tone of Greek tragedy and religious ceremony in general that the play has constantly defied the attempts of naturalistic criticism to rationalize its supernatural realities as at most psychological illusions and no more. The naturalists clearly believe in neither witches nor ghosts, nor do they believe Shakespeare should have. Yet the power witches both have and represent is meant to be accepted automatically by the audience of *Macbeth*. Their power is quite simply the power of evil, both freely chosen and predestined. It is a power for which every evil person, including Macbeth, is totally responsible. That he is not innocently possessed is carefully indicated by Banquo's resistance to similar temptations, the pangs of conscience Macbeth has in carrying out his initial crime, and the goading thus required from his wife. Macbeth is at once the best of men and the worst of men. The same principle of supernatural power and moral responsibility applies to the three sisters as Fates or Parcae. Whatever his "fate," Macbeth, damned in the end, is totally responsible for what he does. This seeming contradiction was, as we know, resolved to the satisfaction of many Christian centuries largely by the writings of Boethius.

The Interior of Hellcastle

Beyond the witches, the other most pervasive image of hell in the play is Macbeth's castle itself, despite the illusion of loveliness. Even though that castle becomes three castles—Macbeth's residence in Inverness as thane, in Forres as king, and in Dunsinane as defender of his crown—the dramatic effect of the play is to move us back and forth from the mouth of hell (attended by the witches) to the interior of hellcastle, most apparent as such in the murder and banquet scenes. From inside hellcastle, however, the passageway to the outside world is the other side of hellmouth, hellgate, guarded by its traditional porter.

The seeming incongruity of a cauldron leading from time and space into eternal hell, combined with a gate isolating hell from the world of temporal creation, is undoubtedly difficult to visualize, let alone accept on a symbolic level. But a clarifying example of medieval iconography illustrates the compatibility of these images to a century earlier than our own. In *The Book of Hours of Catherine of Cleves* (ca. 1435),[32] already referred to in my chapter on *Hamlet,* probably the most stunning illumination in the entire collection shows a series of hellmouths combined with a hellcastle (Plate 28). The lion hellmouth of Revelation is repeated four times if we include the border decoration spewing forth the Seven Deadly Sins as well as the lion face within the gaping mouth of the lower lion in the illumination proper. But the most remarkable juxtaposition for our purpose is the two cauldrons surmounting the furnacelike turrets of hellcastle, turrets separated by a crenelated "upper stage" and a grillwork window flanked by slots for archers. A final hellgate is at the rear of the "upper stage," or battlement. Cauldrons combined with a castle are more stimulant than deterrent to this illuminator. The continuity of these conventions into the Renaissance and on the stage is the well-known manuscript color drawing recording the set of the Valenciennes Passion Play, performed in 1547. The rendering is attributed to Hubert Cailleau and shows a hellcastle station at the extreme right of a horizontal cosmic stage set. The hellgate to the castle is a lion-dragon-whale mouth whose jaws hold a cauldron of sinners. Mâle's thirteenth-century artist's representation of "a boiling cauldron in the open jaws of the monster," quoted above by way of G. K. Hunter, is here repeated with the added combination of a hellcastle. And the multiple conflation occurs in 1547, deep into the sixteenth century. Shakespeare uses a far less literal iconic stage set than the one in the passion play, but the old conventions are nevertheless buried in his props and his verse.

As for the presence of hellgate in *Macbeth*, it is one of the play's most familiar details. Just after the murder of Duncan, in Act II, the servant answering the knocking of Macduff complains aloud to himself, "If a man were porter of hell-gate, he should have old turning the key." And he demands the identity of the knocker "i' th' name of Beelzebub." It has long been recognized that this scene is far more than Hazlitt's "comic relief," or inserted to please the "rude multitudes" once thought to be the Globe's main source of income. The porter to hellgate is derived by Shakespeare from the medieval mystery plays. The porter makes his most frequent appearance in the Harrowing of Hell episode, where he opens the gate to the arisen Christ come to release the saved souls from captivity to Satan. Both the Middle Ages and the Pauline Renaissance believed all men were sinners, and thus all men would share captivity by the devil were it not for the redeeming love of God embodied in Christ, his death, and his resurrection. The medieval porter is a comic figure, but one whose quips have theological implications. In his article on the iconic aspects of the porter scene, Glynne Wickham shows Macbeth to be a type of Lucifer who must be defeated by Macduff as a triumphant Christ in the Harrowing of Hell.[33] Students of the Middle Ages and the Renaissance are fully aware of how nearly every sacred event in history was regarded by Christians as a prefiguration or recollection of other sacred events. The births of Samson and Christ foretold by angels; Jonah in the whale and Christ in hell for three days; the Forbidden Tree in the Garden of Eden and the Cross located at nearly the same geographical spot: endless examples are possible. Thus the arrival of Macduff during the porter scene is a prophetic foretaste of the eschatological conclusion to the play, when Macduff defeats Macbeth at Dunsinane, and "frees the time" from its bondage to sin.

Time images are one of the most complex patterns in the play, and much can be said about Shakespeare's use of the mythic time embodied in all religious ritual. In the "liturgical now," all times are one and all places the same: past, present, and future; heaven, earth, and hell. Christ in his Harrowing of Hell and the Archangel

Michael at the Last Judgment are conflated in Macduff. A
neoclassical parallel is to be found in the Petrarchan Triumph of
Eternity over Time at the end of the world. Time is freed from its
bondage to time by its passage into eternity, where no time is. The
Last Judgment wall painting in Shakespeare's parish church in
Stratford was typical of many that existed throughout England,
and the same theme of the Last Judgment, often linked to the
trumpeted end of time as we know it and the Resurrection of the
sleeping Dead, is contained in the middle of the scene in *Macbeth*
that begins with the aroused porter.[34] After gaining entrance and
discovering the murdered Duncan, Macduff awakens the sleeping
household:

> Awake, awake!
> Ring the alarum bell. Murder and treason!
> Banquo and Donalbain! Malcolm! awake!
> Shake off this downy sleep, death's counterfeit,
> And look on death itself. Up, up, and see
> The great doom's image! Malcolm! Banquo!
> As from your graves rise up, and walk like sprites
> To countenance this horror! Ring the bell.
>   *Lady M.* What's the business,
> That such a hideous trumpet calls to parley
> The sleepers of the house? Speak, speak! (II. iii. 71–81)

In the play's pattern of multiple typology Macbeth suggests Adam,
Lucifer, and Everyman; Macduff Christ, the savior of mankind,
the Archangel Gabriel, who blows the trumpet awakening the
dead, and the Archangel Michael, the general of God's army, who
restores the throne to its rightful successor, Malcolm. By the end of
the action, "the wheel is come full circle" in more than one way.
Early in the play, the iconic stage image of a bell rung toward the
end of the dagger soliloquy was interpreted by Macbeth to be
Duncan's death knell: ". . . for it is a knell / That summons thee
to heaven or to hell." Now in the porter scene we are reminded
that Macbeth also is to be summoned to a last judgment. As Glynn
Wickham says about the conclusion to the play:

> Scotland has been purged of a devil who, like Lucifer, aspired
> to a throne that was not his, committed crime upon crime

first to obtain it and then to keep it, and was finally crushed
within the refuge of his own castle by a saviour-avenger
accompanied by armed archangels. Hell has been harrowed:
'the time is free.'[35]

Shakespeare's porter, as seemingly trivial in dramatic importance as the quips of his progenitor in the mystery plays, has the
paradoxical effect of universalizing the setting, the characters, and
the action. He may even have been iconically costumed in a way
to recall the stock character of medieval drama in whose shoes he
stands. He fully reveals to the audience Macbeth's castle as hell
itself; paradoxically, Macbeth, like Marlowe's Faustus and Milton's Satan, is a resident of hell wherever he may be on earth.
"Hell is its own place": the soul in torment. Yet the play is not an
allegory in the narrow modern sense for two major reasons. The
dramatic events are rendered with the greatest "historical" speci-
ficity, and character, setting, and event are never locked into a
single meaning. Rather they flow in and out of the various
dimensions of history, eternity, and heaven and hell, to say nothing
of multiple levels within each dimension.

The porter scene, for instance, can be viewed in still another
iconic context. More specific than its eschatological implications
are the implied references to the convention of the Seven Deadly
Sins. Macbeth is Satanic not only in the scale of his crimes, but in
the character of his sin. According to the medieval tradition of
clearly defined and classified sins he and Lady Macbeth would be
motivated by the Sins of the Devil, Pride and Envy, leading to
political ambition. The drunken porter, however, is assigned a
speech bringing to mind the Sins of the Flesh, Gluttony, Lechery,
and Sloth. Excess drink brings sexual desire, in turn frustrated by
sleep.

> *Macd.* What three things does drink especially provoke?
>
> *Port.* Marry, sir, nose-painting, sleep, and urine. Lechery,
> sir, it provokes and unprovokes: it provokes the desire, but it
> takes away the performance. Therefore much drink may be
> said to be an equivocator with lechery: it makes him, and it
> mars him; it sets him on, and it takes him off; it persuades
> him, and disheartens him; makes him stand to, and not stand
> to; in conclusion, equivocates him in a sleep, and, giving him
> the lie, leaves him. (II. iii. 26–34)

Shakespeare is not, like Spenser, given to the rendering of virtues and vices in magnificent processions, but he too places the appropriate citizenry in his castles, and in creative ways which would be nonetheless understandable to an audience who could rattle off the Seven Deadly Sins as we do the days of the week. The comic porter, sleepy, drunk, and bawdy, is one of those citizens. His original stage appearance might have recalled not only the medieval guardian of hellgate but also details of costume and makeup used in the production of processions of the Seven Deadly Sins, such as that in Marlowe's *Faustus,* in particular the Sins of the Flesh. With characteristic economy Shakespeare has conflated the porter to hellgate in the mystery plays and three of the standard Sins, stock comic characters from the medieval morality plays.

Malcolm's prudent testing of the newly arrived Macduff later in the play also relies on recalling these same Sins, but the coverage is more complete. Malcolm claims to have fallen prey to the World, the Flesh, and the Devil. When Macduff says, ". . . Not in the legions /Of horrid hell can come a devil more damn'd /In evils to top Macbeth . . . ," Malcolm replies:

> I grant him bloody,
> Luxurious, avaricious, false, deceitful,
> Sudden, malicious, smacking of every sin
> That has a name; but there's no bottom, none,
> In my voluptuousness. . . . (IV. iii. 57–61)

In line 78 Malcolm adds worldly Avarice to fleshly Lust, and we are prepared to hear him conclude by claiming one of the Sins of the Devil, Pride or Envy; but his third speech of false self-accusation simply threatens to "Pour the sweet milk of concord into hell," where, of course, the devil holds sway.

Several characters try to make their escapes from hell. Malcolm and Macduff fly to the wholesome English atmosphere. Lady Macbeth walks in her sleep. On the third night of her restlessness she tries like Pilate to wash her hands in "innocency" (Psalms 26:6), but the smell of blood remains. The candle she carries is the emblem of her own soul in torment, as we are later reminded by Macbeth's "Out, out, brief candle!" But the white nightgown she wears and the taper she carries also identify her as a type of the female penitent, ultimately based on the archetype of Mary Magdalene.[36] The concept has already been more fully developed in my chapter on *The Merchant of Venice.* Lady Macbeth holds the candle to her shames, but only half of her, the unconscious half, repents. She can neither control nor resolve the agonizing conflict, and the conclusion is madness and apparent suicide. How much simpler it would have been had she the courage of her own evil, if only she could have beeen totally convinced that a little water could clear her of the deed. But, as her attendant remarks, "I would not have such a heart in my bosom for the dignity of the whole body." To violate the engraved law of conscience for the hope of something greater is to sacrifice all for nothing.

The tragic conclusion to the play occurs when Macbeth discovers this obvious truth, too late. His spiritually suicidal career begins when he makes a pact with himself to "jump the life to come" (I. vii. 7). Thus he accepts the "deep damnation" of Duncan's murder for the sake of present bliss, Tamburlaine's "sweet fruition of an earthly crown." If the audience misses Macbeth's first reference to his Faustian pact, they are reminded of it when he regrets that he has given his "eternal jewel" to "the common enemy of man" (III. i. 67–68), and all for the sake of Banquo's issue. From the murder of Duncan onward, with few exceptions, he steadily grows in boldness as he decays in feeling, and Macbeth's last words prepare us to accept his life as damnable to the end: ". . . Lay on, Macduff; /And damn'd be him that first cries 'Hold, enough!' "

The Head

When Macbeth's "cursed head" is brought back upon the stage on the sword (or perhaps pike) of Macduff, it is described as the head of a "dead butcher." The detail of the head may be repugnant to us, but it is probably the most important single iconic stage image in the entire play; and the stage directions are perfectly clear: *"Enter Macduffe, with Macbeths head"* (F1—"Trage-dies," p. 151). The head decapitated recalls a long tradition, one already invoked in my chapter on *As You Like It.* That the seed of Adam and Eve were to "bruise" the "head" of the serpent was a familiar detail from Genesis. It was God's punishment of the serpent for tempting Eve that its progeny be killed by "her seed." Another prophecy enters the play as Malcolm promises to "tread

upon the tyrant's head" (IV. iii. 45) when as the Prince of
Cumberland and rightful heir to the throne he returns to Scotland.
Medieval biblical exegesis saw Satan in the serpent and Christ as
Son of Man in the prophetic "seed" of Eve. Thus Christ defeats
the serpent once and for all in the Crucifixion when he assumes the
role of Pauline Second Adam redeeming the losses of the First
Adam. Exegetics saw a similar pattern in biblical decapitations,
not only that of Holofernes by Judith but also in the defeat of
Goliath by a youthful David. Remember Donatello's bronze *David*
(Plate 3), who stands with his foot on the decapitated head of
Goliath, and also Macbeth's repeated emphasis on the youth of
Malcolm and his ominous refusal to "kiss the ground before young
Malcolm's feet" (V. viii. 28). In all these cases the head of God's
enemy is either bruised or cut off. The Renaissance even gave
classical subjects the authority of biblical typology. Perseus is
rendered holding forth the serpent head of Medusa in the famous
bronze by Cellini (1500–71); the mythographers conflated the
serpent in the Garden of Eden with the serpent-hair of the Furies
and the Gorgons, and Medusa was one of the three Gorgons. The
decapitated head of Macbeth reassures the audience that the
kingdom is truly cleansed of an agent of evil.

The potential for gore at this point in the play must surely
offend or attract many a modern director. Shakespeare, on the
other hand, has prepared his audience very carefully for this
moment, not only in the wealth of time imagery culminating in
Macduff's ". . . Behold where stands /Th' usurper's cursed head.
The time is free," but also in Malcolm's earlier promise, cited
above, to "tread upon the tyrant's head." Many other earlier
dramatic elements coalesce at this point as well. A framing effect
to the play is achieved by the early expository report from the
"bloody sergeant" of how Macbeth "unseam'd" MacDonwald,
"And fix'd his head upon our battlements" (I. ii. 23). The motif is
picked up again by the *"Armed Head"* (F1—"Tragedies," p. 144) in
the apparitions scene (IV. i), usually taken by editors to foretell
Macbeth's decapitation. This particular detail of an *"Armed"* head
also suggests what Shakespeare may be doing in the epic arming
scene of Act V, scene ii when Macbeth shouts twice for Seyton to
assist him in the always-difficult task of dressing for battle. The
famous poignant speech between the shouts—". . . My way of life
/Is fall'n into the sear, the yellow leaf"—always springs forth in the

reading, but often overlooked are the details of the arming, which are far more emphatic in dramatic production. The foot-dragging Seyton's answer to Macbeth's demand for his armor is a rude " 'Tis not needed yet." The master must prod twice more, while talking distractedly to the doctor about Lady Macbeth, before Macbeth makes a curious command, ". . . Pull't off, I say," immediately following a line that ends in "echo." Then, a few lines later, Macbeth's exit speech begins with "Bring it after me." What is "it" if not the helmet, possibly misapplied to Macbeth's head by a maladroit Seyton, thus producing a possibly comic "echo" from within the helmet earlier. Shakespeare is certainly not above comic flashes in the midst of tragic self-destruction.

If the helmet is given this kind of stage emphasis in the arming scene, it echoes the *"Armed Head"* of the apparitions scene and, furthermore, suggests how the decapitated head may best be handled at the end of the play. All Macduff need have in the way of a head when he reenters is the helmet, seen first as an apparition, then as a detail of armor, and finally as a "head." The actual grisly head is merely implied within the helmet held forth. The gore is offstage, so to speak, or upstage, in a sense.

Added to the iconic stage image of an implied decapitation is the iconic stage image of a helmet. Geffrey Whitney's *A Choice of Emblemes* (Leyden, 1586) illustrates not only the kind of Renaissance helmet that, once attached, could conceivably hold up within it a head (Plate 29); but this "first of English emblem books" also suggests one possible set of iconographic implications to a warrior's helmet. The motto is "ex bello, pax" (out of war, peace); the emblem shows bees building a hive in an abandoned helmet; and the poem contrasts the productive joys of peace to the bloody and mortal woes of war:

> The helmet stronge, that did the head defende,
> Beholde, for hyue, the bees in quiet seru'd:
> And when that warres, with bloodie bloes, had ende.
> They, hony wroughte, where souldiour was preseru'd:
>> Which doth declare, the blessed fruites of peace,
>> How sweete shee is, when mortall warres doe cease. (p. 138)

The "head" of Macbeth may have been Shakespeare's last compliment to a masque-loving monarch whose motto was "beati pacifici" (blessed peacemakers).

My last chapter on an individual play will also deal with a work whose style of production is deeply influenced by the court masque and where iconic stage imagery is correspondingly important. As we move toward the end of Shakespeare's career we discover a return to the iconic staging so frequent at the beginning and relatively minor in the middle plays, such as *Hamlet*. *The Tempest*, however, probably shows Shakespeare at his most iconic. Just as the medieval craft cycles had possibly shed their lingering style of presentation over the early plays, the fashionable taste for the masque came to influence the symbolic staging of *Macbeth* and the romances.[37]

6

The Tempest: Moment of Calm

Several of the excellent brief critical studies of Shakespeare's last plays have shared two assumptions. First, the romances solve the social, political, and psychological problems left unsolved in the earlier tragedies; second in *Cymbeline, The Winter's Tale,* and *The Tempest,* innocent youth redeems a corrupted older generation. The second assumption, especially, is drawn from Edward Dowden's definition of this period in Shakespeare's career, written over a century ago:

> . . . in these latest plays, the beautiful pathetic light is always present. There are the sufferers, aged, experienced, tired—Queen Katherine, Prospero, Hermione. And over against these are the children, absorbed in their happy and exquisite egotism—Perdita and Miranda, Florizel and Ferdinand, and the boys of old Belarius.[1]

The marriages traditional to the end of romance do largely involve the young rather than the old, and the old have had more opportunity to suffer than the young. Yet Mamillius is hardly happy nor Paulina tired. Ferdinand is deeply absorbed in the loss of a father, and his love for Miranda is neither entirely happy nor is it born of egotism. And Antonio never seems to suffer anything more than frustration.

An alternative pattern does exist, one seriously qualifying the mythic view that these plays share the redemption of age by youth, the triumph over winter by spring. In Shakespeare's tragicomedies, but especially in *The Tempest,* the contrast is not so much between the generations as it is between chaos and calm, between the storm and providential escape from shipwreck, if only for a moment.

The Tempest and *Midsummer Night's Dream* come especially close to the temper and style of the court masque. Both plays stress the scenic element, although *The Tempest* is more inclined to translate description into the literal resources of stage machinery. We know from the Revels Accounts that *The Tempest* was presented at Whitehall before the king on Hallowmas Eve, 1611, shortly after its composition. Inigo Jones, that ingenious designer of royal masques for the Banqueting House at Whitehall, had left his mark during the fifteen years between Shakespeare's two dramatic celebrations of courtly matchmaking.[2] When *The Tempest* begins in the disorder of a storm at sea the audience immediately hears *"A tempestuous noise of Thunder and Lightning"* (F1—"Comedies," p. 1). Toward the end of the play, at the beginning of Act V, the harmony symbolized in the charmed circle drawn by Prospero is expressed by solemn music provided by unseen "elves" and "demi-puppets." The circle is described by Prospero as an "airy charm" which soon "dissolves apace." This may have been a special effect created by smoke forced within a hollow magician's staff and released at the appropriate moment. Between the storm and the circle the most spectacular effect is clearly the enticing banquet suddenly interrupted by Ariel as a harpy. Yet several other devices must have pleased a contemporary audience's taste for stage novelties. The grotesque Caliban is apparently kept in a cave, and perhaps even punished by confinement in a rock of apparent solidity, when he is not needed for domestic chores; a masque of classical deities is invoked by Prospero to celebrate the engagement of Ferdinand and Miranda; and the rebellious servants are driven from a line of rich garments by an antimasque of dogs. These effects undoubtedly created awe, delight, or surprise, but they also had the potential effect of stimulating a host of iconographic associations especially appropriate to another important aspect of the court masque—its allegory.

Clearly, Shakespeare's *Tempest* is not based upon the obvious and often wooden kind of allegory we can expect from the plays of a George Peele. Shakespeare's characters have a vitality and immediacy which push aside any notion that they are no more than allegorical personifications. Yet in *The Tempest* Shakespeare comes closer to the form of allegory than he does in any other play. In the present reassessment of medieval and Renaissance allegory, furthermore, we are beginning to understand how richly complex and understated it could become. The old one-to-one equivalences we came to expect from the form as a result of its nineteenth-century popular exponents do not begin to account for the sophistication of which Renaissance allegory is often capable.[3] The scholarly James I has often been cited as a partial model for Prospero. Even that rather literal-minded and humorless king knew that the allegorical reading of the Bible required consider-able intellectual flexibility. In "A Speech in the Starre-Chamber the xx of June, anno 1616," published in *The Workes of James I* (London, 1616), the king explicates for his ministers the first verse of Psalm 72: "Give thy judgments to the king, O God, and thy righteousness to the king's son." James clarifies two meanings, one "literall" and the other "mysticall," the literal one having to do with David and Solomon and the mystical one having to do with God and Christ, both senses "woven together." James goes on to explain that at other points in the Psalm certain passages "can onely bee properly applied vnto God and Christ," and other passages only "vnto *Dauid* and *Salomon*" (p. 549).[4] This ability to move in and out of mimetic and symbolic realities, to see where they merge and where they stand independent of each other, is essential to the reading of even a universally acknowledged allegory such as the *Faerie Queene*. The emphasis in Shakespeare is far more upon the literal when we compare him to Spenser, but in both at least two worlds merge and separate constantly.

Seeing *The Tempest* partially in allegorical terms is certainly not new. Much criticism has been written on Caliban as brute understanding, Ariel as fancy, and Prospero as imagination;[5] or on the pattern of the four elements embodied in the imagery and the characters, with Caliban as water and earth and Ariel as fire and air;[6] or on Prospero as Art and Caliban as Nature.[7] It is my hope that an iconic approach to some of the stage imagery in the play can add the allegorical emphases created by the action and setting, alert us to the differences between conventional modes of thought and Shakespeare's creative use of them, and perhaps even encour-age a critical sense of when we are in the realm of literal stage action without symbolic overtones. My touchstones will be the emblematic still points created by the storm, the banquet, and the charmed circle drawn by Prospero as Neoplatonic magus; my further purpose is a clarification of the degree of reconciliation in this last romance.

The Storm

The threatened shipwreck amid storm introducing *The Tempest,* seen in the context of literary history, is known to all of us as one of the standard episodes of the Greek prose romance and all its many descendants, for which Heliodorus' *Aethiopica* is a famous progenitor in the fourth century A.D. In *The Tempest* Prospero furthers his plot by raising a storm at sea in order to gather his enemies on the island. But the antiromantic beginning of the action at the end of the story gives the storm an importance it lacks in many other romantic plays of the period. The action in *The Tempest* begins at "the end" by beginning in the middle of a storm. Also, the storm is rendered on stage, rather than merely reported, as Prospero might easily have done as a preface to his long expository speeches. The storm, not his speeches, is the prologue to this unusually strict neoclassical action of three hours' duration. Shakespeare is investing valuable dramatic time in one of his shortest plays for the sake of a reasonably sustained scene showing men confronted by imminent death at sea. It is easy to sense that this storm will take on meaning beyond the literal.

If we consider the text alone the initial stress is upon the principle of the social hierarchy. The gentlemen on board endanger the ship by interfering with the labors of the mariners. Authority is appropriate only in one's place, and the place of aristocrats under the present circumstances is out of the way. The Boatswain is succinct. Speaking of the howling winds, he tells Gonzalo, "What cares these roarers for the name of king? To cabin! silence! Trouble us not." Another emphasis gradually emerges as well, one having to do with the principle of Fate. As others are interfering with the crew or losing emotional self-control, Gonzalo respectfully submits himself to higher powers. At one point he says, "Stand fast, good Fate" and at another, the "wills above be done." The storm scene is a prologue for two of the issues subsequently major to the play: the upsetting of the natural law supporting the principle of hierarchy (in nature and in society as combined on a ship threatened by a storm at sea) and submission of one's will to destiny. A belief in Fate shared by good men is especially appropriate to an action set in pre-Christian times and to a society enjoying only limited Revelation. As we know, the pre-Christian setting is shared by *The Tempest* with Shakespeare's other tragicomedies. In these last plays allusion is often made to oracles (always right even if in unexpected ways), the gods, and Fate as an independent power in the universe, although Fate is also presented as subject to the gods, as we have seen in the case of Gonzalo. In still earlier plays set by Shakespeare in pre-Christian times, such as *Julius Caesar* or *King Lear,* the correct source of reliance is usually the stars. The good trust their power and direction; the evil, like Cassius or Edmund, express cynical disbelief. The basic principle seems to be a form of pre-Christian piety, one properly expressed in a respect for powers in the universe beyond one's control. The storm is seen by Gonzalo as a declaration of divine will to which men can only submit. The one qualification is rendered by the figure of the Boatswain: submission is appropriate after men have served their proper offices in the natural hierarchy.

The storm as an iconic stage image symbolizing the seemingly arbitrary circumstances (Fate) under divine control ("wills above") is consistent with the allegory assigned by Edgar Wind to Giorgione's famous *Tempesta* (Plate 30). In this painting of the Venetian School, executed about 1507 and a monument in the history of art because of its atmospheric coloring, a storm is gathering over troubled waters. The figures on either side are a man leaning on a staff and a woman nursing a baby. The painting has been the object of many interpretations. Some scholars have held that it is no more than a simple pastoral scene; others consider it an allusion to an episode from classical myth or the Bible, such as the birth of Apollo or the finding of Moses; some think it is an allegory, such as of the forces of nature or of Venus Genetrix.[8] The learning of Edgar Wind, who belongs to the allegorical school, lends authority to such an interpretation.[9] For him the painting is a pastoral allegory of Fortezza, Carita, and Fortuna. Fortuna, expressed in the storm gathering over the water, is the spirit of chance we usually associate with the medieval image of a woman turning a wheel. But in the Renaissance the goddess Fortuna was also often rendered with a wind-filled sail, perhaps standing on a slippery globe in the midst of ships threatened by storms at sea. In an allegorical design by Wenceslas Hollar, dated 1625, these Renaissance accretions are comprehensively combined (Plate 31).[10] Nor are these the only attributes assigned Fortune in the Renaissance. The halter of Fortune is one of her characteristics acquired from Nemesis, which as destiny no man can escape. One of Dürer's most famous engravings is alternately called "The Great Fortune" and "Nemesis" (Plate 32). The bridle and reins are in one hand, the cup of bounty in the other. In *The Pilgrimage of Life,* Samuel Chew points out how close this development brings her to the figure of Justice, and remarks on Gonzalo's words about the Boatswain, in the midst of the tempest:[11]

> I have great comfort from this fellow. Methinks he hath no drowning mark upon him; his complexion is perfect gallows. Stand fast, good Fate, to his hanging; make the rope of his destiny our cable, for our own doth little advantage. If he be not born to be hang'd, our case is miserable. (I. i. 26–31)

These same associations occur in the translator Richard Lynche's *Fountaine of Ancient Fiction* (London, 1599), where Fortune, Nemesis, and Justice are described as various forms of the same cosmic power (sigs. Aa4v–5r).[12] The rope of destiny mentioned by Gonzalo above would thus be the halter of Fortune in her role as Fate, Nemesis, and Justice.

By suggesting the power of Fortune through the means of the storm alone, Giorgione has created the atmospheric background that has made his *Tempesta* so famous in the history of art. As for the figures, the one on the left is a man (probably meant to be a soldier), leaning on a staff and standing close to two broken columns slightly in the background.[13] According to Wind, the man is the embodiment of Fortezza, the principle of male strength and constancy, also called Virtus. Apparently the broken columns are the appropriate emblem of this virtue in many Renaissance works of art. On the right of the painting is a woman nursing a child. She is identified as Carita, the principle of female gentleness and love, also called Amor. The painting inspires the conclusion that the vicissitudes of life (Fortuna) demand the cooperation of constancy (Fortezza) and love (Carita). Wind quotes from Pope's *Essay on Man* in order to capture the spirit of concentrated Renaissance allegory rendered by this painting: "The rising tempest puts in act the soul" (II. 105). Wind's interpretation makes of Giorgione's *Tempesta* one of many statements in the Renaissance of the union of Fortezza and Carita. Closely related is the even more famous Renaissance allegory of the love between Mars and Venus. Their love was seen as both conflicting and complementary, the attraction between male aggression and female voluptuousness, sometimes destructive to each other, sometimes creating a new harmony.[14] In *Antony and Cleopatra*, for instance, Shakespeare develops the Mars and Venus ambiguities in several ways underlined by both stage and verbal iconic imagery.[15] Fortezza and Carita, however, are invariably complementary, the one relying on the other.

In *The Tempest* a parallel with Giorgione's *Tempesta* can be seen if we regard Ferdinand and Miranda as loose types of Fortezza and Carita. They are introduced to each other by a storm. Miranda is contrasted to Ferdinand by her astonishing innocence and gentleness. He quickly reveals his male courage and independence when he tries to avoid enslavement by Prospero by drawing the sword so easily enchanted. His constancy is suggested by the "thousands" of logs he pleasurably bears for the sake of Miranda. When the lovers are finally revealed to the others washed on shore, they are shown playing at chess, often seen in the Middle Ages as a romantic game whereby equal opponents are made one. In the Arden edition of the play, in a note on the chess scene (V. i), Frank Kermode reviews the meaning the game had for lovers in the chivalric romances:

> . . . the lady's pieces represent the courtly virtues of the female, the knight's of the male. . . . Chess games between lovers are frequently represented on wedding-chests and mirror-cases, and there is a characteristic mirror-case in the Victoria and Albert Museum . . . ; allowing for the costume, it could be an illustration to *The Tempest*.[16]

Ferdinand and Miranda can be loosely seen as opposites in need of each other if the tempests of life are to be survived (like Fortezza and Carita), whose union is symbolized by the chivalric love-game of chess. Medieval and Renaissance conventions seem to blend perfectly here. But there is clearly no rigidly worked out allegory along these lines in the play. Whatever symbolism there is remains appropriately submerged, and Ferdinand and Miranda are, of course, much more than the abstractions that they may tangentially suggest.

The tempests on sea and land, furthermore, are trials for both Ferdinand and Alonso. Their survival from drowning is the greatest instance of trial in the play. But the dramatic development of the theme of testing is a succession of frustrations and subsequent possibilities of despair woven into the action of the entire play. Both Neapolitan generations risk the consequences of a despairing belief that the other is gone forever, dead and drowned. Later, Ferdinand must be denied too easy access to Miranda as Alonso is denied the tantalizing banquet. In effect, both must learn the fortitude which accepts power beyond one's own, here expressed by the power of Prospero.

The Banquet of Sense

The endangering of Ferdinand by despair seems scarcely developed when we consider what Shakespeare will do with it in the case of his father. Yet something close to despair is the first emotion revealed in Alonso's heir. In his first stage appearance, Ferdinand follows the music of an invisible Ariel:

> Where should this music be? I' th' air or th' earth?
> It sounds no more; and sure it waits upon
> Some god o' th' island. Sitting on a bank,
> Weeping again the King my father's wreck,
> This music crept by me upon the waters,
> Allaying both their fury and my passion
> With its sweet air. . . . (I. ii. 387–93)

Ferdinand's sorrow over the presumed loss of his father brought him close to the excessive grief of a suicidal Hamlet, if we are to trust the implications of a passage paralleling the shipwrecking waves and Ferdinand's passions. Both waves and soul are here brought into harmony by sweet music.

The specifically suicidal aspects of excessive grief, a well-known form of Renaissance despair, are elaborated not with Ferdinand but with his father, beginning in Act III. Alonso's own belief that his son is drowned is briefly stilled, once again by "Marvellous sweet music," this time provided by Prospero to introduce a tantalizing banquet. Alonso's enigmatic statement as he agrees to eat, however, suggests that he plans to make this meal his last one in life: ". . . I will stand to, and feed, /Although my last; no matter, since I feel /The best is past. . . ." After making the banquet vanish, Ariel, in the form of a harpy, accuses Alonso and his companions of the crimes of supplanting Prospero as duke of Milan and of exposing him and Miranda to the sea, then cites the loss of Ferdinand as Alonso's punishment. The combined power of hunger, guilt, and grief drives the King of Naples into clearly defined suicidal despair:

> O, it is monstrous, monstrous!
> Methought the billows spoke, and told me of it;
> The winds did sing to me; and the thunder,
> That deep and dreadful organ-pipe, pronounc'd
> The name of Prosper; it did base my trespass.
> Therefore my son i' th' ooze is bedded; and
> I'll seek him deeper than e'er plummet sounded
> And with him there lie mudded. . . .   (III. iii. 95–102)

Alonso returns to this despairing guilt and grief in Act V after Prospero, who had remained *"on the top (inuisible:)"* (F1—"Comedies," p. 13) during the banquet scene in Act III, finally identifies himself to the most important of his unwilling guests on the island. Prospero's ambiguous statement that he has lost his daughter (V. i. 148), meaning to Ferdinand, is taken by Alonso to mean that she is dead. Thus, despite the earlier mental cure effected by a combination of music and Prospero's magic circle, Alonso reverts obliquely to suicidal despair, when, speaking of Miranda and Ferdinand, he says, "O heavens, that they were living both in Naples, /The King and Queen there! That they were, I wish /Myself were mudded in that oozy bed /Where my son lies. . . ." Alonso wishes himself dead instead. This is not quite the same as despair, but it recalls to an audience his earlier condition. As we are aware, among the greatest fears of Renaissance man was that he would fall victim to a despairing state of mind.[17] It stood directly opposite to all that was good and healthy in the ideal human response to life's inevitable adversity. Despair as the opposite psychological extreme to fortitude represents in this play a danger far greater than assassination, or the sea, or the punishment of Alonso and his companions by a revengeful Prospero. Although these dangers are an important aspect of the play as a tragicomedy, in which disaster is a constant threat but never a reality, despair is the greatest of all threatened disasters, and it is Alonso who is most endangered by it.

The climax in his emotional development comes at the moment for which Shakespeare has reserved his most spectacular stage effect: the banquet in Act III, which *"vanishes"* with a *"quient deuice"* (F1—"Comedies," p. 13).[18] Alonso has reached his lowest point of physical and psychological exhaustion, having given up all hope of finding Ferdinand alive: "Well, let him go." Antonio and Sebastian resolve once more to assassinate Alonso in this weakened condition, both of them "glad that he's so out of hope." The spiritual context here recalls the death of Hamlet senior without the benefits of the last rites, and Hamlet's determination to seek a perfect revenge on Claudius by killing him in the midst of sin, not prayer. The determination of Antonio and Sebastian to kill Alonso in a spiritual condition of being "so out of hope" betrays their utter indifference to his eternal spiritual fate. Although the lost "hope" is specifically the hope that Ferdinand is still alive, it is so closely linked to Alonso's suicidal despair that Shakespeare's audience would almost invariably recall the alternating "comforts" (all based on *hope* for God's mercy) and "temptations" (but especially that of despair) of the ars moriendi.

The subsequent banquet is a device contrived by Prospero to reform his enemies so that they may be forgiven. And the major enemy seems to be the one of highest rank and power, Alonso, rather than Antonio, the one who has harmed Prospero most directly. Having reached his weakest point of hunger, weariness, grief, and vulnerability, Alonso is suddenly offered a lovely meal, which is just as suddenly snatched away by Ariel in the form of a harpy. Because touch and smell are missing in the gratifications promised or provided by the *"strange shapes"* (F1—"Comedies," p. 13), this banquet is an abbreviated Banquet of Sense. It is meant to prove to these men, but especially Alonso, how addicted their lives are to base sense rather than the pursuit of goodness. The motif of the Banquet of Sense is repeated in numerous visual sources in the Renaissance, and it reoccurs in many literary contexts, both poetic and dramatic. Shakespeare himself had earlier employed its conventions in *Timon of Athens,* in the banquet prepared by Timon for his fair-weather friends. Recall the elegant artifice arranged by Timon for the entertainment of his guests, where Cupid speaks the prelude to a masque of Amazons:

> Hail to thee, worthy Timon, and to all
> That of his bounties taste! The five best Senses
> Acknowledge thee their patron, and come freely
> To gratulate thy plenteous bosom. Th' Ear,
> Taste, Touch, Smell, pleas'd from thy table rise;
> They only now come but to feast thine eyes. (I. ii. 117–22)

Everyone is enchanted by both feast and entertainment but Apemantus, the scornful malcontent and misanthrope Timon is to become. Although the reaction of both to the duplicity of men is excessive, the betrayal of host by guests does come, and Timon's second entertainment of his disloyal friends (III. vi) is a parody of the first, with the former's delicacies replaced by the latter's dishes of warm water. Timon is a prodigal who has sacrificed all to an illusion of friendship. In *Timon of Athens* the two major negative implications of the banquet as an emblematic Renaissance device are thus employed. It is both prelude for betrayal, with the Last Supper as the prototype, and associated with prodigality, with the hog trough described in the parable of the prodigal son the most memorable detail for the Renaissance.

More immediate than the Bible as an antecedent for the Banquet of Sense is the Banquet of Sins, alluded to in the entertainment provided Spenser's Red Cross Knight in the House of Pride before the procession of the Seven Deadly Sins (*FQ* I. iv. 15). The Banquet of Sins is illustrated in an iconographic engraving probably executed by Cornelis Anthonisz (Teunissen) about 1540, where the prodigal son eats at a table of labeled personifications, from Vanity and Avarice to the World with his foot upon the head of Conscience.[19] The Banquet of Sins has obvious medieval roots, as does the Banquet of Sense. In a woodcut published in Paris in the fifteenth century to illustrate *Exercitium super pater noster,* Everyman dines with Pride, Gluttony, and Avarice.[20] As a later variation on the medieval Feast of the Seven Deadly Sins, the Renaissance Banquet of the Five Senses usually has negative associations.[21] Perhaps because the Neoplatonists stressed the moral hierarchy of the senses, with sight at the top and touch at the bottom, the Renaissance tended to associate the senses with sinful overgratification. We have seen how the Banquet of

Sense in *Timon of Athens* comes to introduce the gluttony of parasites rather than the community of true friends. We also know that the banquet as occasion for sin or sinful temptation is basic to an understanding of passages in both *Dr. Faustus* and *Paradise Regained.* Faustus and Mephistopheles have "sport" with the papal court on the day of St. Peter's feast. Faustus, invisible, and foreshadowing Ariel as a harpy, tears food from the pope, whose greatest pleasure is in gluttony. In the second book of *Paradise Regained* a banquet is Satan's first temptation of Christ. Satan's feast, like the one in *Timon,* is a banquet of all the five senses. Milton makes the prototype the apple that tempted Eve (*PR* II. 348–50).

Shakespeare clearly wants us to interpret the banquet in *The Tempest* as an emblem of sin. In the original staging of the play, this dramatic purpose may even have been conveyed to the audience by hinting at the conventional stage appearance of the Seven Deadly Sins in the costuming and behavior of the *"strange shapes"* who bring the banquet in, making it a procession like that of the Seven Deadly Sins in *Dr. Faustus.* Or the *"shapes"* may alternatively have suggested the Five Senses. Although the banquet never gratifies more than Antonio's, Sebastian's, and Alonso's sense of sight and hearing (both by sweet music and metaphorically by the "excellent dumb discourse" of the shapes), the emphasis on sin is clearly conveyed by Ariel's first words to these famished men:

> You are three men of sin, whom Destiny,
> That hath to instrument this lower world
> And what is in't, the never-surfeited sea
> Hath caus'd to belch you up; and on this island
> Where man doth not inhabit—you 'mongst men
> Being most unfit to live. . . . (III. iii. 53–58)

The particular sin stressed is Gluttony, underlined by the irony of an always-hungry sea unable to tolerate a meal of evil men. This judgment taken on a literal level is absurd; no matter what they may have done in the past, these men have every right to be hungry now. It is only when we grasp the emblematic quality of the banquet as a dumb show that we are able to associate the Gluttony symbolized by an inviting banquet and the general principle of greed and ambition for more than is rightfully ours, which Ariel accuses Prospero's enemies of having practiced in supplanting the rightful Duke of Milan:

> . . . that you three
> From Milan did supplant good Prospero;
> Expos'd unto the sea, which hath requit it,
> Him, and his innocent child; for which foul deed
> The pow'rs, delaying, not forgetting, have
> Incens'd the seas and shores, yea, all the creatures,
> Against your peace. . . . (III. ii. 69–75)

Ariel as a harpy apparently includes himself among those "creatures" incensed by the powers above. By the time of the Renaissance, harpies had come to convey many literary and symbolic associations. The most famous literary instance at the time was Virgil's *Aeneid.* A banquet spread by Aeneas and his men, who have wandered off course into the islands inhabited by the harpies, is quickly attacked. According to Thomas Phaer's translation of the *Aeneid* (London, 1562), these creatures "Lyke foules with maidens face thei ben, their paunches wyde defilde /With garbage great, their hoked pawes thei sprede, and ever pale /With hungry lookes . . ." (sig. G1r). The food not snatched away is fouled by their "garbage." The Renaissance drew from the descriptions in this and other ancient literary sources (particularly those concerning Jason and the Argonauts) the moral allegory of harpies as symbols of greed.[22] What the harpies did not need for their own use they rendered useless to others. This is the sense in which Molière's Harpagon was named in *The Miser,* and we still call a greedy person a harpy. Many variations on this association between harpies and greed occur in Renaissance graphics, paintings, and emblem books. In 1515 Albrecht Dürer completed the monumental composite of 192 woodcut prints known as *The Triumphal Arch of Maximilian I, Holy Roman Emperor.* In the same year Johannes Stabius, the Emperor's astronomer, poet, and historiographer, issued the descriptive program that had guided the creation of this nearly ten-by-twelve-foot design from the beginning. The three portals of the arch symbolized Maximilian's fame, honor and power, and nobility. The archway of honor and power is flanked by large columns, and at the base of each of these columns are three harpies holding an escutcheon and musical instruments. According to Stabius, these "monstrous, misshapen, pale and miserly . . . [harpies mean that] his Majesty has not permitted them to spoil his riches and his generous pleasures."[23] Maximilian ordered his arch reproduced and distributed throughout Europe.

In the emblem books of the period the emblems showing harpies usually make the same point about greedy men being like harpies, but one emblem in particular makes possible our fuller understanding of Prospero's use of Ariel to bring Alonso into despair. The dominant theme is the despairing effect of sins mirrored back upon the sinner. The emblem of particular interest (Plate 33) first appears in the *Parvus mundus* (1579) of Laurentius Haechtanus, translated by Jacob de Zetter as *Speculum virtutum* (1644).[24] The motto reads "homicida sui ipsius ultor" (the homicide his own greatest avenger). The emblem picture shows three harpies, the traditional number: one killing a man, another looking at its reflected face in a pool of water, and a third lying dead on its back. The accompanying emblem poem in Latin is followed by another one in German. The substance of both is that harpies destroy men by their rapacious greed, but when they see a reflection of their own human faces they believe that they have killed one of their own kind. Thereupon their guilt drives them into suicide. Thus it is with greedy men: they destroy their fellow creatures until they discover their common humanity and are driven into suicidal grief. The function of Ariel is not to destroy himself but to cause Prospero's enemies to see themselves as harpies. In this way Ariel is the mirror image of those he confronts, and the emblematic response for Alonso is suicidal. That this is Prospero's intended purpose in casting Ariel as a harpy is indicated by the "harpy's" words: "You are three men of sin" who are "unfit to live" and thus "I have made you mad." "And even with such-like valour men hang and drown /Their proper selves . . ." (III. iii. 53–60). Yet Prospero never states a desire to see his enemies actually commit suicide; more likely, Shakespeare intends them to reach a bottom of psychological helplessness (such as that of Shylock, Richard II, and Lear) from which true repentance will be possible. Though the process has a positive goal, it brings Alonso into much suffering, and that suffering is both his partial penance and perhaps in a dramatic way Prospero's revenge.

Shakespeare makes reference to Nemesis as "winged vengeance" in *King Lear* (III. vii. 65). We recall that Gonzalo linked Fortune

with Nemesis at the beginning of the *The Tempest* (I. i. 26–31).
Ariel's performance as a harpy also underlines this connection. A
mysterious painting (Plate 34) by Giovanni Bellini (1430–1516),
once again first adequately explained by Edgar Wind, helps us to
understand how the Renaissance received these associations. This
allegorical painting shows a "blindfolded harpy with flying
forelock . . . [who] carries the two jugs of Temperance."[25] Along
with four other allegorical panels, it was probably designed as part
of a mirror frame. Wind titles it "Nemesis," includes it among a
suite of five paintings, and assigns it to the top of the mirror as a
summary statement of the paintings at the four corners.[26] Bellini's
"Nemesis" combines several attributes of the greedy harpy: the
feathered tail, the wings (also often shared with impatient
Fortune), and the griffin's hairy legs and sharp talons. Fortune is
also recalled in several ways: the wings, the slippery gloves, the
flowing water in the background, the alluring upper body and
arms, the streaming forelock so difficult to grasp, and the blindfold
of arbitrary indifference to the merits of men (also shared with an
impartial Justice). The jugs of Temperance further reinforce the
ambiguity of this image. Temperance opposes both greed and
Fortune because it is poured out in equal measure. Wind clarifies
the problem by suggesting that the mirror this image probably
surmounted was being presented to the beholder as a means of
"good or ill" (in much the same ambiguous way the symbolism of
the mirror functions in the deposition scene of *Richard II*). As we
know, Renaissance mirrors could be either instruments of self-
awareness or of vanity.[27] Prospero hopes that Ariel as harpy will be
a mirror of the "three men of sin" bringing self-awareness. The
self-awareness it succeeds in bringing to Alonso also brings him
terrible suicidal suffering, in turn his punishment and the beginning of a penance concluded in the full restoration of Milan to
Prospero.

One of the most interesting aspects of Shakespeare's use of Ariel
as harpy is the complex combination of the many issues summarized, to a degree that leaves perhaps even Bellini on the level of
simplicity. Ariel represents both Nemesis, divine retribution for
past sins, and greedy reflection of the vain sinners being punished.
He also recalls the pattern of sudden turns in Fortune, because the
good fortune of the banquet, so appreciated by Gonzalo, is almost
instantly turned into bad fortune when it is snatched away and

replaced by a harpy. The harpy is a just accuser, who creates despair in Alonso; and he is a foul monster to be hunted down by Sebastian and Antonio, as the harpies were pursued to the Strophedes Islands by the followers of Jason. The despair created by Ariel in Alonso becomes both his punishment and the penitential basis of his forgiveness by Prospero.

It is of final importance to see that only Alonso responds as all three men were apparently intended to, by falling into suicidal despair. Antonio and Sebastian simply determine to rid the island of its monstrous fiends. The effect of the "mirror" on them has been "ill." Their lack of a clear repentance is an aspect of the end of this play often commented upon. In the general scene of reconciliation Antonio, certainly, stands aside silently. Prospero apparently expects no more of them. Perhaps we are meant to feel that he has learned from his experience with Caliban how some natures are largely incapable of change, how they must simply be made to do what is right by means of forcible control. Prospero forgives his unrepentant brother Antonio, but in the same breath insists upon the return of the dukedom, which he knows he "must restore." He can keep both Sebastian and Antonio under permanent control, despite his renunciation of his magic, because of something he holds over them: "But you, my brace of lords, were I so minded, /I here could pluck his Highness' frown upon you, /And justify you traitors; at this time /I will tell no tales . . ." (V. i. 126–29). Obviously, the penalty for plotting the death of the king is death. Prospero's knowledge of the facts will give him great and continuing power over these untrustworthy men even after his abandonment of "rough magic."

It is increasingly clear how many troubling aspects of *The Tempest* elude a comic tone of love and reconciliation created by the innocence of a younger generation. The drift of the play is at least as much toward the sophistication of the innocent young as it is toward the converting of the oversophisticated old. The play opens with the exposition of Miranda's cruel past, and Ferdinand must prove his worthiness of Miranda by more than his youthful innocence. Nor are the old simply lovingly forgiven. Prospero apparently tries to lead several of his virtual prisoners into the depths of suicidal despair before he even fully makes up his mind upon forgiveness. Despair was a terrifying prospect to most Jacobeans, if.we are to believe the innumerable warnings published against it deep into the seventeenth century.[28] The despair in the play does stop short of death, and it is also a stage in the process of Alonso's spiritual regeneration, but the pattern of tragicomic courting of disaster, interrupted by hairbreadth escapes and final reconciliation, will not account for the entire play. Antonio and Sebastian remain villains from beginning to end. They never have the slightest moral qualms about the plot to kill Alonso, even after they know of its discovery by Prospero. Earlier in the play Sebastian is only initially afraid that the plot might not be successful.

The Magic Circle

The iconic stage image of the magic circle drawn by Prospero in the last act marks the point where we discover how ardently Prospero has finally come to value the conversion of all his former enemies, not only Alonso, but Sebastian and Antonio as well. When he draws the enchanted circle in the air with his staff, Prospero hopes that the spellbound guests may reach moral consciousness at the same time that their senses are restored. He expects what James Joyce anachronistically came to call aginbite of inwit. Just as Stephano and Trinculo have been literally pinch-spotted by goblins as they were driven away from the line of alluring garments, Alonso, Sebastian, and Antonio are all assumed by Prospero to have been metaphorically pinched by a reforming conscience:

> Most cruelly
> Didst thou, Alonso, use me and my daughter;
> Thy brother was a furtherer in the act.
> Thou art pinch'd for 't now, Sebastian. Flesh and blood,
> You, brother mine, that entertain'd ambition,
> Expell'd remorse and nature, who, with Sebastian—
> Whose inward pinches therefore are most strong—
> Would here have kill'd your king, I do forgive thee. (V. i. 71–78)

This is the very forgiveness just inspired by Ariel's famous rebuke to Prospero's total power over his spellbound enemies. We all recall how Ariel's remark that his "affections /Would become tender" toward them were he "human" inspires Prospero's reply that ". . . the rarer action is /In virtue than in vengeance; they being penitent, /The sole drift of my purpose doth extend /Not a frown further. . . ." That we are to assume the three major enemies now fully prepared for repentance is implicit in an even earlier remark by Gonzalo. His statement is made after Ariel's speech as a harpy, in Act III, drives Alonso offstage vowing suicide, immediately followed by Sebastian and Antonio: "All three of them are desperate; their great guilt, /Like poison given to work a great time after, /Now gins to bite the spirits. . . ." Were Gonzalo's fears about a despair stimulated by conscience more fully justified at that point, the total outcome of the play might have been far more optimistic. But by the end of the action only Alonso among Prospero's three major enemies is clearly moved by conscience, let alone repentance. Yet Shakespeare has certainly aroused our more hopeful long-range expectations by means of the speeches quoted just above. Perhaps those expectations were aroused so that we might feel even more keenly the concluding absence of perfectly fulfilled repentance, forgiveness, and love.

It is the magic circle, that emphatic iconic stage image of perfection, that probably stimulates those expectations most strongly in an audience intent upon the action of the play. The circle is familiar among the most ancient of symbols, ubiquitous in all ages. It is nearly impossible to confine its separate meanings, and Shakespeare leaves it nearly as broad in implication as he received it, but three observations can be made about the meanings engendered by its dramatic context in *The Tempest*. The emphasis seems to be primarily upon the harmony created by love. A minor aspect of the symbolism is the theme of time and eternity. Finally, the circle used to create a space apart is a protection against danger.

Love, time, and eternity are integrated into the simplest of Renaissance emblems, the perfectly drawn circle. Theodore Beza (1519–1605) was both a humanist scholar and the loving friend in whose arms Calvin died. In Beza's *Icones, id est verae imagines virorum doctrina simul et pietate illustrium* (Geneva, 1580), praise of both Catholic and Protestant Renaissance church reformers is followed by a series of elegantly rendered and printed emblems. The first emblem is a circle set in a seemingly decorative perspective landscape, but the setting is probably meant to suggest the world of time and space as well (Plate 35). A translation of the accompanying Latin quatrain reads:

> Whoever seeks the beginning in an elegant form
> Will find here the beginning in the end.
> Thus whoever has true love in the veneration of Christ
> Will in his last hour end by beginning.[29] (sig. Kk3v)

Love therefore continuously returns to the compassionate lover in a circle of time melting into eternity, where all created things come to rest in elegant perfection of form, beyond time and space, beyond birth and death, where Gonzalo's tears will be wiped forever from his eyes.

As for protection against danger, the circle drawn on the earth was the way the black magician created an inviolable precinct wherein he could conjure devils without fear of harm to himself.[30] In Act V Prospero, practicing a more exalted white magic, draws his iconic circle in the higher element of the air[31] (probably with some kind of vapor concealed in a hollow staff). He also puts his enemies and those mourning their fate within the circle, instead of standing within its protective compass himself. At this point the enemies are more vulnerable than the magician, and he is deeply concerned for them rather than for himself. The sympathy Prospero now feels for those enchanted within the circle is underlined by his tears at seeing Gonzalo's own sympathy for his distraught masters: "Holy Gonzalo, honourable man, /Mine eyes, ev'n sociable to the show of thine, /Fall fellowly drops. . . ." Therein lies the stress upon the loving harmony created by a sense of shared humanity, the emphasis first introduced by the ability of even Ariel at least to imagine tenderness. As a magic circle it is drawn by Prospero the Neoplatonic magus, a white magician, who has not yet entirely abjured his powers.

Because of the recent study of Giordano Bruno made by Frances Yates we now know a good deal about how Renaissance Hermeticism justified the concept of a Neoplatonic magus, who sought to be like God himself by using occult knowledge and power in the service of good.[32] And it has long been suggested that Shakespeare might have known about the contemporary white magician John Dee.[33] Among Prospero's last God-like acts are the drawing with his staff of an "airy charm" (the circle) and the commanding of "heavenly music," both designed to bring himself into final and perfect harmony with his enemies. Prospero has the highest hopes for his last device, in turn an emblem of that final moment out of time and at the end of time when creation melts into eternity and all opposing forces are at last reconciled.[34]

> The charm dissolves apace,
> And as the morning steals upon the night,
> Melting the darkness, so their rising senses
> Begin to chase the ignorant fumes that mantle
> Their clearer reason. . . .
> . . . . Their understanding
> Begins to swell, and the approaching tide
> Will shortly fill the reasonable shore
> That now lies foul and muddy. . . . (V. i. 64–68; 79–82)

These perfectly articulated images draw the entire philosophical setting of the play into a few climactic moments. Yet we already know that the promise these images make will remain only partially fulfilled at the end. Even the whitest of magic can have only a partial success, and that only on the lower levels of human experience. Prospero can constrain obedience in Caliban because of magic, he can protect himself by knowing the plans of his enemies, and he can even construct elaborate existential devices (like those of Portia) designed to bring about self-knowledge and repentance. The actual repentance, however, like the true love of God, can only exist as an expression of man's free will.

One of Shakespeare's most recurrent themes in this play (in contrast to *The Merchant of Venice*) is the issue of freedom, true and false. Just as the important distinction between right reason and wrong reason is a theme crucial to both the *Faerie Queene* and *Paradise Lost,* the difference between freedom as an illusion and freedom as a reality is basic to both Milton's epic and this play. The theme is introduced in Act I when Ariel reminds Prospero of the promise to set him at liberty within the year; Caliban ironically thinks it "freedom" in Act II when he finds a god in Stephano, one whose tyranny is destined to become far worse than the controls imposed by Prospero as a God-like magus; in Act III Ferdinand offers to be the love servant of Miranda and then paradoxically compares his submission to the yearning of bondage after freedom; in the same act Stephano sings a song containing the cliché about the freedom always available to thought, only to have Caliban insist "That's not the tune"; Ariel is finally set free in Act V according to promise, almost immediately after Prospero abjures his magic; and, finally, the very last words of the play are Prospero's plea in the epilogue that the audience show its approval of the performance and thus "set me free."

The issue of freedom is what finally sets this play so clearly apart from the ultimate drift of Hermeticism. It is difficult to create any detailed or systematic relationship between Prospero and the Neoplatonic magus, perhaps because Shakespeare is doing at once so much less and so much more with his protagonist. Beyond the magical control over creatures assigned in a general way to the spheres of the four traditional elements, an initial willingness to use God-like power in the service of good, and the costume and tools of the white magician, Prospero has little in common with the enormously learned, incredibly detailed, and frequently contradictory system of the Hermeticists. Where he exceeds their sophistication, however, is in his sense of the limitations of the system. They were trying to resurrect what they regarded as an extremely ancient, pre-Christian occult wisdom for the purpose of bringing the perfection of Heaven on earth. If all the age-old knowledge lost could be found, if it were carefully made compatible with Christianity, if it were reserved for the use of only the wise and the learned, then man's life on earth could be drawn into the transcendent and harmonious world of perfection beyond the stars, whose own beauty manifests its presence. The attempt to contain all human experience within the system made the system unbelievably complex.

But Prospero goes beyond this goal because of his clear sense of the limitations of power itself. Older than Neoplatonism and the unconscious sources of its symbolism in post-Christian Greek thought is the belief that God reserves even his power for the sake of man's free will. The summit of God's creation is the love he freely gives in the hope that it will be just as freely returned. One of the most fundamental senses in which it was believed that man was created in God's image was man's sharing of God's capacity for unconstrained love. God freely used the power of the creator of all to reserve his power at the point of man's freedom. Prospero's recognition of that mystery is expressed in his abjuration of magic and his freeing of Ariel. He tries to prepare Caliban,

Antonio, and Sebastian for a similar freedom, the one through education and the other two by a moving of conscience, but with these attempts he largely fails. Sebastian is, at most, momentarily impressed by the sudden revelation of Ferdinand and Miranda at chess—"A most high miracle!" (V. i. 177)—but he quickly reverts to his sardonic companionship with Antonio throughout the conclusion to the action. As for Caliban, his conversion is the result of discoveries made entirely on his own about the empty power of drink and the stupidity of folly: ". . . What a thrice-double ass /Was I to take this drunkard for a god, /And worship this dull fool! . . ." Prospero's education failed, was perhaps worse than nothing, where the freely sought familiarity with Stephano and Trinculo succeeded.

By abandoning his magical power at the end, and in taking the risk of success or failure for the sake of man's God-ordained freedom, Prospero becomes truly God-like in a way apparently unimagined by the Hermeticists.

The celestial banquet of love can only be enjoyed by willing guests. By magical means Prospero brings his guests to the door of the Banqueting House, assuming that they will all enter joyfully on their own. His abjuration of his magic, his "rough" and arbitrary power over them, suggests that he knows they must enter consciously and freely if they are to enter at all. But because Prospero is only like a god, yet not God, he can only know what it is reasonable for them to do, not what they will do. Like most men he anticipates too much from other men. Despite his disappointment, nevertheless, he settles for less than the ideal of love among all men by retaining a secular power over Sebastian and Antonio, the threat of exposure. The muted ending rests considerably below the summit of Neoplatonic ascent.

Neither the ending of *The Tempest* nor that of *King Lear* is as reassuring as the endings of most of Shakespeare's other plays. In *Lear* Albany is about to make precisely the same mistake Lear made at the beginning of it all, giving away and dividing the kingdom. He offers it to both Kent and Edgar, when, according to convention, he, as highest ranking survivor, should rule it all. Some balance is restored when a weary Kent (recalling the weary Lear at the beginning) defers the honor, but, even so, Edgar is not the appropriate single ruler. The end of *The Tempest* stands in the same relationship to the endings of the other romances as the end of *Lear* stands to the endings of the other tragedies. It is as if Shakespeare were once again saying, "Speak what we feel, not what we ought to say." We leave a meditative Prospero concerned with preparing for death—"Every third thought shall be my grave"—and able to promise no more about the future than calm seas on the voyage to Naples.

Postscript: Discordia Concors

Shakespeare's ideal world is expressed in Prospero's iconic circle: the melting of time into eternity by a loving reconciliation of opposites. Since Milton, our civilization has tended to withdraw both from the eternal questions and from the ideal of unity. The great cultural reconciliation of the late Middle Ages was the consolidation of Jewish and Christian revelations, a consolidation widely distributed at that time in block-books such as the *Biblia pauperum* and the *Speculum humanae salvationis*. The humanistic Renaissance conflated that reconciliation with the monuments of classical civilization. Spenser and Milton are the great English examples known to us all. The unifying spirit they embody has been clearly summarized by André Chastel in a paragraph defining humanism:

> . . . the association of nature, virtue, beauty, reason, anti-quity and the Christian religion in one and the same intuitive apprehension— . . . purified and reduced to their 'true essence.' An ideal sufficiently powerful to carry all before it, yet, in a certain sense, too 'naive' as to be capable of discursive expression. The invention, the repetition of certain symbols and emblems was appropriate to the expression of such an aspiration, of the pathos of a 'return to the fountain-head'—a 'renaissance,' or rebirth . . . : that is to say the return to the original classical virtue; to the origins of art . . . ; to the original wisdom—that of the sages and

mythic philosophers. Every important discovery was presented as a rediscovery—even that of perspective, which was attributed to the artists of antiquity; even that of America, which was believed to have been converted . . . by the Apostle Thomas. In the humanist concept of history, progress became . . . the recovery of Eden.[1]

In the last one hundred years, however, Nietzsche's dialectic of Apollo and Dionysius has been cast as classical reason against medieval superstition, or romantic individual freedom against repressive social control, or, most recently of all, love against exploitation. These modern stances deeply influence our perception of both Shakespeare and his age. Controversy is vigorous as to whether Shakespeare was orthodox in religion and politics, or skeptical and radical; whether the Renaissance represented the full flowering of the Middle Ages, or the beginning of modern history. The relationship between the Middle Ages and the Renaissance has thus been seen from every extreme. Burckhardt, the secular humanist, has usually been given the credit for the classic distinction. C. S. Lewis, the Christian humanist, denied any real difference. Mario Praz has posited two inconsistent cultures living side by side in the Renaissance. He finds the emblem of the period in Castiglione,

> . . . a pious man, narrowly and rigidly orthodox, and yet, except for certain fleeting references, religion is firmly excluded from the whole construction of his dialogues. As one finds with all the humanists, the plane of worldly wisdom and that of religious dogma . . . are kept severely separate.[2]

As for Shakespeare, Praz says that the Christian element is always there, but always kept in the background. Praz rightly stresses the way in which pagan and Christian worlds existed side by side in the Renaissance, but we need not share his further view that these two worlds were both separate and the basis of unreconciled "contradictions." The Renaissance at its best, in figures like Ficino, Erasmus, and Shakespeare, can be seen as a period of overlap, neither medieval nor modern, but a brief moment in which the best of the last two thousand years and more was unified. It might be refreshing to declare it neutral ground, a free city, where religion and classical humanism lived briefly at peace with one another. As Praz himself goes on to demonstrate concerning the new style of Renaissance church architecture, the principle is one of harmony. He quotes for authority Leon Battista Alberti's fifteenth-century discussion of the correspondence of musical intervals and architectural proportions.

We might add that Christ was not lost in the transition from the medieval church in the form of a cross to the Renaissance church with the proportioned facade of a Roman triumphal arch. The new emphasis on Christ Triumphant rather than Christ Crucified simply stimulated the revival of the classical form. Or, if you wish, the revival of the classical form encouraged a new image of Christ. The intellectual conflict, in Renaissance England at least, was between religious sects, not between religion and secularism. The broad outlines of the traditional religious and moral system, it is true, were not universally accepted throughout Europe. A few very unconventional thinkers—Machiavelli, Montaigne, perhaps Marlowe—quickly come to mind. But the primary challenge was to international Christianity, not to Christianity. Heaven and hell had not yet been replaced by the modern polarities of theism and skepticism, or the individual and the state. Intellectual controversy in Renaissance England was almost entirely confined to polemics against Rome and arguments over the details of orthodoxy. In her later years, Queen Elizabeth expressed a sane response to this state of affairs in her famous comment, "There is only one Christ Jesus and one faith: the rest is a dispute about trifles."

Much scholarly controversy in recent years has centered on the issue of Shakespeare's relationship to the Christian doctrine. Roland M. Frye has warned us against creating Renaissance theology out of whole cloth,[3] but we should also probably be very cautious about accepting the sophisticated beliefs of Luther, Calvin, and Hooker, however seminal their theology, as authority for what Shakespeare or his audience might have thought about religion and its proper relationship to art. These Protestants, like Aquinas before them, were amplifying, correcting, and refining the religious thinking of both their scholarly predecessors and the educated priest or layman. A case in point might be one of the central issues in the present reassessment of *The Merchant of Venice:* whether enforced conversion is as good as any other kind.[4] As I have tried to show in my chapter on this play, such theological dilemmas do not necessarily exist in the plays Shakespeare wrote.

Shylock is probably meant to illustrate how it is possible to be forced into a true conversion, in other words, forced into a situation that fundamentally convinces him of Christian truth. If so, like Gloucester and Alonso, he is existentially converted by dramatic means.

The common understanding of Christianity among the Elizabethans, furthermore, was probably, in certain ways having little to do with theology, very different from that of the average layman today. In the twentieth century, for many Christians as well as for their antagonists, religion has had a formulaic and moralistic cast. We should be careful not to assume automatically that the most formulaic expressions of religion in the past are the proper touchstones for an understanding of Shakespeare. The thought of men such as Luther, Calvin, and Hooker, however brilliant and cogent, is not necessarily the major source of Christianity's survival and effect on the laity over many centuries. Devotional, meditational, and liturgical texts (of the kind found in The Book of Common Prayer, and the works of Bernard of Clairveaux, Bonaventure, and the mystics) preserve a much less intellectually defined tradition of religious experience, one emphasizing the opening of the soul rather than the resolution of theological arguments. At its best, this alternate tradition of affective piety is charitable toward man and awestruck by the mystery of God's creation. When it comes to documenting what Shakespeare's audience might have thought on the subject of Revealed Truth the best source is probably not theology or even sermons but the enormous body of devotional and meditational prose published in the course of the English Renaissance. The history and effect of this kind of writing has been extremely well researched by scholars such as Helen C. White and Louis Martz.[5]

As for Shakespeare, we will probably never know whether he, like so many Englishmen then and since, believed in ghosts, or Christianity, or damnation when he wrote plays such as Macbeth, and Hamlet, and Othello. The documents simply do not exist, as they do for Milton or Donne. I myself am inclined to the paradoxical feeling that this is one of our most valuable sources of ignorance. What does seem reasonably clear, however, is that Shakespeare, that most stage-conscious of all playwrights, wrote as if his audience did believe in such realities. Even here we must make a final qualification. Shakespeare's emphasis almost always remains on man's spiritual and moral existence here and now. It is the life to come that is in the background, but it is left in shadows. The death of Hamlet leaves us with a far stronger sense of his loss to the world than it does with Horatio's vision of "flights of angels." *The Taming of the Shrew,* to use another example, is in structure Shakespeare's most didactic play. Not only is the dominant line of action focused on Petrucchio's methods for teaching Kate to be a good wife, but the play concludes with a long moralizing speech delivered by Kate on the subject of female submission. This speech has the explicitly didactic effect of God's words at the end of *The Castle of Perseverance* or the Doctor's message at the end of *Everyman,* yet Kate's frame of reference is secular, which is to say "of time." Kate uses the parallel of the correct relationship between the subject and his prince for her model of the proper attitude of a wife toward her husband. When Milton returns to the same subject he reestablishes the theological sanctions which even Chaucer had carefully qualified through his narrator in the epilogue to the "Clerk's Tale of the Patient Griselda." For Milton, woman should obey man as man obeys God. Milton is explicit on a point carefully muted by the medieval Chaucer and held to man's life on earth by the Renaissance Shakespeare. Shakespeare's tragic endings are usually also held to time rather than pointed toward eternity. The conventional consolation for grief in his century was the conviction that the soul was freed into eternity. Friar Lawrence, so like Polonius in his stock of commonplaces, pulls the stop on this meditation when consoling Capulet for the "death" of the drugged Juliet:

> Heaven and yourself
> Had part in this fair maid; now heaven hath all,
> And all the better is it for the maid.
> Your part in her you could not keep from death,
> But heaven keeps his part in eternal life.
> The most you sought was her promotion,
> For 'twas your heaven she should be advanc'd;
> And weep ye now, seeing she is advanc'd
> Above the clouds, as high as heaven itself? (IV. v. 66–74)

Yet no such speech occurs at the end, after Juliet's actual death, even though the end would be a more appropriate place for it were *Romeo and Juliet* a morality play or a sermon instead of a romantic tragedy. At the end of the play Shakespeare holds the explicit didacticism to a few comments focused on the need to heal the civil strife in Verona.

In the course of my study I have frequently stated that many of Shakespeare's iconic stage images carry associations with religious symbolism. The candle carried by Jessica in Act II of *The Merchant of Venice* is expressive of penitence; the head of Macbeth brought in at the end by Macduff suggests emblematic heads ranging from that of the serpent in Genesis to that of Medusa; Richard II should probably assume Christ-like postures on more than one occasion. The critical questions I am now raising are concerned with whether these religious values emphasize doctrine or feeling, belief or experience, and whether the overall and conclusive emphasis of Shakespeare's plays is upon this world (spiritually and morally perceived) or the next. It is hardly necessary to conclude that the pattern is feeling, experience, and this world, usually but not necessarily rendered within a traditional religious framework. As for a conflict between the play as a play and religion, formulaic or experimental, none need necessarily exist. As I have already implied, theology and homilies are not the only (or even the primary) way in which the religious sensibility has been communicated from generation to generation. Our awareness of the way in which Renaissance art was organically didactic, furthermore, is also much more sophisticated now than it was some years ago, especially since the work of Rosemund Tuve. And, finally, the fully developed religious sensibility has always provided for mystery, refusal to usurp the judgment of God, and vast areas of paradox.

Shakespeare's Speaking Pictures has thus been unified by two major emphases: iconic study of Shakespeare's verbal and stage imagery, and a thematic analysis of the ways in which his plays serve the "union of contraries." A considerable body of scholarship in recent years has stressed the ubiquitous Renaissance topos of what was usually referred to then as "discordia concors." The authority for this Latin phrase is most frequently given to Horace: "the world corresponds with discord by concord" (Epistles, 1, 12, 19), although Ovid, Lucan, and Lactantius are also often cited.[6] The Latin father Lactantius was the one who brought the concept into the mainstream of Christian theology:

> So . . . heat and moisture . . . have faculties different from and opposed to each other, which God has marvelously

devised for sustaining and supporting all things. . . . Whence certain philosophers and poets have said that 'the world corresponds with discord by concord' but they did not see the plan very thoroughly.[7]

By the Renaissance the "plan" had been worked out in considerable detail and parts of it were to be found throughout both religious and secular literature and the arts, especially in the emblematic combination of Latin mottoes and esoteric pictures. The union of contraries is well illustrated, for instance, in the popular Renaissance motto, "festina lente" (make haste slowly). This phrase has already been discussed in my chapter on *Macbeth*, along with the dolphin and anchor often used to express the motto emblematically. And I have repeatedly returned throughout this book to the way in which a knowledge of Renaissance iconography reveals discordia concors in the plays of Shakespeare, indeed almost everywhere in the art and literature of his day. The paradoxical truths expressed in Shakespeare are also increasingly perceived today by those examining the plays with the tools of the literary critic.[8] Controversy over the meaning and purpose of these plays will always suggest their vitality as art, but some of the controversy can probably be resolved by the knowledge that Renaissance discordia concors harmonized what have come to be seen by subsequent centuries as exclusive categories. In other words, the very presence of intense post-Romantic controversy can indicate the equal presence in Shakespeare of the Renaissance union of contraries. Orlando is both a naïve writer of amatory verse and a sophisticated wit combatant; he is both civilized and refreshed by the green world, as Hymen symbolizes both chastity and love, united in marriage. Richard is both Adam and Christ; he is both the cause of his deposition and violated by it. And Prospero's tempest both punishes and redeems Alonso.

If the reader will forgive my presumption in concluding this study with my translation of Dante's ending to his *Commedia*, these closing tercets bring into perfect focus the reconciliation of the irreconcilable:

> At the final moment of vision I was
> Like the mathematician who struggles
> To compute the circle and fails.

I tried to see how image and circle were one,
But my wings were not sufficiently strong.
Then my soul was assaulted with light.

Power alone never brings full knowledge
Until desire and will are spun upon a wheel,
Evenly and smoothly, by the Love

That moves the sun and the other stars.

Quale e 'l geometra che tutto s'affige
     per misurar lo cerchio, e non ritrova,
     pensado, quel principio ond'elli indige,
tal era io a quella vista nova:
     veder volea come si convenne
     l'imago al cerchio e come vi s'indova;
ma non eran da cio le proprie penne:
     se non che la mia mente fu percossa
     da un fulgore in che sua voglia venne.
All'alta fantasia qui manco possa;
     ma gia volgeva il mio disio e 'l velle,
     si come rota ch' igualmente e mossa,
l'amor che move il sole e l'altre stelle.

Appendix

Othello's Angels: Ars Moriendi
Bettie Anne Doebler

The final scene in the last act of *Othello* invokes the ars moriendi tradition, a popular Renaissance tradition of comfort for the dying, which stands in ironic contrast to Othello's own violent and despairing death. The most familiar prop in the iconography of Renaissance death is the bed, and the bed is the dominant iconic stage image in this scene, a bed that should probably be both well downstage and as massive as possible while still capable of being rolled forward. In many of the woodcuts that accompany the ars moriendi tracts and in the sixteenth-century paintings of deathbed scenes, the bed is inclined to be massive and rectilinear, in contrast to the curvilinear voluptuous couch hung with tentlike draperies which appears in representations of amorous scenes.[1] Supporting this dominant image of Desdemona's deathbed is a network of iconic verbal images, especially those associated with angels and devils, the contestants for a dying man's soul.[2] There is no great elaboration of this theme in *Othello;* the details are commonplaces. By 1604,[3] the probable date of the play's first performance, such a long and popular Christian tradition as the ars moriendi needed only to be hinted at.

The Judeo-Christian view of life as a trial, or series of temptations, is familiar to medieval and Renaissance scholars. The patterns of temptation and fall, or temptation and victory, appear throughout the history of literature. The great archetypes are, of course, biblical. The pattern for tragedy to the Renaissance mind was the narrative of Adam and Eve falling to the devil in the Garden. The tragicomic pattern, however, was exemplified by Job and Christ, both of whom came to ultimate victory over the world, the flesh, and the devil. Some scholars have seen Othello as a type of Adam in his fall through uxoriousness to the temptations of Iago in the main body of the play, but no one has seen Act V, scene ii as a parallel temptation and fall underlined by allusions to the ars moriendi.[4] Shakespeare, by the use of this tradition, intensifies the tragic fall of Othello. As he has lived and fallen earlier to jealousy, embodied in Iago, so he dies, accused by his own sins as they seem to be summarized in Iago, falling into the sin of despair and taking his own life. The most explicit allusion to the ars tradition is made by Gratiano. His words remind the audience of the deathbed struggle between good and evil, in which the stakes are very high:

> Did he [Brabantio] live now,
> This sight would make him do a desperate turn,
> Yea, curse his better angel from his side,
> And fall to reprobance. (V. ii. 209–12)

By the time Gratiano speaks these lines we are conscious that Othello is facing his own struggle with the temptations to despair and suicide, concluding in probable damnation.

Critics have found it impossible to believe that Othello is both damned and heroic. On the one hand, those who see his damnation seem to lose sight of the heroic proportion of his struggle and the very human glory of his ending. On the other hand, those who respond to Shakespeare's dramatic portrayal of the struggle try to minimize the theological implications of his suicide. Somewhere in between are the scholars who discuss the play as something of an allegory of fortunate fall; they see many theological allusions to damnation in the language of the play, but at the same time they find in the final scene a structure of redemption, often built upon Desdemona as a Christ figure and upon Othello's sincere repentance of her murder.[5] All three positions seem to me to ignore at some point the actual text of the play as it would be apprehended by a Shakespearean audience. In his professional knowledge of the theater and of the need to communicate immediately to an audience, Shakespeare often speaks explicitly. When he is using allusions to suggest a dimension other than that of the particular, he frequently gives a summary clue. In *Othello,* perhaps his most carefully wrought play, Gratiano, horrified at the murder of Desdemona, brings explicitly into the context the commonplace ars tradition in his comment on what would have been Brabantio's response to the scene were he alive and present.

The explicit reference to the ars tradition operates dramatically in two ways. It throws into relief the contrast between the tragic suffering of Othello in Act V and the ordinary suffering of one who dies well. By juxtaposing the ideal of dying with something very near its opposite, Shakespeare evokes the risk of Othello's damnation. At the same time, however, by showing the heroic intensity of the struggle, and the suffering that results from the recognition of his guilt (against the conventional background of the ars) Shakespeare evokes great dramatic sympathy for the human Othello. Othello's probable damnation is supported by the references to the ars tradition; paradoxically, he becomes more dramatically sympathetic through the intensity of his spiritual suffering.

In order to appreciate fully what the allusions contribute dramatically, one should know something of the ars moriendi tradition. The first work on the theme of dying well that was more than a chapter in a theological treatise was printed ca. 1450 as a block-book, which included eleven illustrations and accompanying texts, all printed from woodblocks. The purpose of the book was to instruct someone on the art of dying well when no priest was present. There were two early versions of the text, both widely imitated and reprinted in the fifteenth and sixteenth centuries, especially in England, France, and Germany. The conventions of the tradition continued to be expressed in both Catholic and Protestant devotional books of the seventeenth century. Although the instruction had its source on the Continent, it apparently came into England about 1490 with Caxton's translation of the *Tractatus de arte vivendi et moriendi.*[6]

At the heart of the ars tradition is the actual deathbed scene, viewed as a climactic struggle between the forces of evil and the forces of good for the possession of the dying one's soul. In the oldest, simplest, and most iconographic terms, as it is seen in the woodcuts, for example, or in medieval dramas such as *The Castle of Perseverance,* this struggle occurs between one's Good Angel and one's Bad Angel (or the devil). The struggle between the two angels centers on five temptations and five inspirations. The instruction attempts to aid the dying one to overcome the devil and to die peacefully, with the eleventh illustration showing his soul being received out of his mouth and into heaven by the Good Angel.[7] Sections of instruction beyond the temptations and inspirations were usually included, of course, and sometimes in the seventeenth century the central struggle disappeared so that the text consisted of comforts alone.[8] Yet many popular devotional writers, such as Cardinal Bellarmino and the Protestant preacher Christopher Sutton, continued to write ars books which were expansions of the original struggle, including the instruction against temptations.[9] The introduction to an ars book was often an extensive treatise on accepting death as the gateway to life. Also, there were usually instructions for those attending the sick: questions to be asked, prayers to be said.

In spite of the dramatic sympathy which arises from the recognition by the audience that Othello has not fallen through his own malice but rather, like Adam in the Garden, has been tempted by the devil through uxoriousness, the audience could hardly fail to see the manner of his dying against the long and popular tradition of the ars moriendi. The counsel of the ars against impatience in the face of suffering, or against despair that might lead to suicide, could hardly have failed to present a contrast to Othello in his last moments. According to conventional Renaissance theology, Othello dies badly; like Faustus, he does not follow the accumulated wisdom of Christian theology. Roland M. Frye has shown, in *Shakespeare and the Christian Doctrine*, the nearly universal agreement in the sixteenth century that damnation resulted from suicide committed willfully, consciously, and successfully.[10] Shakespeare reminds his audience of this contrast between the ideal death and that of Othello by commonplaces—a technique suggesting that by this time Shakespeare had only to refer to traditional images and themes to bring before the mind's eye of the audience the ordered and optimistic ideal for dying that had come to it through block-books and popular iconography, not to mention the large quantity of pious treatises that were sold in London every day.[11]

The constant injunction to carry the thought of death always in one's mind and ever to be preparing for it could hardly have failed to produce a sensitivity to the subject. Most of the religious devotional books in the ars tradition began with a section on the necessity for accepting death joyfully and preparing oneself for it. As part of this preparation, many writers gave copious advice on how to die to the world. Christopher Sutton's *Disce Mori: Learne to Die*, 5th ed. (London, 1609), reminds us that an essential part of this preparation is self-knowledge:

> Well the perfection of our knowledge is to know God and ourselves: ourselues wee best knowe, when we acknowledge our mortall being. By our dying to the world, Christ is saide to come and liue in vs, and by our dying in the world, we are saide to goe to liue with Christ.[12]

One of the methods used by the devotional writers to encourage meditation on and preparation for death was a warning against just such sudden death as we find in *Othello*. This warning arose out of the recognition that men need a leisurely death in order to prepare their souls. Even so sophisticated a preacher as Richard Hooker said that the virtuous desire leisurely death in old age, both for their own joy and for the example that they can give to those around them:

> . . . because the nearer we draw unto God, the more we are oftentimes enlightened with the shining beams of his glorious presence as being then almost in sight, a leisurable departure may in that case bring forth for the good of such as are present that which shall cause them for ever after from the bottom of their hearts to pray, "O let us die the death of the righteous, and let our last end be like theirs."[13]

Probably the suddenness and violence of the deaths in the last act of *Othello* were in themselves enough to arouse horror in an audience warned against being caught unprepared. At the same time, however, that devotional writers warned men to be on guard against sudden death, they also warned witnesses not to judge the future of the dying one, often referred to as the "moriens." One could not know whether or not the moriens might have time for repentance between apparent dying and the actual going out of the soul. Erasmus, with characteristic acidity, says: "For it may be, that he, whiche for treason, is hanged, drawen, and quartered, passeth into the company of aungelles, where as an nother, the whiche dyeng in a gray friers cote, and relygiously buried, departeth downe vnto hell."[14] Despite these qualifications and although even the sophisticated desired a leisurely death, the tradition in general allowed for a "good" sudden death under only one essential condition: that of a good life. Clearly, this is the justification for Desdemona's good death, and, in less ideal terms, for Emilia's. Neither has time for the traditional preparation, and yet the audience would have seen Desdemona's death in perfect charity as ideal, and Emilia's in heroic truth-telling as something close to ideal.

Clearly, the instructions for deathbed behavior were aimed more surely at those who had doubts about having lived well and therefore at those who envisioned a last epic struggle with the devil. The tradition was designed to be comforting, especially for those who needed the assurance of a ritual. In fact, the great set of eleven illustrations that accompanies the ars block-books narrates what I have earlier regarded as tragicomedy. The final scene illustrates the happy dying of the sick man, with the vanquished demons uttering execrations as the soul flies off into heavenly bliss. In the other ten illustrations, which comprise the struggle between good and evil, five temptations are of the devil: against faith, to despair, to impatience, to vainglory, and to avarice. Alternating with these are the five inspirations of the Good Angel: to faith, against despair, to patience, against vainglory, and against avarice. Central to all of these is the figure of the moriens on his deathbed. All the representations, however, are crowded with figures: in the temptations the dominant figures are naturally demonic, while in the inspirations the Good Angel takes an important place, as do God, Christ, the Virgin, and saints. The effect of the series is not, however, to frighten the reader with the mightiness of the struggle, but rather to reassure him that with the aid of his Good Angel he will be able to overcome the devil. Particularly essential is the patterning of one's death on the Passion of Christ and the remembering of his mercy. The literal expression of this counsel is to fix one's eyes on the figure of Christ on the Cross. In the "Inspiration of the Good Angel against Despair," in the "Inspiration against Avarice," and in the final scene of dying well, the figure of Christ on the Cross is prominent.[15] In an anonymous tract called "The Craft to Know Well to Die," the following advice is given:

> Item [there] ought to be presented to the sick person the image of the crucifix, which always should be among the sick

people, and also the image of our Blessed Lady, and of other saints which the sick man hath most loved and honoured in his life.[16]

Erasmus even goes to the length of suggesting that the crucifix be laid against the eyes of the sick man.[17]

Certainly, compared to the danse macabre and even the memento mori that stemmed from it, the specific ars tradition had a particularly kind and encouraging tone. For the most part the writers of the ars tracts shunned images of damnation and hellfire; they sought to encourage the dying one through the difficult spiritual time of the last illness lest his bodily weakness cause him to fall prey to the devil's temptations, especially the sin against faith and the sin of despair, both of which might lead to suicide.[18] Almost all the authors of these numerous books on the art of dying (which became during the Renaissance a category of courtesy books) attempted to give very practical instructions. In vivid contrast to the optimistic tone of this instruction, the end of *Othello* is filled with passion, murder, recrimination, and a barrage of temptations for Othello, which he is unable to overcome except in dramatic terms. Anyone familiar with the medieval exempla of good Christians facing their deaths (a tradition which reached at least as far into the seventeenth century as Walton's description of Donne's death) would recognize in Othello's ending a near-antithesis of the ideal. But certainly the ironic contrast is the point. Shakespeare is using the tradition to underline the tragedy.

Lest one think that the conventions of the ars had lost their force by the beginning of the seventeenth century, one should remember that the publication of devotional literature was increasing in the early seventeenth century with the Counter-Reformation. Approximately half the books published in England since the beginning of printing had had clearly religious titles, not to mention the many others without such titles which nevertheless expressed an essentially religious point of view.[19] Clearly, the literate Elizabethan was more spiritually sensitive than scholars have realized until recently. More directly related to my theme is the quantity of writing on preparation for death, both in books of popular devotion (such as those of Perkins, Becon, and Sutton) and in the more intellectual books of meditation that came into England with the Continental books influenced by the *Spiritual Exercises* of St.

Ignatius Loyola.[20] To this quantitative argument should be added common knowledge about seventeenth-century life: the plagues, the very high rate of mortality in childbirth and of contagious disease, and the certainty by parents that a high percentage of their children would not live to make old bones.

The popularity of the theme of preparation for death had led, of course, to several sorts of writing on the subject: the ars tradition, with the focus on the struggle, symbolic and visual; the more intellectualized books of meditation; and pious treatises that tended to focus more on practical instructions for setting one's property in order than upon the great spiritual crisis. Shakespeare, with his characteristic sense of dramatic and visual potential, chose to use the ars tradition, with its focus on the central deathbed struggle, a tradition which was still very much alive.

The visual quality of the ars possibly stimulated Shakespeare's iconic imagination. One recalls the woodcuts mentioned above, which had appeared first with the block-books but which had been reproduced and imitated elsewhere up through the sixteenth century. The high artistic quality of the original woodcuts, still famous in their own right among art historians, suggests that they would have imprinted themselves on the imagination of all who saw them. There is evidence that originally many writers considered the cuts themselves as the core of the ars and intended merely to accompany them with a brief text of explanation and instruction. At least we do know from the closing lines of the introduction of one of the early block-books that the author intended the words and pictures to *work together* to teach a man how to die.[21] Since these books were not designed primarily for the clergy but predominantly for the uneducated layman, one may further deduce the primary importance of the illustrations.

For these reasons, one may speculate that the visual dominance of the bed in Act V was for Shakespeare's audience pervasively suggestive of the deathbed scenes of the ars. Also, the gathering of the central dramatic characters about the bed as the scene progresses—first with the entrance of Emilia, after Desdemona's near-death; then with the entrace of Montano, Gratiano, and Iago; and finally with the entrance of Lodovico, Cassio, and Officers—suggests the visually crowded woodcuts, in which the moriens is surrounded by friends and foes of a supernatural or symbolic nature, as well as by members of his family.

Not only does the art of dying suggest the importance of the bed, but it also helps us to understand the overall structure of the scene. Scene ii is divided into two major parallel sections: the first is the murder and "good" death of Desdemona; and the second is the discovery by Othello of his monstrous mistake and his consequent suicide, or theologically "bad" death. In the first section, even a contemporary audience agreed that Desdemona's death was extremely affecting.[22] This was true undoubtedly not only because of her innocence and loveliness but because in exemplifying the ideal of Christian forgiveness she brings into the context of the play a great body of emotional associations with a good death. During the first part of the scene, before he is overcome by jealousy and rage, Othello casts himself as just avenger. Still softened by his first sight of Desdemona asleep and the kiss with which he has wakened her, he himself remembers the advice of the ars tradition that the soul should not depart out of the world unprepared; he admonishes her to think on any crime that she has not as yet confessed because he would not kill her "unprepared spirit," her soul (V. ii. 32). A few lines later he utters the conventional phrase: "Think on thy sins" (43). When, however, Desdemona does not confess, he advises her not to commit the sin of perjury, as she is on her "death-bed" (54). The verbal identification of their connubial bed with the deathbed is, of course, an important support for the iconic stage image of the bed in the scene. The seeming peace of the scene, however, with its echoes of traditional phrases and kindly advice, is merely a thin overlay for the tension as Othello grows increasingly angry at what he believes to be Desdemona's stubborn dishonesty. As the scene builds, Othello shifts his role from that of fatherly adviser or confessor to that of the accusing Bad Angel of the ars series, too overcome by his own passion at the end to allow her even one prayer. Othello regains some sympathy from the audience, however, by his final attempt to keep Desdemona from suffering when she seems slow to die.

The second part of the scene begins with Emilia's entrance and the discovery of the murder, which almost immediately turns her into an accuser. The earlier section, Desdemona's good death, is linked now with the second by her poignant and momentary waking, which critics have long seen as an emblem of perfect Christian forgiveness and a final attempt at reconciliation. Asked by Emilia who has committed the murder, she replies: "Nobody. I

myself. Farewell. /Commend me to my kind lord. O, farewell!"
(V. ii. 127–28). Ironically Othello remarks: "She's like a liar gone
to burning hell" (132). He sees her as having damned herself by
lying on her deathbed. Only as this second section progresses,
however, would the audience begin to see Othello take the place of
Desdemona as the *moriens*. During the earlier part of the second
section one remains conscious of Othello as demonic in his murder
of Desdemona. This consciousness is underlined by Emilia's line:
"O, the more angel she, /And you the blacker devil!" (133–34).
The veriest commonplace of commonplaces,[23] the opposition here
may nevertheless suggest the further implication that Desdemona
as Good Angel has sought to save Othello by means of her
forgiving example, and that in killing her he has played the role
of his own Bad Angel against himself. His shift to the *moriens*
becomes stronger when Gratiano makes the *ars moriendi* tradition
explicit about a hundred lines later in the reference to Brabantio
already cited:

> Did he live now,
> This sight would make him do a desperate turn,
> Yea, curse his better angel from his side,
> And fall to reprobance. (V. ii. 209–12)

Gratiano is glad that Brabantio is dead because the sight of
Desdemona murdered would have brought him to despair, a state
which would cause him to curse his Good Angel from his side and
fall into "reprobance," or reprobation, defined by the OED as "a
state of rejection by God."[24] Thus Gratiano would be ordained to
eternal misery. Here the text makes explicit for the audience one
of the strongest warnings of the *ars* tradition, the avoidance of
despair and suicide.

Gratiano's speech is extremely important in several ways. First,
it makes clear that Shakespeare is thinking of the *ars* tradition and
therefore not using the references to angels and devils in a loose
metaphorical way. Second, through implied analogy, the speech
helps to shift the focus of the audience to someone new as the
dying one, even though Othello has not yet begun to die
physically. Finally, and perhaps this overlaps with the second
effect, the speech sums up symbolically what Othello has done and
foreshadows the tragedy of what he will do. By killing Desdemona,
his Good Angel, he has cursed her from his side, and the full

revelation of his sin in doing so eventually leads him to the despair and suicide which were seen by Renaissance theology as resulting in damnation. Suicide itself is, of course, not mentioned explicitly in Gratiano's speech, but the connection between despair and suicide was very close by Shakespeare's time.[25] For this reason, in the ars tradition there was an almost inordinate emphasis on the temptation to despair and the means of overcoming it. In some measure this explains the increasing emphasis in devotional literature on the comforts for the dying.

That Iago also parallels the devil of the ars (and is thus able to augment Othello by stepping into this role during the second section of the scene) is suggested in a number of places, both before and during the second scene of Act V. The association is most obviously prepared for by Iago's lines early in the play:

> Divinity of hell!
> When devils will the blackest sins put on,
> They do suggest at first with heavenly shows,
> As I do now; . . . (II. iii. 339–42)

Critics have long recognized that Iago is diabolic in his love of evil and deception. Othello's own superstitious response to the depth of deception which Iago has practiced upon him is an explicit suggestion in Act V itself: "I look down towards his feet—but that's a fable. /If that thou be'st a devil, I cannot kill thee" (V. ii. 289–90). One should not press it too far, but Othello, perhaps significantly, finally only wounds him. The association between Iago and the devil is underlined a few lines after the famous reference to the devil's cloven hoof by Othello's calling Iago "demi-devil" and asking him why he has ensnared his "soul and body" (V. ii. 304–5). In terms of the deathbed scene of the ars, Iago becomes for Othello the cause and embodiment of the sins of faithlessness and jealousy that have led him to murder and despair.[26] The discovery of Iago's perfidy is the means by which Othello confronts his own sins. In the "Temptation to Despair" in the early woodcuts the moriens is surrounded by six devils pointing to the sins of his past (Plate 16). One of the six carries a scroll which bears the inscription "Ecce peccata tua" (Behold thy sins). The others point to various representations of those the moriens has sinned against by fornication, avarice, and murder.[27]

The tragic force of the revelation of his own sins finds Othello without any of the supports that are recommended by the *ars* tradition. The leisurely death, with its time for meditation and repentance, is impossible. Desdemona, after one attempt at holy inspiration, is dead. There are no friends around Othello to encourage him by mentioning the thief on the cross beside Christ's or other examples of sinful men who died saved. Indeed, before her death, Emilia lashes out with fury to judge his guilt. Even as the truth is revealed and Iago is shown to be the villain, there is among those present pity for Othello's rashness, but no real comfort for his grief and no mention of Christ's mercy. Because the devilish Iago remains largely inarticulate through the scene, one feels that Othello's despair stems primarily from his own confrontation of his sins.

Othello's despair seems inevitable in these circumstances. It becomes self-evident in several speeches and, of course, in the suicide itself. Othello remarks after he wounds Iago but does not kill him: "I am not sorry neither: I'd have thee live; /For, in my sense, 'tis happiness to die" (V. ii. 292–93). These lines are ironic in terms of the *ars* tradition because the well-prepared soul should be happy to die. The irony is given its despairing cast more specifically, however, by Othello's previous speech:

> Here is my journey's end, here is my butt,
> And very sea-mark of my utmost sail.
> Do you go back dismay'd? 'Tis a lost fear;
> Man but a rush against Othello's breast,
> And he retires. Where should Othello go?
> Now, how dost thou look now? O ill-starr'd wench!
> Pale as thy smock! When we shall meet at compt,
> This look of thine will hurl my soul from heaven,
> And fiends will snatch at it. Cold, cold, my girl!
> Even like thy chastity. O cursed, cursed slave!
> Whip me, ye devils,
> From the possession of this heavenly sight.
> Blow me about in winds, roast me in sulphur,
> Wash me in steep-down gulfs of liquid fire.
> O Desdemona! Dead! Desdemona! Dead!
> O! O! (V. ii. 270–85)

Not only does Othello see himself cast out from heaven, as his earlier lines ironically foreshadowed: "O, I were damn'd beneath all depth in hell /But that I did proceed upon just grounds /To this extremity" (V. ii. 140–42), but he also desires to be cast away from the vision of Desdemona's innocence. At the "compt," the Last Judgment, the sight of Desdemona will hurl him to hell. In spite of his use of what was at one time presumably purgatorial imagery of winds and fiery gulfs, the overall suggestion is that of hell.[28]

It is only a short step from Othello's sense that his sin is unforgivable to suicide. Relevant here is the figure of the demon in the original woodcut "Temptation against Faith"; the demon has his right hand upon the shoulder of the moriens and his scroll reads: "Interfecias te ipsum" (Kill thyself). But before Othello commits suicide, he makes his dying speech, a final justification that redeems him dramatically. Paul Siegel has said that all the imagery of the play, and certainly that of the final scene, suggests Othello's damnation. True as this may be, Othello nevertheless partially regains our human sympathy, and he also assumes the scale of tragic heroism.[29] The dignity of his final speech surely projects the image of a man who was potentially a great hero and thereby a great loss in his tragic fall. That the suicide itself is conventionally unacceptable, however, is suggested by the choric comments of Lodovico and Gratiano:

> *Lod.*   Oh bloody period!
> *Grat.*   All that is spoke is marr'd. (V. ii. 360)

That the dramatic and human dimensions take emotional precedence despite the official disapproval of the suicide is shown in Cassio's comment, which comes in the last and most emphatic position: "This did I fear, but thought he had no weapon; /For he was great of heart" (363–64). Dramatically, one's tragic sympathy remains with Othello, and the indications that he is damned only intensify the tragic loss of potentiality.

The presence of theological commonplaces does not necessarily imply that Shakespeare's audience would be preoccupied with eschatological considerations while it viewed the last act of *Othello*. The play is not an allegory, and one must agree with Roland M. Frye that Shakespeare is primarily concerned with the *now*, the ethical present.[30] Shakespeare's audience was no doubt most immediately involved in the murder of Desdemona, the discovery by Othello of Iago's diabolical scheme, and the recognition by

Othello of his own guilt, leading to suicide. At the same time, however, remembering what scholars have learned from Panofsky and Wind about the Renaissance ability to move back and forth readily between the particular and the universal, one can hardly doubt that the audience was from the beginning aware of universal implications, one of which was that Othello was playing the climactic scene of his life in the scene of his dying. The great bell of the contemptus mundi tradition had rung so insistently across the ages that men knew the scallop shell of the pilgrim as the emblem of life. Erasmus had sounded the subordination of this life to the next in the most conventional phrasing:

> We be wayfarynge men in this worlde, not inhabytantes, we be as straungers in Innes (or to speke it better) in bouthes or tentes, we lyue not in our countrey. This holle lyfe is nothing elles but a rennynge to deathe, and that very shorte, but death is the gate of euerlastyng lyfe.[31]

It is difficult to define precisely the effect of the allusions to the ars moriendi in the final scene of Othello. Clearly the scene is not an allegory of dying badly. The suggestions are neither frequent nor elaborate. It seems to me consistent with Shakespeare's artistry, however, that he deepen the emotional response of his audience to a particular image of life by suggesting analogues from experience and history. In this case the introduction of the ideal for dying sharpens and universalizes the emotional response of the audience to the "tragic loading of the bed."

Arizona State University

Notes

Introduction

1. Jean H. Hagstrum, *The Sister Arts: The Tradition of Literary Pictorialism and English Poetry from Dryden to Gray* (Chicago, 1958), traces the concept of ut pictura poesis from antiquity to the English literature of the eighteenth century. A book focused on the sixteenth century is Robert John Clements, *Picta Poesis: Literary and Humanistic Theory in Renaissance Emblem Books* (Rome, 1960). The classical monograph on the subject, which first appeared as an *Art Bulletin* article in 1940, is Rensselaer W. Lee, *Ut Pictura Poesis: The Humanistic Theory of Painting* (New York, 1967).

2. Wylie Sypher, *Four Stages of Renaissance Style: Transformations in Art and Literature, 1400–1700* (Garden City, 1955), is probably the most widely read study of a zeitgeist uniting the art and literature of the Renaissance. Also vastly influential is Arnold Hauser, *The Social History of Art*, trans. Stanley Godman, 2 vols. (London, 1951). For Hauser's comments on Shakespeare, see especially 1:396–423. Equally impressive is Mario Praz, *Mnemosyne: The Parallel between Literature and the Visual Arts* (Princeton, 1970), the short title recalling the mother shared by the sister Muses; see especially Chap. 1, "Ut Pictura Poesis."

3. *University of London: The Warburg Institute* (London, 1960). This pamphlet, descriptive of the Institute, is available from its location in Woburn Square, London, W.C. 1.

4. Jean Seznec, *The Survival of the Pagan Gods: The Mythological Tradition and Its Place in Renaissance Humanism and Art*, trans. Barbara F. Sessions (New York, 1953), p. 3; 1st pub. in French in 1939.

5. E. M. W. Tillyard, *The Elizabethan World Picture* (1943; rpt. London, 1967). The conclusions reached by Tillyard here were later qualified by him in *The English Renaissance: Fact or Fiction?* (London, 1952).

6. C. S. Lewis, *English Literature in the Sixteenth Century, Excluding Drama* (Oxford, 1954), Vol. 3 of the Oxford History of English Literature.

7. A history of the initial establishment of the Gothic style in art and then reactions for and against it down to the present century is Paul Frankl, *The Gothic: Literary Sources and Interpretations through Eight Centuries* (Princeton, 1960). The Netherlandish style as dominant among the plastic arts during Shakespeare's lifetime is one subject in the Folger Booklet on Tudor and Stuart Civilization by David William Davies, *Dutch Influences on English Culture, 1558–1625* (Ithaca, 1964). Hauser, *Social History*, has observed that English art of the sixteenth century moved directly from Gothic to Mannerist, and that is also my impression of the art of the Lowlands. For parallels with dramatic style see Cyrus Hoy, "Jacobean Tragedy and the Mannerist Style," *Shakespeare Survey* 26 (1973):49–67.

8. Rosemond Tuve, *Elizabethan and Metaphysical Imagery: Renaissance Poetic and Twentieth Century Critics* (Chicago, 1947). Tuve, *A Reading of George Herbert* (London, 1952), continued her attack on the New Criticism, aided by her rich knowledge of medieval and Renaissance iconography.

9. Tuve, *Allegorical Imagery: Some Medieval Books and Their Imagery* (Princeton, 1966). For the work of Émile Mâle, see especially *The Gothic Image: Religious Art in France of the Thirteenth Century*, trans. Dora Nussey from 3d ed. (1913; rpt. London, 1961).

187

10. Notable medieval studies: Morton W. Bloomfield, *The Seven Deadly Sins: An Introduction to the History of a Religious Concept, with Special Reference to Medieval English Literature* (East Lansing, 1952); D. W. Robertson, *A Preface to Chaucer: Studies in Medieval Perspectives* (Princeton, 1962); and Siegfried Wenzel, *The Sin of Sloth: Acedia in Medieval Thought and Literature* (Chapel Hill, 1967).

11. Robert Kellogg and Oliver Steele, eds., *Books I and II of the* Faerie Queene, *the Mutability Cantos and Selections from the Minor Poetry,* by Edmund Spenser (New York, 1965). The Arden *Richard II,* ed. Peter Ure, 4th ed. rev. (Cambridge, Mass., 1956), is a standard text making use of iconography, especially for the interpretation of the mirror episode in the deposition scene. For the use of iconography in the glossing for students of one of Shakespeare's contemporaries in drama, see the New Mermaids edition of Cyril Tourneur's *The Revenger's Tragedy,* ed. Brian Gibbons (New York, 1967), especially p. xxxiii. Neither of these play editions, however, uses iconography in the comprehensive manner of Kellogg and Steele.

12. Another impressively detailed iconographic analysis of *FQ* is Chap. 7, "Iconography in the *Faerie Queene,*" of Paul J. Alpers, *The Poetry of the* Faerie Queene (Princeton, 1967).

13. V. A. Kolve, *The Play Called Corpus Christi* (Stanford, 1966). For an iconic interpretation of stage properties used in a medieval play, see Eugene B. Cantelupe and Richard Griffith, "The Gifts of the Shepherds in the Wakefield *Secunda Pastoral:* An Iconographical Interpretation," *Medieval Studies* 28 (1966):328–35; and Lawrence J. Ross, "Symbol and Structure in the *Secunda Pastorum,*" *Comparative Drama* 1 (1967):122–49. An understanding of staging made possible by a knowledge of medieval plastic arts is extensively employed by Fletcher Collins, Jr., *The Production of Medieval Church Music-Drama* (Charlottesville, 1972).

14. John Shaw, "The Staging of Parody and Parallels in *I Henry IV,*" *Shakespeare Survey* 20 (1967):61–73, has suggested that Shakespeare relies on the technique of theological prefiguration which informs the staging of the medieval mystery plays. *1 Henry IV,* with Falstaff often cast in the role of morality Vice, is clearly an appropriate play for Shakespeare to make use of iconic medieval stage technique.

15. Mary D. Anderson, *Drama and Imagery in English Medieval Churches* (Cambridge, 1963). George R. Kernodle, *From Art to Theatre: Form and Convention in the Renaissance* (Chicago, 1944), sees architectural forms behind the origins of the Renaissance stage. He mounts impressive evidence to show the similarities between Renaissance architectural facade and theater design, but, of course, debate on this issue is far from closed.

16. Henry Green, *Shakespeare and the Emblem Writers: An Exposition of Their Similarities of Thought and Expression, Preceded by a View of Emblem-Literature down to A.D. 1616* (1870; fascim, rpt. New York, 1964). A useful bibliography of the more reliable work done since Green is Samuel Schuman, "Emblems and the English Renaissance Drama: A Checklist," *Research Opportunities in Renaissance Drama* 12 (1969):43–56.

17. Mario Praz, *Studies in Seventeenth-Century Imagery,* 2d ed. (Rome, 1964); 1st ed. pub. in Italian in 1934.

18. Russell A. Fraser, *Shakespeare's Poetics in Relation to* King Lear (London, 1962).

19. See the medieval illuminated MS illustrated by William D. Wixom, *Treasures from Medieval France* (Cleveland, 1967), p. 221. The biblical authority for the "Transfixion" of Mary is Luke 2:34–35. In *The Geneva Bible* (1560; facsim. rpt. Madison, 1969), this passage is glossed, "sorrowes shulde pearce her heart, as a sworde" ("Newe Testament," fol. 28r). See also Yrjö Hirn, *The Sacred Shrine: A Study of the Poetry and Art of the Catholic Church* (Boston, 1957), pp. 380–81. The familiarity of Renaissance Englishmen with what was often in origin Continental and Catholic devotional iconography and literature is a subject I develop in my Chapter 3, on *Richard II,* especially n17.

20. See Harley Granville-Barker, *Prefaces to Shakespeare,* 4 vols. (1946; rpt. Princeton, 1963); and John Russell Brown, *Shakespeare's Plays in Performance* (London, 1966), which are

of particular interest; and also Maurice Charney, *Shakespeare's Roman Plays: The Function of Imagery in the Drama* (Cambridge, Mass., 1961).

21. The call for directing attention to "seen" or "heard" (rather than verbal) imagery was made by Alan S. Downer, "The Life of Our Design: The Function of Imagery in the Poetic Drama," *The Hudson Review* 2 (1949):242–63; and R. A. Foakes, "Suggestions for a New Approach to Shakespeare's Imagery," *Shakespeare Survey* 5 (1952):81–92.

22. As is well known, Caroline F. E. Spurgeon has been both vastly influential and severely attacked for her limitations, particularly her attempt to discover in Shakespeare's frequently used verbal images his personal interests and tastes, his psyche unwittingly revealed. See, for instance, Spurgeon, *Shakespeare's Imagery and What It Tells Us* (1935; rpt. Cambridge, 1958). The first important qualifications to her approach to imagery were made by Wolfgang Clemen, *The Development of Shakespeare's Imagery* (Cambridge, Mass., 1951); 1st pub. in German in 1936. Clemen views the image as meaningful only within the total organic structure of the play. The subsequent history of the subject is comprehensively but concisely reviewed by Kenneth Muir, "Shakespeare's Imagery—Then and Now," *Shakespeare Survey* 18 (1965):46–57.

23. The terms *iconography* and *iconology* have caused much confusion. Erwin Panofsky provides the classic definitions in his introduction to *Studies in Iconology: Humanistic Themes in the Art of the Renaissance* (1939; rpt. New York, 1962). Another useful source is William S. Heckscher, "The Genesis of Iconology," *Acts of the XXIst International Congress of Art History, Bonn, 1964* (Berlin, 1967), pp. 239–62. For Heckscher, "Iconography describes. . . . Iconology interprets" (n. on pp. 260–61). My less specialized use of *iconography* and *iconographic* covers both the description and interpretation of primarily visual Renaissance symbolism. I reserve the adjective form *iconic,* however, to indicate dramatic verbal and stage imagery influenced by Renaissance iconography.

24. Charney, *Roman Plays,* p. 8. For other studies of "presentational" imagery, see Dean Frye, "The Context of Lear's Unbuttoning," *ELH* 32 (1965):17–31; Robert Hapgood, "Speak Hands for Me: Gesture as Language in *Julius Caesar,*" *Drama Survey* 5 (1966):162–70; Alan Dessen, "Hamlet's Poisoned Sword: A Study in Dramatic Imagery," *Shakespeare Studies* 5 (1969):53–59; and Scott McMillin, "The Figure of Silence in *The Spanish Tragedy,*" *ELH* 39 (1972):27–48. An article especially valuable for its critical sophistication is Inga-Stina Ewbank, " 'More Pregnantly than Words': Some Uses and Limitations of Visual Symbols," *Shakespeare Survey* 24 (1971):13–18.

25. Several studies of Shakespeare's references to the plastic arts and his knowledge of them have been made: Margaret F. Thorp, "Shakespeare and the Fine Arts," *PLMA* 46 (1931):672–93; Arthur H. R. Fairchild, *Shakespeare and the Arts of Design: Architecture, Sculpture, and Painting,* University of Missouri Studies, 12, No. 1 (Columbia, Mo.: January, 1937); Samuel C. Chew, *The Virtues Reconciled: An Iconographic Study* (Toronto, 1947); and especially Chew, *The Pilgrimage of Life* (New Haven, 1962), pp. 253–98. Chew, *Virtues,* cites the most famous Shakespearean reference, that to the painter Giulio Romano, in *The Winter's Tale,* and points out that in "performing" the statue of Hermione, Romano has completed it with "the colors of life" (p. 11). Cyrus Hoy, "Jacobean Tragedy," provides valuable additional information about the reference to Romano (pp. 65–66, especially n. 3).

26. Chew, *Virtues,* p. 16. This detail in *1 Henry IV* is elaborated by John M. Steadman, "Falstaff as Actaeon: A Dramatic Emblem," *Shakespeare Quarterly* 14 (1963):230–44. Other plays I have noticed where the cushion occurs in the same iconic context are *2 Henry IV* (V. iv) and Webster's *The White Devil* (I. ii).

27. Chew, *Virtues,* pp. 47–48.

28. The book-length studies using a knowledge of iconic stage imagery have often been directed toward Jonson's masques: the alphabetical catalog by Allan H. Gilbert, *The Symbolic Persons in the Masques of Ben Jonson* (1948; rpt. New York, 1965); Stephen Orgel, *The Jonsonian Masque* (Cambridge, Mass., 1965), leading to the related subject expanded by

Orgel and Roy C. Strong in *Inigo Jones: The Theatre of the Stuart Court*, 2 vols. (London, 1973); and John C. Meagher, *Method and Meaning in Jonson's Masques* (Notre Dame, 1966). A book I was unfortunately unable to see before this one went to press, however, promises an analysis of iconic stage imagery, especially the icon of Time, in *Richard III, Macbeth,* and *King Lear:* Soji Iwasaki, *The Sword and the Word: Shakespeare's Tragic Sense of Time* (Tokyo, 1973).

29. Lawrence J. Ross, "The Meaning of Strawberries in Shakespeare," *Studies in the Renaissance* 7 (1960):225–40. The Ross Ph.D. dissertation is "The Shakespearean *Othello:* A Critical Exposition of Historical Evidence," 3 vols. (Princeton University, 1957). Another study of iconic stage imagery by Ross is "Shakespeare's 'Dull Clown' and Symbolic Music," *Shakespeare Quarterly* 17 (1966):107–28, an article which appeared when others had begun to publish along these lines as well. See, for instance, Richard Knowles, "Unquiet and the Double Plot of *2 Henry IV,*" *Shakespeare Studies* 2 (1966):130–40.

30. Ross, "Strawberries," p. 231.

31. Ross, "Art and the Study of Early English Drama," *Renaissance Drama: A Report on Research Opportunities* 6 (1963):35–46. Lawrence J. Ross informs me that he made the same invitation as early as 1957, in a paper given at the annual MLA meeting: "Shakespearean Drama and the Speaking Picture," delivered before the section on Literature and the Arts.

32. Ross, "Art," p. 37. Recent students of the Elizabethan stage have increasingly stressed the continuity to be found in medieval and Renaissance cosmic theaters. See especially Glynne Wickham, *Early English Stages, 1300–1660,* 2 vols. in 3 thus far (London, 1959–). Wickham deals most specifically with the contemporary documentation of iconic staging in Vol. 2:Part 1:153–324 ("Emblems and Images"). As for recent studies of Shakespeare's stage and stagecraft in general, Thomas J. King, *Shakespearean Staging, 1599–1642* (Cambridge, Mass., 1971) collates stage directions from 276 plays in order to confirm the appearance and function of the stage; he also has a useful appendix reviewing the bulk of important earlier studies (pp. 119–32). For an understanding of theatrical elements characteristic of Shakespeare's stage (costumes, blocking, properties, even the pace of oral delivery), a convenient summary is J. L. Styan, *Shakespeare's Stagecraft* (Cambridge, 1967).

33. Martha Hester Golden [Fleischer], "The Iconography of the English History Play" (Ph.D. dissertation, Columbia University, 1964); and her "stage imagery" in *The Reader's Encyclopedia of Shakespeare,* ed. Oscar James Campbell and Edward G. Quinn (New York, 1966). Fleischer, like Lawrence J. Ross (*n*31 above), has invited greater scholarly interest in iconic staging: Martha Hester Golden [Fleischer], "Stage Imagery in Shakespearean Studies," *Shakespearean Research Opportunities* 1 (1965):10–20; but most of the actual information Fleischer gives in this paper is repeated in her encyclopedia article cited above. Her important dissertation is published with its original title under her new name of Martha Hester Fleischer, as Elizabethan and Renaissance Studies, No. 10 (Salzburg, 1974), gen. ed. James Hogg; part of Salzburg Studies in English Literature, gen. ed. Erwin A. Stürzl. Another Ph.D. dissertation of some interest is Samuel Schuman, "The Theatre of Fine Devices: Emblems and the Emblematic in the Plays of John Webster," (Northwestern University, 1969).

34. Martha Hester Golden [Fleischer], "stage imagery," pp. 819–20. Clifford Lyons has also urged a greater attention to the imagery of production, especially as it is informed and reinforced by verbal imagery: "Stage Imagery in Shakespeare's Plays," in *Essays on Shakespeare and Elizabethan Drama in Honor of Hardin Craig,* ed. Richard Hosley (London, 1963), pp. 261–74. In this article Lyons uses "stage imagery" in exactly the same sense as Maurice Charney uses "presentational" imagery, which conveys a symbolic meaning demanding no knowledge of the conventions of Renaissance iconography.

Confusion of terminology (and subsequently thought) is a continuing problem. Where, for instance, does "illustration" leave off and the "icon" begin in a picture of Cleopatra bitten by asps? My own reading, nevertheless, has turned up Renaissance analogues to the clearly iconic aspects of Shakespeare's paradoxical stage image of Cleopatra's asps. In the Italian Renaissance Vasari painted a fresco of a beautiful woman both threatened by serpents and subdued by Virtue: see André Chastel, *The Crisis of the Renaissance, 1520–1600*, trans. Peter Price (Geneva, 1968), illus. p. 129; and in the French Renaissance Jean Mignon produced a print of Cleopatra's death with both a nursing satyress and an erotic satyr in the border: see Henri Zerner, *The School of Fontainebleau: Etchings and Engravings*, trans. Stanley Baron (New York, 1969), Pl. J.M.31.

35. Dieter Mehl, *The Elizabethan Dumb Show: The History of a Dramatic Convention* (Cambridge, Mass., 1966); 1st pub. in German in 1964.

36. Dieter Mehl, "Emblems in English Renaissance Drama," *Renaissance Drama*, n.s. 2 (1969):39–57. Nicholas Brooke, *Shakespeare's Early Tragedies* (London, 1968), show sensitive critical awareness of how within a single scene Shakespeare can move in and out of mimetic and emblematic modes in a play such as *Titus Andronicus*. This critical sensitivity is fully shared by Mehl. See especially his lucid "Visual and Rhetorical Imagery in Shakespeare's Plays," *Essays and Studies*, n.s. 25 (1972):83–100.

37. The iconic staging of civic pageantry runs parallel to the purpose of this book, but excellent scholarship has been done on the subject: David M. Bergeron, "The Emblematic Nature of English Civic Pageantry," *Renaissance Drama*, n.s. 1 (1968):167–98, since followed by Bergeron's book, *English Civic Pageantry, 1558–1642* (London, 1971), especially Chap. 11, "The Soul." A standard work is Alice Sylvia Venezky [Griffin], *Pageantry on the Shakespearean Stage* (New York, 1951). See also Wickham, *Early English Stages.*

An area separate from both civic entertainment and the court masque is fête, only just recently coming to the attention of scholars. See the preface to Andrew C. Minor and Bonner Mitchell, *A Renaissance Entertainment: Festivities for the Marriage of Cosimo I, Duke of Florence, in 1539* (Columbia, Mo., 1968), especially pp. 40–42, for a useful definition of the emblem tradition and its importance to the fête.

38. At the World Shakespeare Congress held at Vancouver, British Columbia, in August 1971, Dieter Mehl delivered a paper in which he elaborated several cautionary qualifications for the iconic approach to stagecraft, especially the danger of over-subtle analysis of everything on stage.

His healthy skepticism and reserve about Renaissance iconic stagecraft is shared in a different way by John M. Steadman, "Iconography and Renaissance Drama: Ethical and Mythological Themes," *Research Opportunities in Renaissance Drama* 13–14 (1970–71): 73–122. This double issue of *RORD* is a rich mine of information on literature and iconography. See especially William S. Heckscher, "Shakespeare in His Relationship to the Visual Arts: A Study in Paradox," pp. 5–71; and Ann Haaker, *"Non sine causa:* The Use of Emblematic Method and Iconology in the Thematic Structure of *Titus Andronicus,"* pp. 143–68 (both papers kindly sent me by their authors before publication). As for Steadman's warnings, they should be kept well in mind by those of us trained in English: literary criticism and art history "require different skills and diverse techniques; and if the literary scholar *must* encroach on the iconographer's province he must do so with caution—combining the wariness of the poacher with the humility of the amateur" (p. 114).

A further interest in the critical problems created by the contrast in methods characterizing literary and art history can be richly gratified by the articles in the Spring (No. 3) issue of *New Literary History* 3 (1972), especially Svetlana and Paul J. Alpers, *"Ut Pictura Noesis?:* Criticism in Literary Studies and Art History," pp. 437–58.

39. Lawrence J. Ross, "Wingless Victory: Michaelangelo, Shakespeare, and the 'Old Man,'" *Literary Monographs* 2, ed. Eric Rothstein and Richard N. Ringler (Madison, 1969), pp. 3–56, plus 20 pp. of illus., nn. on pp. 197–212.

40. The difficult question of the actual historical links between Tudor culture and the arts of the Continent is best treated to my knowledge by Fritz Saxl and Rudolf Wittkower, *British Art and the Mediterranean* (Oxford, 1948), especially pp. 38–41, with the geographical

movement of specific designs and works of art clearly cited. But much remains to be done in this area.

41. See Frances Ann Shirley, *Shakespeare's Use of Off-Stage Sounds* (Lincoln, 1963).

42. Norman Rabkin, *Shakespeare and the Common Understanding* (New York, 1967).

43. E. H. Gombrich, *"Icones Symbolicae:* The Visual Image in Neo-Platonic Thought," *Journal of the Warburg and Courtauld Institutes* 11 (1948):163–92.

44. The commonplace Renaissance debate between poet and painter (known as the "paragone") is reflected in Sonnet 24 (quoted at the beginning of my introduction). For a full analysis of Shakespeare's use of this debate in *Timon of Athens,* see W. Moelwyn Merchant, "Timon and the Conceit of Art," *Shakespeare Quarterly* 6 (1955):249–57. Leonardo, understandably, argued for art over poetry.

45. Daniel Seltzer, "Shakespeare's Texts and Modern Productions," in *Reinterpretations of Elizabethan Drama,* ed. Norman Rabkin (New York, 1969), p. 106.

46. C. Walter Hodges, *The Globe Restored: A Study of the Elizabethan Theatre,* 2d ed. (London, 1968). p. 77.

47. Seltzer, "Shakespeare's Texts," p. 110.

48. Just as this book was going to press I received three pieces of information, two of them from Mrs. Nati H. Krivatsy, Reference Librarian at the Folger. She reported an unfinished MS by Caroline F. E. Spurgeon at the Library (S.d. 51), called "A Shakespearean Picture Book" and described as a study of the pictures Shakespeare may have seen and their influence on his imagery. I have not seen the MS and know nothing of its usefulness, but establishing specific sources for the iconic in Shakespeare is always suspect. A resource of undoubted value, however, is a Folger project of several years' duration, a card index of subjects illustrated in STC books at the Folger. All the folio volumes have been indexed and all the smaller size books through STC 4500. The file presently holds about forty-two hundred cards distributed among about four hundred fifty subjects.

Another project of potential value for iconic study is under the direction of Alice F. Worsley, of the California State College, Stanislaus, in Turlock. Her project is an index of subjects illuminated in MSS held by the Bodleian, from Europe and Britain and covering the ninth to the sixteenth centuries. Twenty-one categories, broken down into innumerable subheads, presently index five thousand MSS under twenty thousand entries. A brief abstract appears as "Medieval Manuscript Illuminations," *Computers and the Humanities* 7 (1972–73):295–96. The Worsley index includes secular images, unlike the closely related Princeton Index of Christian Art (see *n*22 to my Chapter 4 for the Princeton Index; see *n*3 to my Chapter 2 for the relevance of illuminated MSS to the study of Shakespeare).

A final suggestion is the wealth of material in Otto Schmitt et al., eds., *Reallexikon zur deutschen Kunstgeschichte,* 6 vols. thus far (Stuttgart, 1937–), especially the article on "Emblem, Emblembuch."

Chapter 1

1. Throughout *Shakespeare's Speaking Pictures,* when sources printed before 1700 are the actual basis of citation, place and date of publication are enclosed in parentheses after the short title, with the location of the citation inserted in my text after the quotation or summary. When a secondary source for early material is used (such as Geoffrey Bullough), only the original date of the primary source is indicated in parentheses in my text; the full description of the actual source, including page reference, is reserved for my notes. Exceptions are the appropriately authoritative F1 (ed. Charlton Hinman, Norton facsimile, New York, 1968) and Qq (ed. W. W. Greg, now Hinman, Oxford facsimile series), almost

always cited when quoting stage directions in my text, where place of publication, and the 1623 date of F1, are assumed knowledge.

2. The allegory of Hercules at the Crossroads was familiar to Renaissance England through several sources described by Hallett Smith, *Elizabethan Poetry: A Study in Conventions, Meaning, and Expression* (Cambridge, Mass., 1952), pp. 293–303. The most outstanding source is Cicero, *De officiis*, trans. Nicholas Grimald as *Marcus Tullius Ciceroes three bookes of duties to Marcus his sonne* (London, 1596), Bk. I, fols. 51v–52r. Grimald's is just one of the many editions in which this famous passage may be found. Nine editions were printed between 1553 and 1600. Another important source is Richard Lynche's partial translation of the 1580 edition of Vincenzo Cartari's *Le imagini de i' dei* (1556; Venice, 1580; 1647 ed. rpt. Graz, Austria, 1963), called *The Fountaine of Ancient Fiction* (London, 1599), STC 4691, sigs. T2r–v. The importance and contents of Cartari are fully discussed by Don Cameron Allen, *Mysteriously Meant: The Rediscovery of Pagan Symbolism and Allegorical Interpretation in the Renaissance* (Baltimore, 1970), pp. 228–33. For a listing of pictorial representations of Hercules at the Crossroads, as well as a description of the moral allegory, see Guy de Tervarent, *Attributs et symboles dans l'art profane, 1450–1600: Dictionnaire d'un langage perdu* (Geneva, 1958), cols. 209–10; and Erwin Panofsky, *Hercules am Scheidewege und andere antike Bildstoffe in der neueren Kunst* (Leipzig, 1930).

3. Smith, *Elizabethan Poetry*, cites the medieval mythographer Fulgentius as the original source of the interpretation "of Hercules' victory over Antaeus as the conquest of fleshly lust" (p. 295). For the details of the original classical body of myth, see Robert Graves, *The Greek Myths*, 2 vols. (London, 1955), 2:146–47. For the complementary ideal of Hercules as the champion of true justice, see Jane Aptekar, *Icons of Justice: Iconography and Thematic Imagery in Book V of the* Faerie Queene (New York, 1969), especially pp. 153–214.

4. Illus. pp. 133–35 of Charles Seymour, Jr., *Masterpieces of Sculpture from the National Gallery of Art* (Washington, 1949); commentary, p. 181. For commentary on other examples of the same subject, see John Pope-Hennessey, *Renaissance Bronzes from the Samuel H. Kress Collection: Reliefs, Plaquettes, Statuettes, Utensils and Mortars* (London, 1965); and his *An Introduction to Italian Sculpture*, 3 vols. in 5 (London, 1955–63), 2, *Italian Renaissance Sculpture* (1958), Pl. 90 (Pollaiuolo) and fig. 142 (Antico).

5. *Honor Triumphant over Falsehood* illus. John Pope-Hennessey, *An Introduction*, Vol. 3, 3 parts in 1 vol., *Italian High Renaissance and Baroque Sculpture* (1963), Part 2, *Plates*, no. 77. Vasari is cited in Part 3, *Catalogue*, p. 78.

6. Richard Knowles has written an important article on the parallels between *As You Like It* and, among other things, the story of Hercules and Antaeus: "Myth and Type in *As You Like It,*" *ELH* 33 (1966):1–22. His conclusions are very reserved.

That not all wrestling matches with allegorical implications are handled in so subliminal a way in the English Renaissance, however, is to be seen from a painted *Allegory* (1571), by Joris Hoefnagel, an Antwerp painter visiting England between 1569 and 1571. Two headless nude men struggle before an audience of Elizabethan courtiers in the countryside outside Windsor. According to the commentary privately printed by the Burlington Fine Arts Club along with an illustration of the painting, the wrestlers represent brute force and fraud: *Catalogue of an Exhibition of Late Elizabethan Art, in Conjunction with the Tercentenary of Francis Bacon* (London, 1926). For yet another artistic expression of allegorical wrestling applicable to Shakespeare, see Lawrence J. Ross, "Wingless Victory."

7. The battle is described under the heading of "Antheus." A facsimile reprint of Thomas Cooper, *Thesaurus* (London, 1565), is that of the Scolar Press (Menston, 1969). As for Shakespeare's familiarity with the classical mythology to be found in Renaissance dictionaries, especially Cooper, see DeWitt Talmage Starnes and Ernest William Talbert, *Classical Myth and Legend in Renaissance Dictionaries: A Study of Renaissance Dictionaries in Their Relation to the Classical Learning of Contemporary English Writers* (Chapel Hill, 1955), especially Chap. 5, "Shakespeare and the Dictionaries."

8. *Narrative and Dramatic Sources of Shakespeare,* ed. Geoffrey Bullough, 7 vols. thus far (London, 1957–), Vol. 2, *The Comedies, 1597–1603* (1958), p. 170

9. Ibid., p. 171.

10. F1 is the authoritative text; its stage directions are meager but appear to originate in the notes of a bookkeeper annotating a prompt-copy.

11. Cited by O. J. C. (Oscar James Campbell), in *The Reader's Encyclopedia of Shakespeare,* ed. Campbell and Quinn, p. 43.

12. Quoted by Arthur Colby Sprague, *Shakespeare and the Actors: The Stage Business in His Plays, 1660–1905* (Cambridge, Mass., 1944), p. 32.

13. Illus. *The Complete Work of Michaelangelo,* ed. Mario Salmi, 2 vols. (London, 1966), 2:464.

14. STC 16318.

15. This passage is cited by Knowles, "Myth and Type," before he elaborates in greater detail Hercules as the type of Christ (pp. 14–18). I have also discovered a scholarly Renaissance pamphlet developing Hercules as the Christian soldier and Antaeus as the devil: Nicolaus Wynman, *Hercules cum Antaeo pugnae allegorica ac pia interpretatio* (Nuremberg, 1537). The title page has a woodcut showing the match. Wynman was a lector in linguistics at the Ingolstadt university.

16. *The Book of Hours of Catherine of Cleves,* ed. John Plummer (New York, 1964), shows hellmouth as the jaws of a lion, no. 26. The MS is ca.1435.

17. Colin Eisler, "The Athlete of Virtue: The Iconography of Asceticism," in *De Artibus Opuscula XL: Essays in Honor of Erwin Panofsky,* ed. Millard Meiss, 2 vols. (New York, 1961), 1:82.

18. Ibid., p. 90.

19. Ibid., p. 85.

20. Ibid., p. 86.

21. Bullough, *Sources,* 2:148.

22. H. W. Janson, *The Sculpture of Donatello,* 2 vols. (Princeton, 1957), 2:84.

23. John Pope-Hennessey, *An Introduction,* 2:264.

24. Edgar Wind, *Bellini's Feast of the Gods: A Study in Venetian Humanism* (Cambridge, Mass., 1948), cites this Renaissance mode of thought: "the union of contraries—that great commonplace of Renaissance thought which pervades Cusanus' *Docta Ignorantia* as it does Politan's *Panepistemon . . .*" (p. 13).

25. Illus. André Chastel, *The Age of Humanism: Europe, 1480–1530,* trans. Katherine M. Delavenay and E. M. Gwyer (London, 1963), P1. 7. Sforza looks no more than eight or nine years old.

26. See *The Oxford Dictionary of the Christian Church,* ed. Frank Leslie Cross (1957; rpt. with corrections, London, 1958), pp. 374–75.

27. Illus. Arthur Henkel and Albrecht Schöne, *Emblemata: Handbuch zur Sinnbildkunst des XVI. und XVII. Jahrhunderts* (Stuttgart, 1967), col. 1850. Valuable supplements to Henkel and Schöne's extensive bibliographies are the appendices to a review of their *Emblemata,* by William S. Heckscher and Cameron F. Bunker, *Renaissance Quarterly* 23 (1970):59–80.

28. The excesses of the pastoral school have been succinctly characterized by Harold Jenkins, *"As You Like It,"* *Shakespeare Survey* 8 (1955):40–51: *"As You Like It* has been too often praised for its idyllic quality alone, as though it were some mere May-morning frolic prolonged into a lotus-eating afternoon" (p. 43). Marco Mincoff, "What Shakespeare Did to *Rosalynde,"* *Shakespeare-Jahrbuch* 96 (1960):78–89, points out that in comparison to his source Shakespeare has softened the violence, the cruelty, *and* the pastoralism.

29. For a discussion of the tradition of Renaissance prodigal son plays and a parody of them by Francis Beaumont and Ben Johnson, see my "Beaumont's *The Knight of the Burning Pestle* and the Prodigal Son Plays," *Studies in English Literature, 1500–1900,* 5 (1965):333–44.

30. Madeleine Doran, " 'Yet am I inland bred,' " *Shakespeare Quarterly* 15, No. 2 (Spring

1964):99–114, is an exhaustive scholarly and critical examination of the nature-nurture theme of the play.

31. Among the many long moralizing speeches in Shakespeare's source, the one on fortune is of particular interest to the play: see Bullough, *Sources*, 2:194–95. For a critical discussion of Rosalind's I. ii speech on the relatedness of fortune to nature, see John Shaw, "Fortune and Nature in *As You Like It*," *Shakespeare Quarterly* 6 (1955):45–50. According to Shaw, "the fundamental plot conflict . . . [is] Nature 'combatting against Fortune.' . . . The court quickly becomes the habitat of the treacherous adherents of Fortune, while the magical forest shields the contented worthy followers of Nature" (p. 48). I am trying to show how these forces cooperate as well.

32. See Chew, *The Pilgrimage of Life*, pp. 144–73; and Raimond van Marle, *Iconographie de l'art profane au Moyen-Age et à la Renaissance, et la décoration des demeures*, 2 vols. (1931; rpt. New York, 1971), 2:159 ff.

33. Thomas Marc Parrott, *Shakespearean Comedy* (New York, 1949), p. 174.

34. Jaques as object of satire rather than satirist is neatly defined by Oscar James Campbell, *Shakespeare's Satire* (London, 1943), pp. 48 ff. The fashion for melancholia in the Renaissance is clearly explained by Rudolf and Margot Wittkower, *Born under Saturn: The Character and Conduct of Artists . . . from Antiquity to the French Revolution* (1963; rpt. New York, 1969), especially pp. 102 ff.

35. Both the Alciati and the Haechtanus emblems are cited by Henkel and Schöne, *Emblemata*, col. 1703. Haechtanus was translated by Jacob de Zetter into German in 1644, the source of Henkel and Schöne. Martha Hester Fleischer suggested the Anchises parallel to me in the course of private correspondence.

36. Henry A. Hargreaves uses the juxtaposition here in *As You Like It* as a prefatory example in an article about "Visual Contradiction in *King Lear*," *Shakespeare Quarterly* 21 (1970):491–95. This article is excellent on the subject of stage images within their dramatic context.

37. Eugene Waith, *The Herculean Hero in Marlowe, Chapman, Shakespeare, and Dryden* (New York, 1962), p. 54. See also Jean MacIntyre, "Spenser's Herculean Heroes," *Humanities Association Bulletin* 17, No. 1 (Spring 1966):5–12.

38. To be listed in the *Short-Title Catalogue* (but already included among University Microfilms, Reel 602): STC 24567b, a Vaenius edition containing love emblems with verses in Latin, English, and Italian; and one of three trilingual versions published in Antwerp, 1608? Vaenius is often cited as Otto van Veen. The first English emblem book is invariably cited as Geffrey Whitney, *A Choice of Emblemes and other Devices* (Leyden, 1586; facsim. rpt. New York, 1969); subsequently followed by P.S., *Heroical Devices . . . of M. Claudius Paradin* (London, 1591), trans. of Claude Paradin, *Devices heroiques* (Lyons, 1551); Andrew Willet, *Sacrorum emblematum centuria una* (Cambridge, 1591–92?), with verses in Latin and English; Thomas Combe, *The Theatre of Fine Devices* (ent. 1593: 1st extant ed. London, 1614), trans. of Guillaume de la Perrière, *Le theatre des bons engins* (Paris, 1539; facsim. rpt. Gainesville, 1964, intro. Greta Dexter); the Vaenius cited above (1608?; facsim. rpt. Hildesheim, N.Y., 1970); and Henry Peacham, *Minerva Britanna, or a Garden of Heroical Devices* (London, 1612). The Peacham probably derives its color symbolism from an extremely common source of Renaissance iconography: Cesare Ripa, *Iconologia* (Rome, 1593; 1603 illus. ed. rpt. Hildesheim, N.Y., 1970, intro. Erna Mandowsky). Ripa was not translated into English until 1709, but he made his way into England much earlier by other means, and he is also a summary of much that precedes him. In like manner, the English emblem books listed above are largely dependent upon Andrea Alciati, *Emblematum liber* (Augsburg, 1531), and innumerable later revised Alciati editions. See Rosemary Freeman, *English Emblem Books* (London, 1948). An editio optima of Alciati has been translated into English by Virginia W. Callahan and William S. Heckscher; it awaits publication.

39. For more about Cartari and Lynche see *n2* above. For more about Hymen see G. K.

Hunter, *William Shakespeare: The Late Comedies:* A Midsummernight's Dream, Much Ado About Nothing, As You Like It, Twelfth Night (London, 1962); and Enid Welsford, *The Court Masque: A Study in the Relationship between Poetry and the Revels* (1927; rpt. New York, 1962), Chap. 15, "Hymen." I am indebted to the kindness of Lidia Haberman for the translation of the Italian passage from Cartari, as I am for assistance with the Latin mottoes translated throughout this book. The original Cartari passage reads:

> Questi da gli antichi fu fatto in forma di bei giouane coronato di diuersi fiori, e di verde persa, che teneua vna vacella accesa nella destro mano, e nella sinistra haueua quel velo rosso, o giallo che fosse, col quale si copriuano il capo, e la faccia le nuoue spose la prima volta, che andauano à marito. E la ragione, che poco di sopra promisi dire di ciò, è tale, che le mogliere de i Sacerdoti appresso de gli antichi Romani vsauano di portare quasi sempre vn simile velo: &, perche à questi non era concesso, come à gli altri, di fare vnqua dinortio, coprendo la sposa con quel velo, si veniua à monstrare di desiderare, che matrimonio non hauesse da sciogliersi mai. Ma questo non vieta pero, che il medisimo non mostrasse anco la honesta vergogna della sposa, come ho detto: quale potiamo dire che fosse una cosa stressa con il Pudore, hauuto in tanto rispetto da gli antichi, che fu come Dio adorato.
>
> Vincenzo Cartari, *Le imagini de i' dei* (Lyons, 1581), p. 165.

40. Peter G. Phialas, *Shakespeare's Romantic Comedies: The Development of Their Form and Meaning* (Chapel Hill, 1966), p. 214.

41. Knowles, "Myth and Type," p. 20. The words and phrases in quotation marks in my text are Knowles' quotation of Arrowsmith (from the essay on "The Comedy of T. S. Eliot").

Chapter 2

1. On the question of the play's coherence, the positions are reviewed by Graham Midgley, *"The Merchant of Venice:* A Reconsideration," *Essays in Criticism* 10 (1960):119–33.

2. Considerable work has been done on the theological background to the play. An article leading to further scholarship is Allan Holaday, "Antonio and the Allegory of Salvation," *Shakespeare Studies* 4 (1968):109–18. Holaday, like others, wants to castigate Antonio for his presumed ill treatment of Shylock. Much more sympathetic toward the drama's Christianity are Norman Rabkin (who nevertheless also stresses an unusual degree of critical consensus on the play), "Meaning and Shakespeare," in *Shakespeare 1971: Proceedings of the World Shakespeare Congress, Vancouver, August, 1971,* ed. Clifford Leech and J. M. R. Margeson (Toronto, 1972), pp. 89–106; and Albert Wertheim, "The Treatment of Shylock and Thematic Integrity in *The Merchant of Venice,"* *Shakespeare Studies* 6 (1970):75–87.

3. Described and illus. Mâle, *The Gothic Image,* pp. 188 ff. See also Lewis Edwards, "Some English Examples of the Medieval Representation of Church and Synagogue," *Transactions of the Jewish Historical Society of England, 1953–1955,* 18 (London, 1958):63–75; and Wolfgang S. Seiferth, *Synagogue and Church in the Middle Ages: Two Symbols in Art and Literature,* trans. Lee Chedeayne and Paul Gottwald (New York, 1970). As for the familiarity of the English Renaissance man of letters and collector (such as John Dee) with medieval MS iconography, see Rosemond Tuve, "Spenser and Some Pictorial Conventions . . . ," in *Essays by Rosemond Tuve: Spenser, Herbert, Milton,* ed. Thomas P. Roche, Jr. (Princeton, 1970), pp. 112–38. It is my opinion that Shakespeare might have had increasing access to such collections, especially as his dramatic company was patronized by court circles.

4. The popular Renaissance image of the melancholy man as revealed in the portraits of the day is delineated by Roy Strong, *The English Icon: Elizabethan and Jacobean Portraiture* (London, 1969), pp. 352–53. Strong draws heavily upon Shakespeare as well. Indeed,

Strong's entire book is a valuable source for the study of iconography. In a self-portrait by George Gower, the balances (to be seen in the hand of Shylock later in the play) are used to symbolize the weighing of conflicting values. In the case of Gower the compasses of the painter's craft outweigh the arms of gentle birth (p. 170). Strong has also written an expanded study of English Renaissance portraits: *Tudor and Jacobean Portraits,* 2 vols. (London, 1969).

5. Recall *Richard III,* the Lady Anne at the villain (I. ii. 144); *Measure for Measure,* Mistress Elbow at Froth (II. i. 80); *Richard II,* Mowbray at Bolingbroke (I. i. 60) and Fitzwater at Surrey (IV. i. 75). In *As You Like It* Rosalind even describes how a lady might be expected to spit at an unwelcome suitor (III. ii. 383).

6. Shylock as the English spelling of the Hebrew *Shallach,* the word for cormorant, was first suggested by Israel Gollancz, "Bits of Timber: Some Observations on Shakespearean Names—'Shylock'; 'Polonius'; 'Malvolio,' " in *A Book of Homage to Shakespeare,* ed. Israel Gollancz (London, 1916), pp. 171–72. According to John Russell Brown, ed., Arden *The Merchant of Venice,* 7th ed. rev. (Cambridge, Mass., 1959), T. Wilson, *A Discourse upon Usury* (1572), describes usurers as "greedie cormoraunte wolfes" (Brown, p. xxiv).

7. Dieter Mehl, "Emblems in English Renaissance Drama," cites the allegorical tableau as the second major way in which the emblematic frame of mind influenced Renaissance drama. Mehl regrets that he had not developed this relationship more in his *The Elizabethan Dumb Show.*

8. To his earlier widely known works on the subjects of blackness in the English Renaissance, Eldred Jones has added "Racial Terms for Africans in Elizabethan Usage," *Review of National Literatures* 3, No. 2 (Fall 1972):54–89. For Professor Jones, Morocco is "tawny" and thus closer to white than black. Whatever his "complexion," however, Portia dislikes it. Jones's earlier monographs are *Othello's Countrymen: The African in English Renaissance Drama* (London, 1965); and *The Elizabethan Image of Africa* (Charlottesville, 1971), a Folger Booklet on Tudor and Stuart Civilization.

9. See the fully documented paper by G. K. Hunter, "Othello and Colour Prejudice," *Proceedings of the British Academy, 1967,* 53 (London, 1968):139–63, especially pp. 147–48.

10. Observed long ago by John Weiss, *Wit, Humour, and Shakespeare: Twelve Essays* (Boston, 1876), p. 312.

11. Such watches occasionally appear for sale and are illustrated from time to time in magazines catering to collectors. The elaborately engraved skull watch said to have been owned by Mary, Queen of Scots, is illustrated in *The Connoisseur* 175, No. 704 (October 1970):112. This watch bears a quotation from Horace and Chronos/Kronos eating his children, engraved on the face of the dial. A sixteenth-century memento mori ring at the British Museum is illustrated by Charles Hercules Read, *The Waddesdon Bequest: Jewels, Plate, and other Works of Art Bequeathed by Baron Ferdinand Rothschild,* 2d ed. (London, 1927), p. 42.

12. Chew, *The Pilgrimage of Life,* describes the conventions of the Three Living and the Three Dead, citing many iconographic instances. As a woodcut the subject appears in Caxton's *The Fifteen Oes* (1491?) and eight other books using the same cut: illus. Edward Hodnett, *English Woodcuts, 1480–1535* (London, 1935), no. 378. Wynkyn de Worde was the first to use another cut of the same subject, one employed in Richard Fox's *The Contemplation of Sinners* (Westminster, 1499). The Three Dead are variously represented as standing, lying in their coffins, or pursuing the Three Living. For several earlier Continental MS examples, see Marle, *Iconographie,* 2:384–93.

13. Sigmund Freud, "The Theme of the Three Caskets," in *Collected Papers,* trans. Joan Riviere, 5 vols. (1924–25; rpt. New York, 1959), 4:244–56. Freud saw the female sexual organ in the caskets, concluded that the choice was originally of three women, with the right choice that of the most unassuming woman (or casket). This third woman, often silent, was the third Fate, or death, who is reputedly conflated by primitive people with love.

Freud's reasoning is that the Goddess of Death and the Goddess of Love become one in Mother Earth, who both creates and receives our bones.

14. See especially John R. Cooper, "Shylock's Humanity," *Shakespeare Quarterly* 21 (1970):117–24. Cooper has his finger precisely on the theological pulse of the play.

The Pauline emphasis within English Renaissance religion, stressed in my subsequent discussion of the play's Christology, is clearly revealed in *Certayne Sermons,* Bk. I (London, 1547) and Bk. II (London, 1563). These sermons were appointed by the Crown to be read from every pulpit. They were published thirty-eight times between 1547 and 1640, not including one edition of both books in Welsh (1606). See STC 13639–78. I suspect Shakespeare and his audience heard many more sermons (church attendance being compulsory) than they read books of theology.

15. Chew, *The Virtues Reconciled,* provides full guidance to the theology, literature, and iconography associated with the Four Daughters of God. According to Chew, Shylock assumes the role of Justice; Bassanio Mercy, especially when he offers to die in Antonio's stead; and Portia Sapience, a character from the morality play tradition of the debate, who leans first to Justice, then to Mercy (p. 48).

16. Described and illus. ibid., pp. 66–68 and Pl. 8.

17. Another iconic aspect of the trial scene that possibly bears investigation is the ritualized anatomy implied by the demand for a pound of flesh. Jewish anatomists were famous in the Renaissance. An art historian with a strong interest in Shakespeare has suggested that punitive dismemberments plus slanders about ritual murders committed by Jews were medieval background to Shylock's demand for a pound of flesh: William S. Heckscher, *Rembrandt's Anatomy of Dr. Nicolaus Tulp: An Iconological Study* (New York, 1958), pp. 100–2; and Heckscher's "Shakespeare in His Relationship to the Visual Arts," pp. 22–24.

18. Chew, *Virtues,* p. 48.

19. See Marle, *Iconographie,* 2:Chap. 1 for a dozen or so examples.

20. Described and illus. Marle, 2:103, 106.

21. Ulrich Thieme and Felix Becker, *Allegemeines Lexikon der bildenden Künstler von der Antike bis zur Gegenwart,* 37 vols. (Leipzig, 1907–50), 22:595. Thieme-Becker is an invaluable encyclopedic source of information about obscure artists in all media.

22. Hans Holbein, *Les simulachres et historiees faces de la mort* (1538), sig. E1r; facsim. rpt. *Hans Holbein's Todtentanz* (Munich, 1903). Shakespeare elaborates this commonplace theme of the corrupt judge in *Lear,* IV. vi. 154–71, and elsewhere.

23. E. M. W. Tillyard, "The Trial Scene in *The Merchant of Venice,*" *Review of English Literature* 2, No. 4 (October 1961):51–59.

24. Ibid., p. 53.

25. Martha Hester Golden [Fleischer], "stage imagery," p. 820.

26. Very sophisticated studies have been made of the philosophical meaning music had for the Renaissance. Particularly interesting are Peter J. Ammann, "The Musical Theory and Philosophy of Robert Fludd," *Journal of the Warburg and Courtauld Institutes* 30 (1967):198–227; and D. P. Walker, "Kepler's Celestial Music," *Journal of the Warburg and Courtauld Institutes* 30 (1967):228–50. See also John Hollander, *The Untuning of the Sky: Ideas of Music in English Poetry, 1500–1700* (Princeton, 1961); and the works of F. W. Sternfeld, most recently "Shakespeare and Music," in *A New Companion to Shakespeare Studies,* ed. Kenneth Muir and Samuel Schoenbaum (Cambridge, 1971), Chap. 11. Sternfeld identifies the lute with domesticity, the oboe with egotism, and the strings with heavenly harmony.

Chapter 3

1. Cf. Brents Stirling, "Bolingbroke's 'Decision,'" *Shakespeare Quarterly* 2 (1951):27–34. Stirling sees three points of decision behind Bolingbroke's career: the deposing, imprison-

ment, and murder of Richard; in the Flint Castle, deposition, and Exton scenes respectively.

2. The best critical study I have seen on the verbal imagery of this play is Richard Altick, "Symphonic Imagery in *Richard II,*" *PMLA* 62 (1947):339–65. He is inclined, however, to center the play on England (the relevant images being "earth," "land," and "ground"), whereas I see the center in Richard the King. Altick cites additional variations on blushing-paleness imagery on pp. 347–48. Some scholars have sought an origin for Richard's changes of color in Holinshed or Froissart, but Peter Ure, in his note to ll. 118–19 on pp. 57–58 of the Arden *Richard II,* explains the thinness of these connections.

For a comparative study of imagery, see also Madeleine Doran, "Imagery in *Richard II* and in *Henry IV,*" *Modern Language Review* 37 (1942):113–22. Doran concludes that the images in *Richard II* are precise and clear (and often allegorical), and those in *1 Henry IV* vague and open-ended.

3. Arthur Watson, *The Early Iconography of the Tree of Jesse* (London, 1934).

4. See George Wingfield Digby, *Elizabethan Embroidery* (New York, 1964), especially pp. 45–50, for the currency and meaning of the emblems most frequent in Elizabethan needlework. Praz, *Mnemosyne,* regards architecture and costume as "the clearest indications" of an age because these are the most commonplace artifacts in their time (p. 109).

The symbolism of red and white roses is first developed by the Tudors in their escutcheon, made into iconic ritual by Shakespeare in the Temple Garden scene of *1 Henry VI* (II. iv), and finally used as the metaphor behind the phrase "Wars of the Roses" in Sir Walter Scott's *Anne of Geierstein* (1829).

5. Wickham, *Early English Stages,* 2:216–17 and n.

6. An article treating the links between older religious iconography and the newer political stage imagery in Marlowe and Shakespeare is Muriel C. Bradbrook "Shakespeare's Primitive Art," *Proceedings of the British Academy, 1965,* 51 (London, 1966):215–34.

7. According to *The Oxford Dictionary of the Christian Church,* three divisions in the Coronation appear throughout the history of this English rite. The second division is "the consecration and anointing of the king" (p. 344). Consecration is defined as the "separation of a thing or person for Divine service" (p. 332), as in the bread and wine of the eucharist, bishops, and altars, churches, and eucharist vessels. Consecration, as distinct from dedication or blessing, is "irrevocable."

For the fluctuations in the history of sacred kingship in England, see Norman F. Cantor, *The English: A History of Politics and Society to 1760* (New York, 1967).

8. The authority behind the original seven was affirmed by the Councils of Florence (1439) and Trent (1545–63). Anglican theologians since the Renaissance have tended to return to the definition of the seven as established at Trent: see *The Oxford Dictionary of the Christian Church,* under various headings.

9. The importance of Starkey's contributions to the new doctrine of the Tudor state was not fully understood until the publication of William Gordon Zeeveld, *Foundations of Tudor Policy* (Cambridge, Mass., 1948). See especially pp. 3–4, and pp. 128 ff. The phrases I quote from Starkey are quoted by Zeeveld, p. 149.

10. The painting is fully placed within the context of the "Tudor myth" by Roy C. Strong, *Holbein and Henry VIII* (London, 1967). Strong also has a great deal to say in general about Whitehall as the new cathedral of state and about the Tudor historians as embarked on a deliberate program of shifting the values of an entire culture from religious ones to political ones. Strong cites *The Tudor Constitution: Documents and Commentary,* ed. Geoffrey R. Elton (1960; rpt. Cambridge, 1972), as a full documentation of the thesis that the politico-religious issue in the Tudor period was the most serious crisis in English history since the Norman Conquest.

As for my point about the "new Donation of Constantine," Strong (p. 7) uses Polydore Vergil's *Anglica historia* (Basel, 1534) to illustrate the Tudor view that their imperium descended from the reign of Constantine to the Kings of England, the idea being that when Constantine ruled both church and state the original purity of the church was still intact.

An invaluable source of legal documentation for the Tudor concept of the king's sacred person is Ernst Kantorowicz, *The King's Two Bodies: A Study in Medieval Political Theology* (Princeton, 1957). In defining the concept of a natural body and an immortal body politic, "Elizabethan jurists sometimes had to proceed with the caution and circumspection of theologians defining a dogma" (p. 12.). Kantorowicz's chapter on *Richard II* sees the title character presented by Shakespeare as king, fool, and God.

11. J. Dover Wilson, ed., New Cambridge *Richard II* (Cambridge, 1939), p. xiii. One of the most interesting areas of critical discussion concerning this play centers on the relationship between its formal, ritualistic style and whether that makes the play more medieval or more Renaissance than Shakespeare's other history plays. In his extremely influential *Shakespeare's History Plays* (London, 1944), E. M. W. Tillyard presents Richard II as the last medieval king, enjoying the hereditary right to rule de jure, rather than de facto as with his successors, who all seized the throne or inherited it from someone who had. Thus the play consistently renders a medieval world in which ceremony and form are ends in themselves, soon to be replaced by hard, modern realism. This particular view is challenged by Peter G. Phialas, "The Medieval in *Richard II,*" *Shakespeare Quarterly* 12 (1961):305–10, who points out that even if the forms are empty they are being contrasted to those of an earlier medieval period, that of the Black Prince, Richard's father. The issues here, as in all Shakespeare's histories, emerge from the politics of the Tudors. The scenery is Elizabethan, according to Phialas, "whatever the nominal *locus* of his plays" (p. 305). My own view is that Shakespeare's implied political philosophy accommodates the "Tudor myth," but that he enlarges its assumptions to include moral principles (the sacredness of an oath in particular) which would restrain the Tudors.

For a book taking the "Tudor myth" head on, cf. Robert Ornstein, *A Kingdom for a Stage: The Achievement of Shakespeare's History Plays* (Cambridge, Mass., 1972), which questions the "myth" as the basic assumption of Shakespeare's history plays.

12. Stanley Stewart, *The Enclosed Garden: The Tradition and the Image in Seventeenth-Century Poetry* (Madison, 1966), charts the history of the convention of the hortus conclusus from the Song of Songs. The initial medieval associations are with the womb of the Virgin Mary.

13. Paul never uses precisely the phrase "Second Adam," but he does call Adam "the figure" of Christ (Romans 5:14) and Christ "the last Adam" (1 Corinthians 15:45). On these hints a medieval typology of Adam and Christ was elaborated. See Mâle, *The Gothic Image,* pp. 186–88. See also Joseph B. Trapp, "The Iconography of the Fall of Man," in *Approaches to Paradise Lost,* ed. C. A. Patrides (London, 1968), pp. 223–65. An interesting further refinement of the pattern by the Tudors and James I is of a First and Second Brutus: see Glynne Wickham, "From Tragedy to Tragi-Comedy: *King Lear* as Prologue," *Shakespeare Survey* 26 (1973):34–48.

14. See the fourteenth-century *Holkham Bible Picture Book,* ed. W. O. Hassall, 2d ed. (London, 1954), p. 8. A recent article on the iconic stage tree is Werner Habicht, "Tree Properties and Tree Scenes in Elizabethan Theatre," *Renaissance Drama,* n.s. 4 (1971): 69–72.

15. The phrase "Behold the man," occurs in John 19:5. The episode is described there and in Matthew 25:15–26; Mark 15:6–15; and Luke 23:11–25.

16. See Louis Réau, *Iconographie de l'art chrétien,* 3 vols. in 6 (Paris, 1955–59), 2:Part 2:459–61, for the currency of this subject on the Continent. The most encyclopedic source of Christian iconography has become Engelbert Kirschbaum, *Lexikon der christlichen Ikonographie,* 5 vols. thus far (Rome, 1968–). Kirschbaum subsumes Réau, and much more, with the added advantage of perfect clarity of organization. Wolfgang Braunfels continues the project, starting with Vol. 5 (the first in a series on hagiolatry).

The *Engraved Passion* series is described in Erwin Panofsky, *The Life and Art of Albrecht Dürer,* 4th ed. (1943; rpt. Princeton, 1955), pp. 139–45.

17. In England the ecce homo appears as a woodcut with accompanying devotional text

in the extremely popular *Sarum Missal.* The woodcut and text were confirmed in STC 16206 (Paris, 1527), fols. 74r–76v. The same subject reappears late in the sixteenth century, despite the Reformation, once again illustrated, in Richard Hopkins, trans., *Of Prayer and Meditation* (1st pub. Paris, 1582; rpt. 8 more times before 1633, at regular intervals). The Hopkins instance of the ecce homo was confirmed in STC 16912 (Douay, 1612), fols. 101v–5r. Hopkins is a translation of Luis de Granada, *Libro de la oración y meditación* (1554). As for the popularity of Continental devotional literature, such as the Hopkins translation, in Renaissance England, see Chap. 8 of Louis B. Wright, *Middle-Class Culture in Elizabethan England* (1935; rpt. Ithaca, 1958). Wright mentions Luis de Granada in the following context: "Frances Meres in *Granados Devotion* (1958) and *The Sinners Guyde* (1598), and Thomas Lodge in *The Flowers of Lodowicke of Granado* (1601), pillaged from Catholic Spain material for the benefit of Protestant readers" (p. 252).

That Shakespeare derived his iconic staging from specific sources, however, even broadly defined ones, is always tenuous at best. The chance of Shakespeare getting the conventions of the ecce homo from the production of mystery plays seen possibly in youth, for instance, is strengthened by Muriel C. Bradbrook, "An 'Ecce Homo' of the Sixteenth Century and the Pageants and Street Theatres of the Low Countries," *Shakespeare Quarterly* 9 (1958):424–26.

18. Listed and described by J. D. Passavant, *Le peintre-graveur, contenant l'histoire de la gravure sur bois, sur métal et au burin jusque vers la fin du XVI. siècle . . . .*, 6 vols. (Leipsig, 1860–64), 6:239:79. The application of the image of Fortune and her wheel to the play has long been recognized. See Raymond Chapman, "The Wheel of Fortune in Shakespeare's Historical Plays," *Review of English Studies,* n.s. 1 (1950):1–7. The seminal book on Dame Fortune (rich in iconography) is Howard Rollin Patch, *The Goddess Fortuna in Medieval Literature* (1927; rpt. New York, 1967). See also Willard Farnham, *The Medieval Heritage of Elizabethan Tragedy* (1936; rpt. with corrections New York, 1956).

19. The pattern of sun imagery in the play has been dealt with critically by S. K. Heninger, Jr., "The Sun-King Analogy in *Richard II,*" *Shakespeare Quarterly* 11 (1960):319–27. According to Heninger, the fall of Richard disrupts the cosmic order, as it disrupts England as a Garden of Eden, symbolized at Langley.

20. Innumerable Renaissance instances of visual renderings of the falls of Phaeton and Icarus can be cited. Perhaps the most famous is Brueghel's *Fall of Icarus* (ca. 1555). The falls of both Phaeton and Icarus are two in the suite of four pagan falls (including Tantalus and Ixion) etched by Henrik Goltzius (1558–1616). The Tantalus fall is dated 1588 and all four are cited by Adam Bartsch, *Le peintre-graveur,* 21 vols. in 17 (Vienna, 1803–13), 3:78–79. The Warburg Institute, on Woburn Square in London, has photographs of many of the graphics cited by Bartsch, as supplemented by Passavant, *Le peintre-graveur.* The Institute has the photographs arranged in volumes keyed into these classic compilations. The four falls by Goltzius are among those photographed. Several universities in America subscribe to these photographs as they are produced over the years by the Warburg Institute and by the Institute of Fine Arts, New York University, but individual copies can be ordered by anyone. These photographs are an invaluable source for the study of Renaissance iconography because Bartsch and Passavant represent the most comprehensive listings of the most widely distributed of Renaissance art forms: the graphic. The Transfixion of the Virgin, for instance (cited in my introduction, *n*19), is illustrated by a graphic listed in Bartsch, 8:475:item 14.

A far less comprehensive source of graphic material, but one occasionally useful for England, is Arthur Hind, *Engraving in England in the Sixteenth and Seventeenth Centures: A Descriptive Catalogue with Introductions,* 3 vols. (Cambridge, 1952–64).

21. Eleven episodes belong to the series, the last the death of the moriens (dying man). The first edition of these woodcuts, by the Master E.S., with explanatory Latin text, was published in Germany, ca. 1450; and a facsimile reprint of the BM copy is *The ars moriendi,*

ed. W. Harry Rylands (London, 1881), where each episode is described and explained in the introduction. See also Henri Zerner, "L'Art au morier," *Revue de l'art* 2 (1971):7–30, for the facts about the woodcuts important to the art or intellectual historian. Caxton printed an abridged English translation of another version of the original Latin text in 1490. Several other English versions followed and they stimulated a whole body of devotional literature on the craft of holy dying (see the appendix of the present volume).

An application of the conventions of the ars moriendi to another history play by Shakespeare is Bettie Anne Doebler, " 'Dispaire and Dye': The Ultimate Temptation of Richard III," *Shakespeare Studies* 7 (1974):75–85.

22. Henkel and Schöne, *Emblemata,* cols. 1346–53, show many instances of mirrors pictured in Renaissance emblem books. Most of the mirrors shown are convex.

23. Chew, *The Virtues Reconciled,* pp. 14–15 (for "Bellini's painting," see my Chapter 6, *n*26). Much scholarship has been devoted to the mirror as a Renaissance symbol. See especially Gustav F. Hartlaub, *Zauber des Spiegels: Geschichte und Bedentung des Spiegels in der Kunst* (Munich, 1951); Heinrich Schwarz, "The Mirror in Art," *Art Quarterly* 15 (1952):97–118; Sister Ritamary Bradley, "Backgrounds of the Title *Speculum* in Mediaeval Literature," *Speculum* 29 (1954):100–15; and Peter Ure, "The Looking Glass of *Richard II,"* *Philological Quarterly* 34 (1955):219–24. Ure's Arden *Richard II* gives still further references (n. 1 on p. lxxxii). Hartlaub, *Zauber,* and Schwarz, "The Mirror," contain many illustrations of convex Renaissance mirrors.

24. See Heckscher, "Shakespeare in His Relationship to the Visual Arts," pp. 10–21, for an explanation of "anamorphoses"—the distorted projections of Mannerist art, known to Shakespeare, and best known to us through Holbein's *The Ambassadors* (1533).

25. A parallel to Richard's multiple shifts in personality and role is to be found in the well-known imagery patterns of sun and water. The sun imagery is gradually transferred to Bolingbroke and the water imagery gradually transferred to Richard: see Kathryn M. Harris, "Sun and Water Imagery in *Richard II:* Its Dramatic Function," *Shakespeare Quarterly* 21 (1970):157–65.

26. Arthur P. Rossiter, *Angel with Horns, and Other Shakespeare Lectures,* ed. Graham Storey (New York, 1961), pp. 28–29.

Chapter 4

1. J. Dover Wilson, *What Happens in* Hamlet, 3d ed. (Cambridge, 1951), pp. 145–46.

2. Meyer Shapiro, " 'Muscipula Diaboli,' the Symbolism of the *Mérode Altarpiece,"* *The Art Bulletin* 27 (1945):182–87. The entire triptych is illustrated by Erwin Panofsky, *Early Netherlandish Painting: Its Origins and Character,* 2 vols. (Cambridge, Mass., 1953), 2:Pl. 91. Panofsky also provides an analysis of the iconography of the painting, but warns against finding a meaning in every object (1:143). For an even fuller analysis, however, see *The Metropolitan Museum of Art Bulletin,* n.s. 16, No. 4 (December 1957), especially Margaret B. Freeman, "The Iconography of the *Mérode Altarpiece,"* pp. 130–39. The object on the window ledge of St. Joseph's workshop is identified by Shapiro and Freeman as a completed mousetrap, but it has been shown to be a carpenter's plane by Irving L. Zupnick, "The Mystery of the Mérode Mousetrap," *Burlington Magazine* 108 (1966):126–33. The only mousetrap in the panel is the one in the process of manufacture, the one in which St. Joseph is boring holes. Another example of the mousetrap demanding holes and pegs and manufactured by St. Joseph in a Nativity scene is shown by Panofsky, *Early Netherlandish Painting,* 2:fig. 110.

3. Migne, *Pat. Lat.,* Vol. 38, col. 1210; trans. Shapiro, " 'Muscipula Diaboli,' " p. 182, who says that the mousetrap metaphor occurs three times in Augustine's sermons: the cited instance; Sermo CXXX, col. 726; and Sermo CXXXIV, col. 745.

4. Shapiro, " 'Muscipula Diaboli,' " p. 182. Shapiro goes on to state that some theologians believed that the devil knew all along, but in the latter Middle Ages most of them, "following Ignatius, . . . held that the Virgin was married to Joseph precisely in order to conceal the birth of Christ from the devil, who thought the child was begotten by Joseph. This . . . interpretation . . . occurs in the writings of Bernard, Bonaventure, and Thomas, in the mystery plays, and in the *Speculum humane salvationis*" (Shapiro, p. 185).

5. Ent. 1567/68; STC 3546. The woodcut appears first in R. Pynson's edition: STC 3545 (London, 1509), fol. CCCLIIr.

6. Described and illus. Panofsky, *Hercules am Scheidewege,* fig. 60 and pp. 119–20. I wanted to include the Saenredam interpretation of the subject among my illustrations, but a search of several print collections, including those at the Warburg Institute and the British Museum, failed to turn it up. It can be seen in the Panofsky study cited above or seen as Pl. 2 in my "The Play within the Play: The *Muscipula Diaboli* in *Hamlet,*" *Shakespeare Quarterly* 23 (1972):161–69. For a description of the full Hercules allegory, see John Rupert Martin, *The Farnese Gallery* (Princeton, 1965). The Carracci version of the subject (1595–97), mentioned earlier in my text, is illustrated by Donald Posner, *Annibale Carracci: A Study in the Reform of Italian Painting around 1590,* 2 vols. (London, 1971), 2:Pl. 93a.

7. For the box-shaped mousetrap as an emblem of vice readily converted to a hellmouth, see Pieter Brueghel's *The Triumph of Death* (Prado), illustrated by Bob Claessens and Jeanne Rousseau, *Our Bruegel,* trans. Haakon Chevalier (Antwerp, 1969), Pl. 55.

8. For Shakespeare's degree and kind of education, see Thomas W. Baldwin, *William Shakespeare's Small Latine and Lesse Greeke,* 2 vols. (Urbana, 1944); and Virgil K. Whitaker, *Shakespeare's Use of Learning: An Inquiry into the Growth of His Mind and Art* (1953; rpt. San Marino, 1964). As for the possibility that he might have known the writings of St. Augustine, see Ann Livermore, "Shakespeare and St. Augustine," *Quarterly Review* 303 (1965):181–93.

9. Shakespeare alternated between the Geneva and Bishops' versions of the Bible (1560 and 1568 respectively), as demonstrated by Richmond Noble, *Shakespeare's Biblical Knowledge and Use of the Book of Common Prayer, as Exemplified in the Plays of the First Folio* (London, 1935); but I have cited from the King James version for the sake of easy reference. The differences are slight and are unrelated to the points I make.

10. Robertson, *Preface to Chaucer,* p. 99. The material in my text within quotation marks is Holcot's citing of the Bible; the rest is Robertson's paraphrase of Holcot. I regret that I was unable to see the original Holcot passage (on pp. 539–40 according to Robertson).

11. *The Book of Hours of Catherine of Cleves.* The two illuminations cited are nos. 48 and 11 in this edition.

12. Green, *Shakespeare and the Emblem Writers.*

13. Most scholars rightly have mixed feelings about Green, especially the way he tries to specify particular emblems, themselves commonplaces, as the actual sources of Shakespeare's iconic imagery. A skillful article which both reviews the emblematic approach to Renaissance literature and warns of its pitfalls is Peter M. Daley, "Trends and Problems in the Study of Emblematic Literature," *Mosaic* 5, No. 4 (Summer 1972):53–68.

14. *Three Chapters of Letters Relating to the Suppression of the Monasteries,* ed. Thomas Wright (London, 1843), p. 133.

15. George Gascoigne, "The Adventures of Master F. J.," in *The Complete Works,* ed. John W. Cuncliffe, 2 vols. (1907–10; rpt. New York, 1969), 1:388–89.

16. See Tervarent, *Attributs et symboles,* p. 322. Two such mice gnawing at the Tree of Life are illustrated in Stewart, *The Enclosed Garden,* fig. 34. For a description of Michelangelo's original plans for the Medici Tomb in the light of this tradition, see Erwin Panofsky, "The Mouse that Michaelangelo Failed to Carve," in *Essays in Memory of Karl Lehmann,* ed. Lucy Freeman Sandler (New York, 1964), pp. 242–51.

17. Orgel and Strong, *Inigo Jones,* 2:688, fig. 354. See 2:660–703 for the full context, visual and literary.

18. Ibid., 2:664.

19. For a useful summary of critical approaches to the dumb show that is the argument for the subsequent "Mouse-trap," see Mehl, *The Elizabethan Dumb Show,* pp. 110–25.

20. Levin L. Shücking, *The Meaning of* Hamlet, trans. Graham Rawson (1937; rpt. New York, 1966), p. 132; 1st pub. in German in 1935.

21. Harry Levin, *The Question of* Hamlet (New York, 1959), p. 18.

22. Whether the associations are well established before the fifteenth century is difficult to know. Virtually all my examples have been drawn from the period after 1400. Rosalie B. Green, the Director of the Index of Christian Art, sponsored by the Department of Art and Archaeology at Princeton University, reported that no mousetraps have been identified before 1400, the date the Index terminates. A duplicate of the Princeton Index is housed at the Art Library, UCLA, Laura F. Franklin, Curator. A brief and charming, but learned, recent study of the bestiaries, both medieval and Renaissance, quotes Rabanus Maurus as saying that "mice signify men who in their breathless eagerness for earthly gains filch their booty from another's store": Beryl Rowland, *Animals with Human Faces: A Guide to Animal Symbolism* (Knoxville, 1973), p. 129.

23. John Cranford Adams, *The Globe Playhouse: Its Design and Equipment,* 2d ed. (New York, 1961), gives the classic argument supporting the existence of an "inner stage." Cf. Donald F. Rowan, "The 'Swan' Revisited," *Research Opportunities in Renaissance Drama* 10 (1967):33–48, for a review and evaluation of more recent opinion. The so-called inner stage is now generally regarded as something that never was, although I am inclined to accept the theory of a shallow recess. I wish to make acknowledgment here to Donald F. Rowan in another matter. It was he who, as a fellow worker at the Folger Shakespeare Library, first drew my attention to the mousetrap in *Hamlet* as a possible symbol by asking me the appearance and meaning of such traps in Renaissance England. A case for staging "The Mouse-trap" in the round is made by Styan, *Shakespeare's Stagecraft,* pp. 130–32.

24. Edward Topsell, *The Historie of Foure-Footid Beastes* (London, 1607), describes many varieties of Renaissance mousetraps, the most common for catching them alive being boxlike, with a "percullis" at one end (pp. 509–12). Such traps are clearly illustrated in Zupnick, "Mystery," figs. 24 and 25. See also C. Roth, "Medieval Illustrations of Mouse-traps," *Bodleian Library Record* 5 (1956):244–52.

25. The degree of Shakespeare's reliance on traditional Christian symbols and values is the subject of continuing vigorous debate. For an overview, especially of the concept of providence, see William R. Elton, King Lear *and the Gods* (San Marino, 1966); and the postscript of the present volume.

26. Illustrated and described in Arthur B. Chamberlain, *Hans Holbein the Younger,* 2 vols. (London, 1913), 1:Pl. 61 and pp. 193–96. This border is later used for the title page of Strabo's *Geographicorum* (1523): illustrated and described by Marle, *Iconographie,* 2:fig. 182 and pp. 151–52. A very large woodcut imitation by David Kandel occurs in the *Cebes Thebanus,* by Epictetus, ed. Hieronymus Wolf (1563): illustrated and described in *Catalogue 146* (March 1971), p. 22, of the modern London antiquarian bookseller E. P. Goldschmidt, 64 Drayton Gardens, S.W.10. Goldschmidt's profusely illustrated and learnedly annotated catalogs are a valuable source of information about medieval and Renaissance iconography, especially that in Continental books. The *Table* appears at least as late as 1642, when Joris van Schooten paints his *Tabula Cebetis:* illus. Horst Gerson, *Rembrandt Paintings,* trans. Heinz Norden, ed. Gary Schwartz (Amsterdam, 1968), p. 32.

27. The *Table* itself was "widely used in Elizabethan grammar schools": Allen, *Mysteriously Meant,* p. 281. Allen's study is enormously rich in the knowledge and understanding of the sources of Renaissance symbolism, particularly when the sources are Continental books, usually in Latin, such as those by Martianus Capella, Fulgentius, and

Isidore of Seville; Giraldi, Natalis Comes (Natale Conti), and Cartari. Because of what is known in general about Shakespeare's inclination to confine his own reading to works in English, I have for the most part used esoteric medieval and Renaissance scholars only when they are known to have been used in Elizabethan grammar schools or were available to him in some form of Renaissance translation into his own vernacular, such as Stephen Bateman, *The Golden Booke of the Leaden Goddes* (London, 1577), or Richard Lynche, *The Fountaine of Ancient Fiction* (London, 1599).

28. Rabkin, *Shakespeare and the Common Understanding,* has pointed out that the critics have finally reached a consensus on only one aspect of this play, its mysterious ambiguity and continual contradictions (pp. 4 ff.). Even if we recall that this is an "editor's play," sewn together from Q2 (1604–5) and F1, the pervasiveness of unresolved problems based on the text, taken together with important details of motivation long withheld from the audience, makes this a unique play in the canon.

29. Norman Rabkin, ed., *Reinterpretations of Elizabethan Drama* (New York, 1969), calls for a limited "paradigm" of analysis: "The play as it impinges on the audience, as it is experienced" from moment to moment (p. vii). For an application of this approach to *Hamlet,* see Stephen Booth, "On the Value of *Hamlet,*" in Rabkin, *Reinterpretations,* pp. 137–76.

30. See Chamberlain, *Holbein,* 1:204–26, for illustration of both the *Dance of Death* woodcuts and the comparatively minor *Alphabet of Death* series. The classic study of the theme (and a fascinating book in its own right) is Leonard P. Kurtz, *The Dance of Death and the Macabre Spirit in European Literature* (New York, 1934). But see also James M. Clark, *The Dance of Death in the Middle Ages and the Renaissance* (Glasgow, 1950).

An increasing interest in death as an independent subject within the play is indicated by recent articles: Bridget Gellert, "The Iconography of Melancholy in the Graveyard Scene of *Hamlet,*" *Studies in Philology* 67 (1970):57–66; and Harry Morris, "*Hamlet* as a *memento mori* Poem," *PMLA* 85 (1970):1035–40.

31. Louis Martz, *The Poetry of Meditation: A Study in English Religious Literature of the Seventeenth Century* (New Haven, 1954), Yale Studies in English, 125.

Chapter 5

1. A. C. Bradley, *Shakespearean Tragedy: Lectures on* Hamlet, Othello, King Lear, Macbeth, 2d ed. (1905; rpt. London, 1937), especially pp. 333–34.

2. G. Wilson Knight, *Shakespearean Production, with Especial Reference to the Tragedies* (Evanston, 1964), p. 131.

3. Guy de Tervarent, *Attributs et symboles,* cols. 147–48; the diamond, with accompanying motto, was used in sixteenth-century France as a personal device (or impresa) by both Claude Micard and the Bering brothers. The complex Renaissance mixture of base and ideal associations with personal ornament is applied critically to stage imagery by Samuel Schuman, "The Ring and the Jewel in Webster's Tragedies," *Texas Studies in Literature and Language* 14 (1972):253–68.

4. STC 13569. A readily accessible text is *Shakespeare's Holinshed: An Edition of Holinshed's Chronicles, 1587, Source of Shakespeare's History Plays,* King Lear, Cymbeline and Macbeth, ed. Richard Hosley (New York, 1968). Hosley makes available important passages not found in Geoffrey Bullough, *Sources.*

5. Gillian Tindall, *A Handbook on Witches* (New York, 1966), gives a full account of the assassination plan. Behind it was the infamous Bothwell, aspirant to the throne, who planned the use of poison should witchcraft fail (pp. 88–91). For the possible and probable instances of topicality in *Macbeth,* see Henry N. Paul, *The Royal Play of* Macbeth: *When, Why and How It Was Written by Shakespeare* (New York, 1950).

6. Documentation for this aspect of English history, subject to the strongest emotions of modern historians, is difficult to come by, but I found the following useful: Montague Summers, *The Geography of Witchcraft* (1927; rpt. New York, 1965), Chap. 2; and Henry C. Lea, *Materials toward a History of Witchcraft*, 3 vols. (New York, 1957). Lea lists the laws passed in England against witches (3:1306–7). The most important and strictest was enacted in 1604, two years before the probable composition date of *Macbeth.*

7. Tindall, *Handbook,* pp. 20–25, gives a fuller account of the events I have summarized. If anything, Tindall is inclined to adopt a tolerant attitude toward these events: "A picture has grown up of a poor old wisewoman . . . being brutally set upon by a neurotic rabble. . . . But, in England . . . the typical witch brought to court seems to have been neither aged, lonely, nor especially pathetic" (p. 12). As for the extent of witchcraft, see Katherine M. Briggs, *Pale Hecate's Team: An Examination of the Beliefs on Witchcraft and Magic among Shakespeare's Contemporaries and His Immediate Successors* (London, 1962).

8. *The Reader's Encyclopedia of Shakespeare,* ed. Campbell and Quinn, provides a description of the occasion (p. 483). James' descent from Banquo was, of course, pure legend.

9. The extensive discussion among the critics and scholars regarding the authenticity of various parts of the witch scenes is clearly summarized by Kenneth Muir, ed., Arden *Macbeth,* 9th ed. (1962; rpt. London, 1970), pp. xxiv–xxv.

10. Starnes and Talbert, *Classical Myth and Legend,* pp. 343 ff.

11. See Zerner, *The School of Fontainebleau,* p. 14 and Pl. P.M.3.

12. The main lines in the debate were drawn by A. C. Bradley, who insisted that the witches are completely powerless and Macbeth totally free *(Shakespearean Tragedy),* pp. 340–41); and Kittredge, who saw the weird sisters as Scandinavian Norns determining a fate for Macbeth. The full history of this debate is outlined by G. K. Hunter, *"Macbeth* in the Twentieth Century," *Shakespeare Survey* 19 (1966):1–11. A third school of thought, which defines the three sisters as Furies, is represented by Arthur R. McGee, *"Macbeth* and the Furies," *Shakespeare Survey* 19 (1966):55–67. McGee sees the Furies as demonic agents of despair bringing Macbeth to damnation; for the Furies had serpents twined in their hair, and they were thus easily regarded as agents of sin and damnation.

Cf. John Velz, *Shakespeare and the Classical Tradition: A Critical Guide to Commentary, 1660–1960* (Minneapolis, 1968), who sees an unresolved tension between Christian and pagan worlds in the play. Just as *Macbeth* combines two forms of tragedy—Christian de casibus and Senecan revenge—the play combines the three sisters as witches and as Parcae (item 2079).

13. Closely related to the union of contraries is the paradox, whereby the seeming contradiction is shown to be a single truth. An impressive list of variations on the theme of paradox in *Macbeth,* as reinforced by the play's language, is provided by Francis Fergusson, *"Macbeth* as the Imitation of an Action," *English Institute Essays, 1951* (New York, 1952), pp. 31–43.

14. The motto was "attributed (wrongly) in the Renaissance to Augustus," according to Rhoda Ribner, "The Compasse of this Curious Frame: Chapman's *Ovids Banquet of Sence* and the Emblematic Tradition," *Studies in the Renaissance* 17 (1970):233–58; quote on p. 244. This article is a very reliable introduction to the emblematic frame of reference. As Ribner points out, "The fashion for emblems as well as their availability was reaching its height in England in the last decade of the sixteenth century" (p. 233).

15. Ibid., p. 238.

16. Arthur Colby Sprague, *The Stage Business in Shakespeare's Plays: A Postscript* (1953; rpt. Folcroft, Pa., 1969), pp. 26–27.

17. Sprague, *Shakespeare and the Actors,* reports an early nineteenth-century acting text in which one of the witches in the cauldron scene (contrary to the stage directions in F1) makes her *exit·*through the cauldron: Cumberland's *British Theatre* (ca. 1829), where the

second witch "gets into the C.," and the other two "retire to R." shortly thereafter (Sprague, p. 227). As for the rapidity with which the complex action of exit and entrance through traps might be accomplished, see Nicola Sabbattini, "Manual for Constructing Theatrical Scenes and Machines" (1638), trans. John H. McDowell, in *The Renaissance Stage: Documents of Serlio, Sabbattini and Furttenbach,* ed. Barnard Hewitt (Coral Gables, 1958), pp. 43–177, especially pp. 119–25.

18. G. K. Hunter, "The Theology of Marlowe's *The Jew of Malta," Journal of the Warburg and Courtauld Institutes* 27 (1964):234. The edition of *The Kalender of Shepardes* I confirmed was STC 22415. The cauldron is shown as the fate awaiting "Covetous men and women" (sig. F1r).

19. Sprague, *Shakespeare and the Actors,* tells how the "veteran Macklin is represented satirically in *St. James Chronicle,* October 19–21, 1773, as interrupting a rehearsal of his production of Macbeth with 'and hark you, you Witches! Manage your Broomsticks with Dignity. . . .' " Sprague goes on with descriptions of later productions. By the nineteenth century the intention of the original F1 stage directions (having them vanish) is achieved by scrim (Sprague, p. 225).

20. Quoted by Sprague, *The Stage Business,* p. 23.

21. Adams, *The Globe Playhouse,* pp. 209–11.

22. See Welsford, *The Court Masque,* for a description of *The Masque of Queens* as "a turning-point in the history of the masque, for it marks the acceptance of the antimasque as an integral part of the performance. . ." (p. 183).

23. Even the speeches of the witches are written in Shakespeare's trochaic tetrameter of song, as the prevailing style of chanting them indicates.

24. The inventories of the Master of the Revels are reprinted as *Documents Relating to the Office of the Revels in the Time of Queen Elizabeth,* ed. Albert Feuillerat (Louvain, 1908). Another volume edited by Feuillerat for the reigns of Edward VI and Queen Mary also appears in the same series: Materialien zur Kunde des alteren englischen Dramas, gen. ed. W. Bang.

25. Cécile de Banke, *Shakespearean Stage Production, Then and Now: A Manual for the Scholar-Player* (New York, 1953), p. 70. Sprague, *Shakespeare and the Actors,* records the handling of the daggers, real and imaginary, in several productions (pp. 237 ff.). The overwhelming tendency, of course, is to make the "dagger of the mind" just that, no more.

26. Chew, *The Pilgrimage of Life,* illustrates the Deadly Sin of Wrath with an engraving of a woman holding a dagger (fig. 85). His source is Philip Galle, *VII peccatorum capitalium imagines elegantissime* (1600?).

27. The dagger's association with Cain is well documented by Martha Hester Golden [Fleischer], in her dissertation: "The Iconography of the English History Play" (Columbia University, 1964), pp. 135 ff. This Ph.D. dissertation is now published under the name of Martha Hester Fleischer (see my introduction, *n*33).

28. Allardyce Nicoll, *Studies in Shakespeare* (London, 1927), calls Banquo's ghost "but an hallucination of Macbeth's own mind. . . . utilized by Shakespeare for the purpose of intensifying the particular atmosphere of the drama. . . . a mere vision called forth from Macbeth's diseased and disordered imagination" (p. 120).

29. William Winter, *Shakespeare on the Stage* (New York, 1911), pp. 461 ff. Sprague, *Shakespeare and the Actors,* describes several other productions, including that of Edwin Forrest, in 1845, and how the ghost is handled in each (pp. 254 ff.).

30. The authenticity of the diary, discovered by the infamous Collier, was confirmed to most scholars' satisfaction by J. Dover Wilson and R. W. Hunt in 1947. Even if the diary is reliable as a Renaissance document, however, its confusions between Holinshed and the play leave the reliability of Forman as an eyewitness to a performance in some question. See Leah Scragg, "Macbeth on Horseback," *Shakespeare Survey* 26 (1973):81–88.

31. That the watch sees the ghost of Hamlet senior in I. i is required by the action of the play and not in the same category as the other instances under discussion. Shakespeare

writes by scenes and is capable of shifting his expressive forms as dramatic necessity requires: see Mark Rose, *Shakespearean Design* (Cambridge, Mass., 1972). Yet a general pattern, the one under discussion in my text, does emerge.

32. *The Book of Hours of Catherine of Cleves.* The mouth-of-hell illumination to which I subsequently refer is no. 99 in Plummer's edition and comes from the Office of the Dead.

33. Glynne Wickham, "Hell-Castle and Its Door-Keeper," *Shakespeare Survey* 19 (1966):68–74; reprinted as part of Chap. 13 in Wickham, *Shakespeare's Dramatic Heritage: Collected Studies in Mediaeval, Tudor, and Shakespearean Drama* (London, 1969). Earlier, Muir developed his reasoning about this scene along much the same lines (Muir, Arden *Macbeth,* pp. xxv–xxxii).

As for the document preserving a record of the hellmouth of the Valenciennes Passion Play, mentioned in my text a little earlier (MS. 12536, fol. 2v, at the Bibliothèque Nationale), it is illustrated by Phyllis Hartnoll, *The Concise History of Theatre* (New York, 1968), illus. 36.

34. That the Stratford mural escaped Tudor whitewashing iconoclasm is a possibility well argued by Mary Lascelles, " 'King Lear' and Doomsday," *Shakespeare Survey* 26 (1973):69–79. Lascelles gives Renaissance examples of selective iconophobia. In one Last Judgment, for instance, only the Papal indulgence in the scale with a saved soul was painted out.

35. Wickham, "Hell-Castle," p. 74.

36. Martha Hester Golden [Fleischer], "Stage Imagery in Shakespearean Studies," especially pp. 15–16.

37. A very perceptive article charting the variations in Shakespeare's use of iconic staging as his career develops is Dieter Mehl, "Visual and Rhetorical Imagery." If I were to recommend only one article on the subject of Shakespeare's iconic stage imagery to the reader, this one would be it.

Chapter 6

1. Edward Dowden, *Shakespeare: A Critical Study of His Mind and Art* (1875; rpt. New York, 1900), p. 370. Noteworthy among the critical studies are E. M. W. Tillyard, *Shakespeare's Last Plays* (1938; rpt. London, 1964); the especially influential G. Wilson Knight, *The Crown of Life: Essays in Interpretation of Shakespeare's Final Plays* (1948; rpt. London, 1965); Derek Traversi, *Shakespeare: The Last Phase* (New York, 1955); and Kenneth Muir, *Last Periods of Shakespeare, Racine, Ibsen* (Detroit, 1961). Cf. Howard Felperin, *Shakespearean Romance* (Princeton, 1972), who challenges the drift of the mythic approach by relating the tragicomedies to the morality play tradition.

2. Welsford, *The Court Masque,* Chap. 3, discusses the relationship of these two plays to the changing conventions of the court masque around the turn of the sixteenth century. The masquelike aspects of *The Tempest* are critically examined by R. A. Foakes, *Shakespeare: The Dark Comedies to the Last Plays, from Satire to Celebration* (Charlottesville, 1971), pp. 156–63.

3. An edition fully sophisticated in its practice of allegorical interpretation is Kellogg and Steele, eds., *Books I and II of the* Faerie Queene, *the* Mutability Cantos *and Selections from the Minor Poetry.* Kellogg and Steele sum up the issue as it is now seen: " . . . if . . . the Renaissance could think of . . . the epics of Homer and Virgil, the impassioned love letters of Ovid's *Heroides,* and the Greek tragedies as being allegorical, they meant something different by the term than do . . . contemporary hand-books when they include only such . . . works as *Piers Plowman* and *Pilgrim's Progress* under 'allegory' " (p. 6). The notes to Kellogg and Steele (especially to pp. 6–10) cite seminal works important in the current reevaluation of Renaissance allegory.

4. Ed. James Montagu. STC 14344.

5. James R. Lowell, quoted by Dowden, *Shakespeare*, n. on pp. 377–78.

6. Nevill Coghill, "The Basis of Shakespearean Comedy," *Essays and Studies*, n.s. 3 (1950):26–27. The idea of interpreting *The Tempest* in terms of the four elements originated in A. W. von Schlegel (1767–1845).

7. Frank Kermode, ed., Arden *The Tempest*, 6th ed. (1958; rpt. Cambridge, Mass., 1971), pp. xxxiv–lix. Fully as old as the allegorical interpretations is the familiar biographical approach of seeing the play as Shakespeare's farewell to the stage in particular and life in general. Dowden, *Shakespeare*, Chap. 8, is the best known touchstone of this view. For important qualifications to both the allegorical and biographical schools, see Elmer E. Stoll, "*The Tempest*," *PMLA* 47 (1932):699–726.

8. A summary of these interpretations and a bibliography of their sources is Terisio Pignatti, *Giorgione* (London, 1971), pp. 101–2.

9. Edgar Wind, *Giorgione's* Tempesta, *with Comments on Giorgione's Poetic Allegories* (Oxford, 1969), pp. 1–4 and nn.

10. Illus. ibid., Pl. 57. The sail is a curious development of the draperies associated with the birth of Venus in the sea. Fortune is an alluring woman and thus conflated with Venus as an ideal of feminine beauty.

11. Chew, *The Pilgrimage of Life*, p. 58. Chew cites several visual sources beyond Dürer (including the title page of Bacon's *Life of King Henry VII*) for the association of Fortune with the halter of Nemesis. Originally, the halter symbolized the restraint the fear of revenge imposed on potential wrongdoers. See also David M. Greene, "The Identity of the Emblematic Nemesis," *Studies in the Renaissance* 10 (1963):25–43.

Lawrence J. Ross informs me of an article of his on the general subject under discussion, due to appear in *Shakespeare Quarterly:* "The Ship, Storm, and Pilot Motif in *Othello*."

12. STC 4691; partial trans. of Vincenzo Cartari, *Le imagini de i' dei* (Venice, 1580).

13. Pignatti cites the description of the painting by Michiel, who saw it twenty-three years after its execution (ca. 1507): "The little landscape on canvas with the tempest with the gipsy and soldier . . ." (Pignatti, *Giorgione*, p. 101). Wind, *Giorgione's* Tempesta, questions the identification of the woman as a gypsy, but shows many pictorial parallels having to do with broken columns and supporting the idea of the man rendered by Giorgione as a soldier symbolizing Fortezza.

14. See Kellogg and Steele's introduction, pp. 48–73, and nn. to Bk. II of the "Faerie Queene." Kellogg and Steele identify the allegorized myth of Mars and Venus as the controlling metaphor of the adventures of Sir Guyon, and illustrate the metaphor with Veronese's painting *Mars and Venus United by Love*, at the Metropolitan Museum of Art (Pl. 2 in Kellogg and Steele). This painting expresses the harmony of the male and female principles.

15. See Raymond B. Waddington, "Antony and Cleopatra: 'What Venus did with Mars,' " *Shakespeare Studies* 2 (1966):210–27.

16. Kermode, Arden *The Tempest*, n. on p. 123.

17. See Kathrine Koller's documentation of the spiritual dangers which overwhelm Sir Terwin: "Art, Rhetoric, and Holy Dying in the *Faerie Queene*, with Special Reference to the Despair Canto," *Studies in Philology* 61 (1964):128–39.

18. For much of the documentation of the following discussion of the banquet scene I am indebted to my student and colleague Robert Nordlie. I have confirmed and expanded the investigations undertaken by him as part of his work in a graduate seminar in Shakespearean Iconography offered at Arizona State University in the fall of 1970.

19. Illustrated and commented upon by Chew, *Pilgrimage*, fig. 77 and pp. 93–94. The emblematic implications of the Banquet of Love becoming the Feast of Pride are developed in Chap. 3 of Robert David Greenberg, "The Image of the Devouring Beast: Its Dramatic Use in Selected Works of Shakespeare" (Ph.D. dissertation, University of California, Berkeley, 1968).

20. See Chew, *Pilgrimage,* fig. 78 and p. 94, for illustration and commentary.

21. The five senses as a medieval trope were rendered positively, however, in the lovely set of six tapestries known as *The Lady and the Unicorn,* which are preserved in a circular room at the Cluny Museum in Paris. Each sense is symbolized in turn by a lady on an island of green, participating in an appropriate activity. The sixth panel, "A mon seul desir," may represent a generalized compliment to the lady alluded to in the other five. In other words, she totally satisfies all five senses. See Pierre Verlet and Francis Salet, *The Lady and the Unicorn,* trans. R. D. Chancellor (London, 1961). For the Renaissance phase in the development of the iconography of the Banquet of Sense, see Rhoda Ribner, "The Compasse."

As for my subsequent references to the Seven Deadly Sins, the following sources are basic: Adolf Katzenellenbogen, *Allegories of the Virtues and the Vices in Medieval Art, from Early Christian Times to the Thirteenth Century,* trans. Alan J. P. Crick (1939; rpt. New York, 1964); and Bloomfield, *The Seven Deadly Sins.*

See also Samuel C. Chew, "Spenser's Pageant of the Seven Deadly Sins," in *Studies in Art and Literature for Belle da Costa Green,* ed. Dorothy Miner (Princeton, 1954), pp. 37–54.

22. Guy de Tervarent, *Attributs et symboles,* col. 209, lists harpies as symbols of greed and provides a number of instances in Renaissance Continental art where this is the case. See also under "Griffes," col. 206, where on the authority of Dante (*Inferno.* XIII: 13–14) harpies are assigned the taloned feet of the griffin as a further symbol of their rapacity.

23. Panofsky, *Dürer,* pp. 177–78. For other examples of harpies as both decorative and, at the same time, emblematic elements, see Rudolf and Margot Wittkower, *Born under Saturn,* pp. 290–91 and figs.

24. Illustrated by means of the Jacob de Zetter translation (Frankfurt, 1644) of Haechtanus, in Henkel and Schöne, *Emblemata,* cols. 1634–37.

25. Wind, *Bellini's Feast,* p. 48. For the rest of Wind's exposition, see n. 14 on pp. 48–49, and Pls. 49–52.

26. All five panels are at the Academy, Venice. "Nemesis" is smaller than the other four, which would thus be appropriate for the corners of the frame. The four are "Vana gloria" (ill fame of woman), "Fortuna amoris" (good fortune of woman), "Servitudo aceccliae" (ill fame of man), and "Comes virtutis" (good fortune of man). "Vana gloria" holds a glass globe; "Fortuna amoris" a convex mirror.

27. Wind, *Bellini's Feast,* pins these connections down with two Alciati emblems: on the role of Nemesis as winged goddess of chance, retribution, and temperance, see Alciati (1531), sig. A7r; on the combination of Nemesis with a mirror, see Alciati (1542), no. 79.

28. Nancy Lee Beaty, *The Craft of Dying: A Study in the Literary Tradition of the Ars Moriendi in England* (New Haven, 1970), carries her study of the ars moriendi from its medieval beginnings until Jeremy Taylor's *Holy Dying* (1651).

29. The original Latin passage reads:

> Principium in tereti quaeris quincunque figura,
> Principium invenies hîc ubi finis erit.
> Sic Christum vero quisquis revereris amore,
> Quae vitam hora tibi finiet, incipiet.
>   Theodore Beza, *Icones*
>   (Geneva, 1580), sig. Kk3v.

For the relationship of the rainbow to the end of the world and eternity, as applied to the betrothal masque of Juno, Ceres, and Iris in *The Tempest,* see René Graziani, "The 'Rainbow Portrait' of Queen Elizabeth I and Its Religious Symbolism," *Journal of the Warburg and Courtauld Institutes* 35 (1972):247–59. Graziani suggests that the rainbow of Iris [undoubtedly a stage property of some sort] iconically corrects the earlier storm, just as the sweet music of Ariel corrects his cacophonies. Pointing in the other direction, toward the end of the play and of time and space, the rainbow prepares for the moment when sublunary creation will melt "into air, into thin air" (pp. 253–54). Graziani promises a "forthcoming paper" on the play (n. 17 on pp. 253–54) developing this intriguing hypothesis.

30. Famous in the history of English drama are the practices occurring in *Dr. Faustus* and *Friar Bacon and Friar Bungay.* For further details on the protective circle of the black magician, see Émile Angelo Grillot de Givry, *Witchcraft, Magic, and Alchemy,* trans. J. Courtenay Locke (1931; rpt. New York, 1954), pp. 104–9.

31. Frances A. Yates, *Giordano Bruno and the Hermetic Tradition* (Chicago, 1964), compares and contrasts black and white forms of magic in the Renaissance; see especially pp. 17–19 and 81–82. The locus classicus of this distinction in the Renaissance is Pico della Mirandola (1463–94), *Oration on the Dignity of Man,* toward the end. Recent studies are David Woodman, *White Magic and English Renaissance Drama* (Rutherford, 1973), and Wayne Shumaker, *The Occult Sciences in the Renaissance: A Study in Intellectual Pattterns* (Berkeley, 1972).

32. Yates, *Giordano Bruno.* Her book has been applied to *The Tempest* in general terms by David G. James, *The Dream of Prospero* (Oxford, 1967), Chap. 3.

33. Dr. John Dee was astrologer to Queen Elizabeth, as well as an alchemist, mathematician, geographer, and practitioner of white magic. He came under the influence of one Edward Kelly, an imposter who claimed the power of necromancy. See Grillot de Givry, *Witchcraft,* pp. 168–71, and Peter J. French, *John Dee: The World of an Elizabethan Magus* (London, 1972).

34. For the serpent biting its tail as an ambiguous Neoplatonic symbol of both time and eternity (time consumes itself in the eternity from which it springs), see Edgar Wind, *Pagan Mysteries in the Renaissance* (1958; rev. rpt. Baltimore, 1967), pp. 265–67. The symbol appears countless times in the popular emblem books as well. Panofsky, *Studies in Iconology,* provides an extremely useful chapter on "Father Time," pp. 69–93 and plates, in which he elaborates the principle of time as creative eternity, or Aion (see especially n. 12, p. 74). Lynche, trans., *The Fountaine of Ancient Fiction* (London, 1599), carries over some of the materials found in his source, Vincenzo Cartari (1580), to elaborate the iconographic serpent of eternity for an English audience:

> Eternitie . . . sits incircled and involved in her selfe, as wee have alreadie discovered in the former description by the form of a Serpent, who continually with her taile in her mouth, turneth her selfe round with as great slownesse or leisure as is possible, shewing thereby that Time with a creeping and unseen pace, steales by little and little cleane from us. (Lynche, sigs. C4r–v)

Postscript

1. Chastel, *Age of Humanism,* p. 17. Friedrich Nietzsche, *The Birth of Tragedy,* next to be cited (obliquely) in my text, was written between 1870 and 1871.

2. Praz, *Mnemosyne,* p. 81.

3. Roland M. Frye, *Shakespeare and the Christian Doctrine* (Princeton, 1963). Frye's thesis is that Shakespeare was a dramatist first and an intelligent layman in theology second.

A study of Shakespeare and religion which has been very influential is Elton, King Lear *and the Gods.* In his richly documented and critically refined book, Elton concludes that *Lear* is more skeptical than religious. The Voice out of the Whirlwind in the Book of Job, however, would not regard these categories as mutually exclusive, quite the contrary; nor, I think, would some Renaissance Christianity, including that in *Lear.*

4. Roland M. Frye, *Shakespeare,* pp. 20–22.

5. Especially valuable is Martz, *The Poetry of Meditation.* Martz not only makes important

distinctions among concepts such as meditation, devotion, and contemplation, but he also outlines the history of the conflict between theology and affective piety. This controversy, first between Abelard and Bernard, and then between Aquinas and Bonaventure, was resolved for the Renaissance by Gerson (Martz, pp. 112 ff.). Finally, Martz's book also provides a wealth of information about Renaissance English literature of private religious experience.

See also two important histories of such books by Helen C. White: *English Devotional Literature, 1600–1640* (1931; rpt. New York, 1966) and *The Tudor Books of Private Devotion* (Madison, 1951).

A history of the Anglican prayer book (especially as it took form during the Renaissance) is Daniel Evans, *The Prayer Book: Its History, Language, and Contents* (London, 1900?). Of some additional interest is A. Tindal Hart, *The Man in the Pew, 1558–1600* (London, 1966).

6. See Wind, *Bellini's Feast,* p. 13 and n. Wind more fully develops the history of the concept of discordia concors in *Pagan Mysteries,* pp. 85–112.

The union of contraries is even the basis of a trope called "syntasis," defined by Frank L. Huntley in an essay on Milton as the union of two complementary opposites, a dichotomy, with one universal regarded as superior to the other. Huntley lists the major figures important to the development of this mode of thought: Plotinus, the Cabbala, Hermes Trismegistus, Augustine, Ficino, but primarily Socrates and Paul, and thus the Christian humanists of the Renaissance. See Frank L. Huntley, "Before and after the Fall: Some Miltonic Patterns of Syntasis," in *Approaches to* Paradise Lost, ed. C. A. Patrides (London, 1968), pp. 1–14.

For other important aspects of the Renaissance philosophy of emblems as expressions of transcendant unity (for instance, that the whole is greater than the sum of the parts), see Minor and Mitchell, *A Renaissance Entertainment,* especially p. 41; and Mehl, "Emblems in English Renaissance Drama," especially p. 41.

7. Lactantius, *The Divine Institutes, Books I–VII,* trans. M. F. McDonald (Washington, 1964), pp. 136–38.

8. See, for instance, Rabkin, *Shakespeare and the Common Understanding,* p. 12.

Appendix

1. See Lawrence J. Ross, "The Use of a 'Fit-up' Booth in *Othello,*" *Shakespeare Quarterly* 12 (1961): 359–70, for an interesting discussion of the staging of the bed. Although I am not entirely convinced that a booth was used, I agree that it is highly unlikely that the bed was originally in an "inner stage."

In the sixteenth century the four-poster was the bed par excellence. A paneled tester, it was the most important piece of furniture in the house and passed on from one generation to another as a valuable inheritance. See *The Tudor Period, 1599–1603,* ed. Ralph Edwards and L. G. G. Ramsey (London, 1956), p. 37.

For the iconographic distinction between the "family bed" (the childbirth bed or the deathbed) and the "bed of luxury," see Gabriel Chappuys, *Figures de la bible* (Lyons, 1582). In this illustrated Bible there is only one bed of luxury, curved and voluptuous, belonging to Potiphar's wife, while there are numerous representations of massive rectilinear deathbeds or (upon occasion) beds of birth.

2. These images belong both to the early medieval drama of the Psychomachia and to the nondramatic and visual tradition of the ars. The popularity and pervasiveness of the ars instruction, however, would make associations with the tradition immediate to a theater audience.

3. E. K. Chambers, *The Elizabethan Stage,* 4 vols. (Oxford, 1923), 3:487.

4. R. N. Hallstead, "Idolatrous Love: A New Approach to *Othello,*" *Shakespeare Quarterly*

19 (1968):107–24. Hallstead argues that Othello's jealousy arises from idolatrous love, but he sees the suicide as a final act of penance.

5. Paul N. Siegel, "The Damnation of Othello," *PMLA* 68 (1953):1068–79. Cf. Kenneth O. Myrick, "The Theme of Damnation in Shakespearean Tragedy," *Studies in Philology* 38 (1941):221–45, who does not see Othello as damned. An example of the third point of view is Irving Ribner, *Patterns in Shakespearean Tragedy* (London, 1960).

6. See Sister Mary Catharine O'Connor, *The Art of Dying Well: The Development of the Ars Moriendi* (New York, 1942), for the Continental history of the ars tradition; and Helen C. White, *English Devotional Literature*, for an understanding of the literature of popular devotion in England.

7. *The ars moriendi* (edito princeps, ca. 1450), facsim. rpt. ed. W. Harry Rylands (London, 1881). This block-book edition contains twelve leaves without page signatures and with illustrations scattered throughout.

8. See Launcelot Andrewes, *A Manual of Directions for the Sick* (London, 1648).

9. See, for instance, Roberto Bellarmino, *The Art of Dying Well*, trans. E. Coffin (London, 1622). An indication of the hold on the popular imagination of the ars tradition is suggested by the practice of recording the deaths of great or popular men of the day; this little book contains an account of Bellarmino's sickness, death, and burial in Rome. See also Christopher Sutton, *Disce Mori: Learne to Die*, 5th ed. (London, 1609).

10. Roland M. Frye, *Shakespeare and the Christian Doctrine*, p. 25. In Thomas Becon, *The Sycke Mans Salue* (London, 1561), we find the traditional use of Cain as an illustration of one who fell into desperation, believing his sin was too great to be forgiven, and was damned. For a full discussion of *Dr. Faustus* in relation to the ars and the question of despair, see Beach Langston, "Marlowe's Faustus and the *Ars Moriendi* Tradition," in *A Tribute to George Coffin Taylor*, ed. Arnold Williams (Chapel Hill, 1952), pp. 148–67.

11. Wright, *Middle-Class Culture in Elizabethan England.*

12. Sutton, *Disce Mori*, p. 8.

13. Richard Hooker, "The Laws of Ecclesiastical Polity," in *The Workes*, 7th ed. rev., ed. R. W. Church and F. Paget, 3 vols. (Oxford, 1888), 1:195–97.

14. Erasmus, *Preparation to Deathe* (London, 1538), sig. D2v.

15. *The ars moriendi*, ed. Rylands.

16. "The Craft to Know Well to Die," in *The Book of the Craft of Dying, and Other Early English Tracts Concerning Death*, ed. Frances M. M. Comper (London, 1917), pp. 77–78. Réau also notes in his *Iconographie*, 2:Part 2:657, the continuing popularity of the injunction to model one's death on that of Christ. Réau mentions the thirty-nine stamps attributed to Romeyn de Hooghe which illustrate the death of the Franciscan David de la Vigne. Each scene in the process of dying is paralleled by an episode from the Passion of Christ.

17. Erasmus, *Preparation to Deathe*, sig. F3v.

18. By the end of the sixteenth century the temptations against faith and to despair seem to have merged in the popular mind. The point is often made in the devotional literature that despair indicates a lack of faith in the mercy of God. For excellent discussions of despair, see Susan Snyder, "The Left Hand of God: Despair in Medieval and Rennaissance Tradition," *Studies in the Renaissance* 12 (1965):18–59: and Koller, "Art, Rhetoric, and Holy Dying," pp. 128–39. Koller's article summarizes a wealth of background materials. In the original ars woodcuts, however, it is the temptation against faith which shows the demon with the scroll advising the moriens to kill himself; lower in the picture is the representation of a man about to cut his throat. The knife is usually associated with suicide: Sir Trevisan in the *Faerie Queene* has a rope around his neck, but the Red Crosse knight almost takes his life with a dagger.

Lewis Bayly, in the extremely popular devotional book, *The Practice of Pietie*, 12th ed. (London, 1620), pp. 649–717, has a meditation against despair, but no separate one against loss of faith.

19. Roland M. Frye, *Shakespeare and the Christian Doctrine,* p. 63.

20. One has only to note the frequency of editions of popular devotional books to see evidence of this quantity. For the discussion of the art of meditation and its influence, see Martz, *The Poetry of Meditation.*

21. O'Connor, *The Art of Dying Well,* p. 44.

22. We even have a Latin letter given in an article by Geoffrey Tillotson, *"Othello* and *The Alchemist* at Oxford in 1610," *The Times Literary Supplement,* July 20, 1933, p. 494, which describes the way in which the audience was moved, especially by Desdemona's death scene: "cum in lecto decumbens spectantium misericordiam ipso vultu imploraret."

23. In a tract called "The Lamentation of the Creature," in *The Book of the Craft of Dying,* p. 139, we see a characteristic use of the opposition:

> The Complaint of the Dying Creature to the Good Angel:
>
> O my GOOD ANGEL, to whom our Lord took me to keep, where be thee now? Me thinketh ye should be here, and answer for me; for the dread of death distroubleth me, so that I cannot answer for myself. Here is my bad angel and is one of my chief accursers, with legions of fiends with him. I have no creature to answer for me. Alas it is an heavy case!

24. OED, 8:488. The dictionary gives as one of its illustrations the following quotation from Sir Thomas More: "To fall in Despicions upon Gods eleccion, . . . and eternall sentence of reprobation." Apparently, the term was used often in opposition to *election.*

25. Traditional advice against suicide is given by the popular preacher, Christopher Sutton, in *Disce Mori,* in Chap. 25, entitled: "An admonition for all such as finde themselves troubled with euill motions, to commit faithlesse and fearfull attemptes against themselues." In the third paragraph of the chapter (pp. 337–38), Sutton makes explicit the connection between despair and suicide:

> Abridge the time we may not, we must not for all the disgraces, iniuries, and obloquies, the crosses and losses this world can lay upon us: fie uppon that discontment [sic], that should make any cowardly to runne away, or distrustfully to giue ouer his standing, before he be called by the Generall of the field: fie upon that dispaire that should make any cast away themselues, and forget they have soules to saue.

26. In Bayly, *The Practice of Pietie,* p. 694, the strategy of the devil is commented upon:

> It is found by continuall experience, that neere the time of death, (when the Children of God are weakest) then Sathan makes the greatest flourish of his strength: and assailes them with his strongest temptations. . . . And therefore he will now bestirre himselfe as much as he can, and labour to set before their eyes all the grosse sinnes which euer they committed, and the *Iudgements* of GOD which are due vnto them: thereby to driue them if hee can, to despaire which is a grieuouser sinne then all the sinnes that they committed, or he can accuse them of.

27. *The ars moriendi,* sig. B3v. See also the painting by Hieronimus Bosch, *The Death of the Miser,* the National Gallery of Art, Washington, D.C., for a deathbed ars combined with "the whole armor of God."

28. John E. Hankins, "The Pains of the Afterworld: Fire, Wind, and Ice in Milton and Shakespeare," *PMLA* 71 (1956):482–95. This article, on the basis of some sound background materials, distinguishes between purgatorial and hell imagery, but my own reading indicates that in the sixteenth and seventeenth centuries the distinction is not necessarily made.

29. Siegel, "The Damnation of Othello," pp. 1068–79. Irving Ribner, in *Patterns in Shakespearean Tragedy,* is recognizing this dramatic redemption in his argument that although Othello dies expecting damnation, Desdemona as a symbol of mercy has prepared

the audience for his salvation. But although I see the critical problem of the final dignity of Othello that it seeks to answer, Professor Ribner's argument does not appear to take cognizance of the strength of Renaissance theological opinion on suicide.

   30. Roland M. Frye, *Shakespeare and the Christian Doctrine,* p. 63.
   31. Erasmus, *Preparation to Deathe,* sig. A4v.

Bibliography

Adams, John Cranford. *The Globe Playhouse: Its Design and Equipment.* 2d ed. New York: Barnes & Noble, 1961.

Alciati, Andrea. *Emblematum liber.* Augsburg: H. Steynerum, 1531.

―――. *Omnia emblemata.* Antwerp: Christopher Plantin, 1577.

Allen, Don Cameron. *Mysteriously Meant: The Rediscovery of Pagan Symbolism and Allegorical Interpretation in the Renaissance.* Baltimore: Johns Hopkins University Press, 1970.

Alpers, Paul J. *The Poetry of the* Faerie Queene. Princeton: Princeton University Press, 1967.

Alpers, Svetlana, and Alpers, Paul J. *"Ut Pictura Noesis?:* Criticism in Literary Studies and Art History." *New Literary History* 3 (1972):437–58.

Altick, Richard. "Symphonic Imagery in *Richard II."* *PMLA* 62 (1947):339–65.

Ammann, Peter J. "The Musical Theory and Philosophy of Robert Fludd." *Journal of the Warburg and Courtauld Institutes* 30 (1967):198–227.

Anderson, Mary D. *Drama and Imagery in English Medieval Churches.* Cambridge: Cambridge University Press, 1963.

Andrewes, Launcelot. *A Manual of Directions for the Sick.* London: Humphrey Moseley, 1648. Wing A3132.

Aptekar, Jane. *Icons of Justice: Iconography and Thematic Imagery in Book V of the* Faerie Queene. New York: Columbia University Press, 1969.

The ars moriendi. Edited by W. Harry Rylands. 1450? Facsimile reprint. London: Holbein Society, 1881. 4th ed. Augsburg: Günther Zainer, 1465.

Baldwin, Thomas W. *William Shakespeare's Small Latine and Lesse Greeke.* 2 vols. Urbana: University of Illinois Press, 1944.

Banke, Cécile de. *Shakespearean Stage Production, Then and Now: A Manual for the Scholar-Player.* New York: McGraw-Hill, 1953.

Bartsch, Adam. *Le peintre-graveur.* 21 vols. in 17. Vienna: J. V. Degan, 1803–13.

Bateman, Stephen. *The Golden Booke of the Leaden Goddes.* London: Thomas Marshe, 1577. STC 1583.

Bayly, Lewis. *The Practice of Pietie.* 12th ed. London: J. Hodgetts, 1620. STC 1604.

Beaty, Nancy Lee. *The Craft of Dying: A Study in the Literary Tradition of the Ars Moriendi in England.* New Haven: Yale University Press, 1970.

Becon, Thomas. *The Sycke Mans Salue.* London: J. Day, 1561. STC 1757.

Bellarmino, Roberto. *The Art of Dying Well.* Translated by E. Coffin. London: St. Omer, 1622. STC 1839.

Bergeron, David M. "The Emblematic Nature of English Civic Pageantry." *Renaissance Drama,* n.s. 1 (1968):167–98.

―――. *English Civic Pageantry, 1558–1642.* London: Edward Arnold, 1971.

Beza, Theodore. *Icones, id est verae imagines virorum doctrina simul et pietate illustrium.* Geneva: Joannes Laon, 1580.

Bloomfield, Morton W. *The Seven Deadly Sins: An Introduction to the History of a Religious Concept, with Special Reference to Medieval English Literature.* East Lansing: Michigan State College Press, 1952.

The Boke of Common Praier. 30th ed. London: Deputies of C. Barker, 1594. STC 16318. 33d ed. London: Deputies of C. Barker, 1596. STC 16321.

The Book of Hours of Catherine of Cleves. Edited by John Plummer. New York: Pierpont Morgan Library, 1964.

The Book of the Craft of Dying, and Other Early English Tracts Concerning Death. Edited by Frances M. M. Comper. London: Longmans-Green, 1917.

A Booke of Christian Prayers. London: J. Daye, 1578. STC 6429.

Booth, Stephen. "On the Value of *Hamlet.*" In *Reinterpretations of Elizabethan Drama,* edited by Norman Rabkin, pp. 137–76. New York: Columbia University Press, 1969.

Bradbrook, Muriel C. "An 'Ecce Homo' of the Sixteenth Century and the Pageants and Street Theatres of the Low Countries." *Shakespeare Quarterly* 9 (1958):424–26.

———. "Shakespeare's Primitive Art." *Proceedings of the British Academy, 1965,* 51:215–34. London: Oxford University Press, 1966.

Bradley, A. C. *Shakespearean Tragedy: Lectures on* Hamlet, Othello, King Lear, Macbeth. 2d ed. 1905. Reprint. London: Macmillan and Co., 1937.

Bradley, Sister Ritamary. "Backgrounds of the Title *Speculum* in Mediaeval Literature." *Speculum* 29 (1954):100–15.

Brant, Sebastian. *The Shyp of Folys.* Translated by Alexander Barclay. London: R. Pynson, 1509. STC 3545. 2d ed. London: J. Cawood, 1570? STC 3546.

Briggs, Katherine M. *Pale Hecate's Team: An Examination of the Beliefs on Witchcraft and Magic among Shakespeare's Contemporaries and His Immediate Successors.* London: Routledge & Kegan Paul, 1962.

Brooke, Nicholas. *Shakespeare's Early Tragedies.* London: Methuen & Co., 1968.

Brown, John Russell. *Shakespeare's Plays in Performance.* London: Edward Arnold, 1966.

———, ed. *The Merchant of Venice,* by William Shakespeare. 7th ed. rev. The Arden Shakespeare. Cambridge, Mass.: Harvard University Press, 1959.

Bullough, Geoffrey, ed. *Narrative and Dramatic Sources of Shakespeare.* 7 vols. thus far. London: Routledge & Kegan Paul, 1957– .

Campbell, Oscar James. *Shakespeare's Satire.* London: Oxford University Press, 1943.

———, and Quinn, Edward G., eds. *The Reader's Encyclopedia of Shakespeare.* New York: Thomas Y. Crowell, 1966.

Cantelupe, Eugene B., and Griffith, Richard. "The Gifts of the Shepherds in the Wakefield *Secunda Pastoral:* An Iconographical Interpretation." *Medieval Studies* 28 (1966):328–35.

Cantor, Norman F. *The English: A History of Politics and Society to 1760.* New York: Simon and Schuster, 1967.

Cartari, Vincenzo. *Le imagini de i' dei.* 1556. Reprint. Lyons: Bartholomeo Honorati, 1581. Facsimile reprint of 1647 edition. Graz, Austria: Walter Koschatzky, 1963. 1580 reprint translated by Lynche, q.v.

Catalogue of an Exhibition of Late Elizabethan Art, in Conjunction with the Tercentenary of Francis Bacon. London: Burlington Fine Arts Club, 1926.

Certayne Sermons [Book I]. London: R. Grafton, 1547. [Book II]. London: R. Jugge, 1563. STC 13639 and 13663.

Chamberlain, Arthur B. *Hans Holbein the Younger.* 2 vols. London: G. Allen, 1913.

Chambers, E. K. *The Elizabethan Stage.* 4 vols. Oxford: Clarendon Press, 1923.

Chapman, Raymond. "The Wheel of Fortune in Shakespeare's Historical Plays." *Review of English Studies,* n.s. 1 (1950):1–7.

Chappuys, Gabriel. *Figures de la bible.* Lyons: Estienne Michel, 1582.

Charney, Maurice. *Shakespeare's Roman Plays: The Function of Imagery in the Drama.* Cambridge, Mass.: Harvard University Press, 1961.

Chastel, André. *The Age of Humanism: Europe, 1480–1530.* Translated by Katherine M. Delavenay and E. M. Gwyer. London: Thames & Hudson, 1963.

———. *The Crisis of the Renaissance, 1520–1600.* Translated by Peter Price. Geneva: Skira, 1968.

Chew, Samuel C. *The Pilgrimage of Life.* New Haven: Yale University Press, 1962.

———. "Spenser's Pageant of the Seven Deadly Sins." In *Studies in Art and Literature for Belle da Costa Green,* edited by Dorothy Miner, pp. 37–54. Princeton: Princeton University Press, 1954.

————. *The Virtues Reconciled: An Iconographic Study.* Toronto: University of Toronto Press, 1947.

Claessens, Bob, and Rousseau, Jeanne. *Our Bruegel.* Translated by Haakon Chevalier. Antwerp: Mercatorfonds, 1969.

Clark, James M. *The Dance of Death in the Middle Ages and the Renaissance.* Glasgow University Publications, 86. Glasgow: Jackson, 1950.

Clemen, Wolfgang. *The Development of Shakespeare's Imagery.* Cambridge, Mass.: Harvard University Press, 1951. (First published in German in 1936.)

Clements, Robert John. *Picta Poesis: Literary and Humanistic Theory in Renaissance Emblem Books.* Rome: Edizioni di Storia e Letteratura, 1960.

Coghill, Nevill. "The Basis of Shakespearean Comedy: A Study in Medieval Affinities" *Essays and Studies,* n.s. 3 (1950):1–28.

Collins, Fletcher, Jr. *The Production of Medieval Church Music-Drama.* Charlottesville: University Press of Viriginia, 1972.

Combe, Thomas, trans. *The Theatre of Fine Devices.* Entered 1593. First extant edition. London: R. Field, 1614. Translation of Perrière, q.v.

The Complete Work of Michaelangelo. Edited by Mario Salmi. 2 vols. London: Macdonald, 1966.

Cooper, John R. "Shylock's Humanity." *Shakespeare Quarterly* 21 (1970):117–24.

Cooper, Thomas. *Thesaurus.* London: Henricum Wykes, 1565. STC 5686. Facsimile reprint. Menston, Eng.: Scolar Press, 1969.

Daley, Peter M. "Trends and Problems in the Study of Emblematic Literature." *Mosaic* 5, No. 4 (Summer 1972):53–68.

Davies, David William. *Dutch Influences on English Culture, 1558–1625.* Folger Booklet on Tudor and Stuart Civilization. Ithaca: Cornell University Press, 1964.

Dessen, Alan. "Hamlet's Poisoned Sword: A Study in Dramatic Imagery." *Shakespeare Studies* 5 (1969):53–59.

Digby, George Wingfield. *Elizabethan Embroidery.* New York: T. Yoseloff, 1964.

Documents Relating to the Office of the Revels in the Time of Queen Elizabeth. Edited by Albert Feuillerat. Materialien zur Kunde des alteren englischen Dramas, gen. ed. W. Bang, 21. Louvain: A. Uystpruyst, 1908.

Doebler, Bettie Anne. " 'Dispaire and Dye': The Ultimate Temptation of Richard III." *Shakespeare Studies* 7 (1974):75–85.

————. "Othello's Angels: The Ars Moriendi." *ELH* 34 (1967):156–72.

Doebler, John. "Beaumont's *The Knight of the Burning Pestle* and the Prodigal Son Plays." *Studies in English Literature, 1500–1900,* 5 (1965):333–44.

————. "Orlando: Athlete of Virtue." *Shakespeare Survey* 26 (1973):111–17.

————. "The Play within the Play: The *Muscipula Diaboli* in *Hamlet.*" *Shakespeare Quarterly* 23 (1972):161–69.

Doran, Madeleine. "Imagery in *Richard II* and in *Henry IV.*" *Modern Language Review* 37 (1942):113–22.

————. " 'Yet am I inland bred.' " *Shakespeare Quarterly* 15, No. 2 (Spring 1964):99–114.

Dowden, Edward. *Shakespeare: A Critical Study of His Mind and Art.* 1875. Reprint. New York: Harper, 1900.

Downer, Alan S. "The Life of Our Design: The Function of Imagery in the Poetic Drama." *The Hudson Review* 2 (1949):242–63.

Edwards, Lewis. "Some English Examples of the Medieval Representation of Church and Synagogue." *Transactions of the Jewish Historical Society of England, 1953–1955,* 18:63–75. London: Jewish Historical Society, 1958.

Eisler, Colin. "The Athlete of Virtue: The Iconography of Asceticism." In *De Artibus Opscula*

XL: Essays in Honor of Erwin Panofsky, edited by Millard Meiss. 2 vols. 1:82–97. New York: New York University Press, 1961.

Elton, William R. *King Lear and the Gods.* San Marino, Calif.: Huntington Library, 1966.

Erasmus, Desiderius. *Preparation to Deathe.* London: T. Bertheleti, 1538. STC 10505.

Evans, Daniel. *The Prayer Book: Its History, Language, and Contents.* London: Wells, 1900?

Ewbank, Inga-Stina. " 'More Pregnantly than Words': Some Uses and Limitations of Visual Symbols." *Shakespeare Survey* 24 (1971):13–18.

Fairchild, Arthur H. R. *Shakespeare and the Arts of Design: Architecture, Sculpture, and Painting.* University of Missouri Studies, 12, No. 1. Columbia: University of Missouri Press, 1937.

Farnham, Willard. *The Medieval Heritage of Elizabethan Tragedy.* 1936. Reprint with corrections. New York: Barnes & Noble, 1956.

Felperin, Howard. *Shakespearean Romance.* Princeton: Princeton University Press, 1972.

Fergusson, Francis. *"Macbeth* as the Imitation of an Action." *English Institute Essays, 1951,* pp. 31–43. New York: Columbia University Press, 1952.

Foakes, R. A. *Shakespeare: The Dark Comedies to the Last Plays, from Satire to Celebration.* Charlottesville: University Press of Virginia, 1971.

———. "Suggestions for a New Approach to Shakespeare's Imagery." *Shakespeare Survey* 5 (1952):81–92.

Fox, Richard. *The Contemplation of Sinners.* Westminster: Wynken de Worde, 1499. STC 5643.

Frankl, Paul. *The Gothic: Literary Sources and Interpretations through Eight Centuries.* Princeton: Princeton University Press, 1960.

Fraser, Russell A. *Shakespeare's Poetics in Relation to* King Lear. London: Routledge & ·Kegan Paul, 1962.

Freeman, Margaret B. "The Iconography of the *Mérode Altarpiece." The Metropolitan Museum of Art Bulletin,* n.s. 16, No. 4 (December 1957):130–39.

Freeman, Rosemary. *English Emblem Books.* London: Chatto & Windus, 1948.

French, Peter J. *John Dee: The World of an Elizabethan Magus.* London: Routledge & Kegan Paul, 1972.

Freud, Sigmund. "The Theme of the Three Caskets." In *Collected Papers,* translated by Joan Riviere. 5 vols. 1924–25. 5:244–56. Reprint. New York: Basic Books, 1959.

Frye, Dean. "The Context of Lear's Unbuttoning." *ELH* 32 (1965):17–31.

Frye, Roland M. *Shakespeare and the Christian Doctrine.* Princeton: Princeton University Press, 1963.

Gascoigne, George. *The Complete Works.* Edited by John W. Cunliffe. 2 vols. 1907–10. Reprint. New York: Greenwood Press, 1969.

Gellert, Bridget. "The Iconography of Melancholy in the Graveyard Scene of *Hamlet." Studies in Philology* 67 (1970):57–66.

The Geneva Bible: A Facsimile of the 1560 Edition. Introduction by Lloyd E. Berry. Madison: University of Wisconsin Press, 1969.

Gerson, Horst. *Rembrandt Paintings.* Translated by Heinz Norden. Edited by Gary Schwartz. Amsterdam: Reynal, 1968.

Gesner, Conrad. *Lexicon graeco-latinum.* 1543. Reprint. Basel: Hieronymi Curionis, 1545.

Gibbons, Brian, ed. *The Revenger's Tragedy,* by Cyril Tourneur. The New Mermaids. New York: Hill & Wang, 1967.

Gilbert, Allan H. *The Symbolic Persons in the Masques of Ben Jonson.* 1948. Reprint. New York: AMS Press, 1965.

Golden [Fleischer], Martha Hester. "The Iconography of the English History Play." Ph.D. dissertation, Columbia University, 1964. [Published 1974.]

———. "stage imagery." In *The Reader's Encyclopedia of Shakespeare,* edited by Oscar James Campbell and Edward G. Quinn. New York: Thomas Y. Crowell, 1966.

———. "Stage Imagery in Shakespearean Studies." *Shakespearean Research Opportunities* 1 (1965):10–20.

Gollancz, Israel. "Bits of Timber: Some Observations on Shakespearian Names—'Shylock'; 'Polonius'; 'Malvolio.' " In *A Book of Homage to Shakespeare*, edited by Israel Gollancz. London: Oxford University Press, 1916.

Gombrich, E. H. *"Icones Symbolicae:* The Visual Image in Neo-Platonic Thought." *Journal of the Warburg and Courtauld Institutes* 11 (1948):163–92.

Granville-Baker, Harley. *Prefaces to Shakespeare.* 4 vols. 1946. Reprint. Princeton: Princeton University Press, 1963.

Graves, Robert. *The Greek Myths.* 2 vols. London: Penguin Books, 1955.

Graziani, René. "The 'Rainbow Portrait' of Queen Elizabeth I and Its Religious Symbolism." *Journal of the Warburg and Courtauld Institutes* 35 (1972):247–59.

Green, Henry. *Shakespeare and the Emblem Writers: An Exposition of Their Similarities of Thought and Expression, Preceded by a View of Emblem-Literature down to A.D. 1616.* 1870. Facsimile reprint. New York: Burt Franklin, 1964.

Greenberg, Robert David. "The Image of the Devouring Beast: Its Dramatic Use in Selected Works of Shakespeare." Ph.D. dissertation, University of California, Berkeley, 1968.

Greene, David M. "The Identity of the Emblematic Nemesis." *Studies in the Renaissance* 10 (1963):25–43.

Grillot de Givry, Émile Angelo. *Witchcraft, Magic, and Alchemy.* Translated by J. Courtenay Locke. 1931. Reprint. New York: Frederick, 1954. (First published in French in 1922.)

Grimald, Nicholas, trans. *Marcus Tullius Ciceroes three books of duties to Marcus his sonne.* 7th ed. London: Thomas Este, 1596. STC 5286.

Haaker, Ann. *"Non sine cause:* The Use of Emblematic Method and Iconology in the Thematic Structure of *Titus Andronicus." Research Opportunities in Renaissance Drama* 13–14 (1970–71):143–68.

Habicht, Werner. "Tree Properties and Tree Scenes in Elizabethan Theatre." *Renaissance Drama,* n.s. 4 (1971):69–72.

Haechtanus, Laurentius. *Parvus mundus.* Antwerp: Gerardum de Jodel, 1579. Translated by Jacob de Zetter, q.v.

Hagstrum, Jean H. *The Sister Arts: The Tradition of Literary Pictorialism and English Poetry from Dryden to Gray.* Chicago: University of Chicago Press, 1958.

Halle, Edward. *The Vnion of . . . Lancastre & Yorke.* 3d ed. London: R. Grafton. 1550. STC 12723.

Hallstead, R. N. "Idolatrous Love: A New Approach to *Othello." Shakespeare Quarterly* 19 (1968):107–24.

Hankins, John E. "The Pains of the Afterworld: Fire, Wind, and Ice in Milton and Shakespeare." *PMLA* 71 (1956):482–95.

Hapgood, Robert. "Speak Hands for Me: Gesture as Language in *Julius Caesar." Drama Survey* 5 (1966):162–70.

Hargreaves, Henry A. "Visual Contradiction in *King Lear." Shakespeare Quarterly* 21 (1970):491–95.

Harris, Kathryn M. "Sun and Water Imagery in *Richard II:* Its Dramatic Function." *Shakespeare Quarterly* 21 (1970):157–65.

Hart, A. Tindal. *The Man in the Pew, 1558–1660.* London: Baker, 1966.

Hartlaub, Gustav F. *Zauber des Spiegels: Geschichte und Bedentung des Spiegels in der Kunst.* Munich: R. Piper, 1951.

Hartnoll, Phyllis. *The Concise History of Theatre.* New York: Harry N. Abrams, 1968.

Hauser, Arnold. *The Social History of Art.* Translated by Stanley Godman. 2 vols. London: Routledge & Kegan Paul, 1951.

Heckscher, William S. "The Genesis of Iconology." *Acts of the XXIst International Congress of Art History, Bonn, 1964,* pp. 239–62. Berlin: Gebrüder Mann, 1967.

———. *Rembrandt's Anatomy of Dr. Nicolaus Tulp: An Iconological Study.* New York: New York University Press, 1958.

———. "Shakespeare in His Relationship to the Visual Arts: A Study in Paradox." *Research Opportunities in Renaissance Drama* 13–14 (1970–71):5–71.

———, and Bunker, Cameron F. "Review of *Emblemata,* by Arthur Henkel and Albrecht Schöne." *Renaissance Quarterly* 23 (1970):59–80.

Heninger, S. K., Jr. "The Sun-King Analogy in *Richard II.*" *Shakespeare Quarterly* 11 (1960):319–27.

Henkel, Arthur, and Schöne, Albrecht. *Emblemata: Handbuch zur Sinnbildkunst des XVI. und XVII. Jahrhunderts.* Stuttgart: J. B. Metzlersche, 1967.

Herrad of Landsberg. *Hortus deliciarum.* 11 fascs. Strasbourg: Trübner, 1879–99.

Hind, Arthur. *Engraving in England in the Sixteenth and Seventeenth Centuries: A Descriptive Catalogue with Introductions.* 3 vols. Cambridge: Cambridge University Press, 1952–64.

Hirn, Yrjö. *The Sacred Shrine: A Study of the Poetry and Art of the Catholic Church.* Boston: Beacon Press, 1957.

Hodges, C. Walter. *The Globe Restored: A Study of the Elizabethan Theatre.* 2d ed. London: Oxford University Press, 1968.

Hodnett, Edward. *English Woodcuts, 1480–1535.* London: Oxford University Press, 1935.

Holaday, Allan. "Antonio and the Allegory of Salvation." *Shakespeare Studies* 4 (1968): 109–18.

Holbein, Hans. *Les simulachres et historiees faces de la mort.* 1538. Facsimile reprint: *Hans Holbein's Todtentanz.* Munich: G. Hirth, 1903.

Holinshed, Raphael. *Chronicles.* 2 vols. London: George Bishop, 1577. STC 13568a. 2d ed. 3 vols. London: J. Harrison, 1587. STC 13569.

———. *Shakespeare's Holinshed: An Edition of Holinshed's Chronicles, 1587, Source of Shakespeare's History Plays,* King Lear, Cymbeline, *and* Macbeth. Edited by Richard Hosley. New York: G. P. Putnam's Sons, 1968.

Holkham Bible Picture Book. Edited by W. O. Hassall. 2d ed. London: Dropmore Press, 1954.

Hollander, John. *The Untuning of the Sky: Ideas of Music in English Poetry, 1500–1700.* Princeton: Princeton University Press, 1961.

Hooker, Richard. *The Workes.* 7th ed. rev. Edited by R. W. Church and F. Paget. 3 vols. Oxford: Clarendon Press, 1888.

Hopkins, Richard, trans. *Of Prayer and Meditation.* 5th ed. Douay: J. Heigham, 1612. STC 16912. Translation of Luis de Granada, *Libro de la oración y meditación,* 1554. Facsimile reprint of 1582 Hopkins edition. Menston, Eng.: Scolar Press, 1971.

Hoy, Cyrus. "Jacobean Tragedy and the Mannerist Style." *Shakespeare Survey* 26 (1973):49–67.

Hunter, G. K. "*Macbeth* in the Twentieth Century." *Shakespeare Survey* 19 (1966):1–11.

———. "Othello and Colour Prejudice." *Proceedings of the British Academy, 1967,* 53:139–63. London: Oxford University Press, 1968.

———. "The Theology of Marlowe's *The Jew of Malta.*" *Journal of the Warburg and Courtauld Institutes* 27 (1964):211–40.

———. *William Shakespeare: The Late Comedies:* A Midsummernight's Dream, Much Ado About Nothing, As You Like It, Twelfth Night. London: Longmans, Green and Co., 1962.

Huntley, Frank L. "Before and after the Fall: Some Miltonic Patterns of Syntaxis." In *Approaches to "Paradise Lost,"* edited by C. A. Patrides, pp. 1–14. London: Edward Arnold, 1968.

Iwasaki, Soji. *The Sword and the Word: Shakespeare's Tragic Sense of Time.* Tokyo: Shinozaki Shorin, 1973.

James, David G. *The Dream of Prospero.* Oxford: Clarendon Press, 1967.

James I. *Daemonologie.* Edinburgh: R. Walde-grave, 1597. STC 14364.

————. *The Workes.* Edited by James Montagu. London: R. Barker, 1616. STC 14344.

Janson, Horst Woldemar. *The Sculpture of Donatello.* 2 vols. Princeton: Princeton University Press, 1957.

Jenkins, Harold. *"As You Like It."* Shakespeare Survey 8 (1955):40–51.

Jones, Eldred. *The Elizabethan Image of Africa.* Folger Booklet on Tudor and Stuart Civilization. Charlottesville: University Press of Virginia, 1971.

————. *Othello's Countrymen: The African in English Renaissance Drama.* London: Oxford University Press, 1965.

————. "Racial Terms for Africans in Elizabethan Usage." *Review of National Literatures* 3, No. 2 (Fall 1972):54–89.

The Kalender of Shepardes. Translated by R. Copland. 7th ed. London: J. Wally, 1570? STC 22415.

Kantorowicz, Ernst. *The King's Two Bodies: A Study in Medieval Political Theology.* Princeton: Princeton University Press, 1957.

Katzenellenbogen, Adolf. *Allegories of the Virtues and the Vices in Medieval Art, from Early Christian Times to the Thirteenth Century.* Translated by Alan J. P. Crick. 1939. Reprint. New York: W. W. Norton, 1964.

Kellogg, Robert, and Steele, Oliver, eds. *Books I and II of the* Faerie Queene, *the* Mutability Cantos *and Selections from the Minor Poetry,* by Edmund Spenser. New York: Odyssey Press, 1965.

Kermode, Frank, ed. *The Tempest,* by William Shakespeare. 6th ed. The Arden Shakespeare. 1958. Reprint. Cambridge, Mass.: Harvard University Press, 1971.

Kernodle, George R. *From Art to Theatre: Form and Convention in the Renaissance.* Chicago: University of Chicago Press, 1944.

King, Thomas J. *Shakespearean Staging, 1599–1642.* Cambridge, Mass.: Harvard University Press, 1971.

Kirschbaum, Engelbert. *Lexikon der christlichen Ikonographie.* 5 vols. thus far. Rome: Herder, 1968–

Knight, G. Wilson. *The Crown of Life: Essays in Interpretation of Shakespeare's Final Plays.* 1948. Reprint. London: Methuen & Co., 1965.

————. *Shakespearean Production, with Especial Reference to the Tragedies.* Evanston: North-western University Press, 1964.

Knowles, Richard. "Myth and Type in *As You Like It.*" *ELH* 33 (1966):1–22.

————. "Unquiet and the Double Plot of *2 Henry IV.*" *Shakespeare Studies* 2 (1966):130–40.

Koller, Katherine. "Art, Rhetoric, and Holy Dying in the *Faerie Queene,* with Special Reference to the Despair Canto." *Studies in Philology* 61 (1964):128–39.

Kolve, V. A. *The Play Called Corpus Christi.* Stanford: Stanford University Press, 1966.

Kurtz, Leonard P. *The Dance of Death and the Macabre Spirit in European Literature.* New York: Columbia University Press, 1934.

Lactantius. *The Divine Institutes, Books I-VII.* Translated by M. F. McDonald. Washington: Catholic University of America Press, 1964.

Langston, Beach. "Marlowe's Faustus and the *Ars Moriendi* Tradition." In *A Tribute to George Coffin Taylor,* ed. Arnold Williams, pp. 148–67. Chapel Hill: University of North Carolina Press, 1952.

Lascelles, Mary. *"King Lear* and Doomsday." *Shakespeare Survey* 26 (1973):69–79.

Lea, Henry C. *Materials toward a History of Witchcraft.* 3 vols. New York: T. Yoseloff, 1957.

Lee, Rensselaer W. *Ut Pictura Poesis: The Humanistic Theory of Painting.* New York: W. W. Norton, 1967.

Levin, Harry. *The Question of* Hamlet. New York: Oxford University Press, 1959.

Lewis, C. S. *English Literature in the Sixteenth Century, Excluding Drama.* Oxford History of English Literature, 3. Oxford: Clarendon Press, 1954.

Livermore, Ann. "Shakespeare and St. Augustine." *Quarterly Review* 303 (1965):181–93.

Lynche, Richard, trans. *The Fountaine of Ancient Fiction.* London: Adam Islip, 1599. STC 4691. Partial translation of Venice, 1580, reprint of Cartari, q.v.

Lyons, Clifford. "Stage Imagery in Shakespeare's Plays." In *Essays on Shakespeare and Elizabethan Drama in Honor of Hardin Craig,* edited by Richard Hosley, pp. 261–74. London: Routledge & Kegan Paul, 1963.

McGee, Arthur R. *"Macbeth* and the Furies." *Shakespeare Survey* 19 (1966):55–67.

MacIntyre, Jean. "Spenser's Herculean Heroes." *The Humanities Association Bulletin* 17, No. 1 (Spring 1966):5–12.

McMillin, Scott. "The Figure of Silence in *The Spanish Tragedy." ELH* 39 (1972):27–48.

Mâle, Émile. *The Gothic Image: Religious Art in France of the Thirteenth Century.* Translated by Dora Nussey from 3d ed., 1913. Reprint. London: Fontana Library, 1961.

Marle, Raimond van. *Iconographie de l'art profane au Moyen-Age et à la Renaissance, et la décoration des demeures.* 2 vols. 1931. Reprint. New York: Hacker Art Books, 1971.

Martin, John Rupert. *The Farnese Gallery.* Princeton: Princeton University Press, 1965.

Martz, Louis. *The Poetry of Meditation: A Study in English Religious Literature of the Seventeenth Century.* Yale Studies in English, 125. New Haven: Yale University Press, 1954.

Meagher, John C. *Method and Meaning in Jonson's Masques.* Notre Dame: University of Notre Dame Press, 1966.

Mehl, Dieter. *The Elizabethan Dumb Show: The History of a Dramatic Convention.* Cambridge: Harvard University Press, 1966. (First published in German in 1964.)

——. "Emblems in English Renaissance Drama." *Renaissance Drama,* n.s. 2 (1969):39–57.

——. "Visual and Rhetorical Imagery in Shakespeare's Plays." *Essays and Studies,* n.s. 25 (1972):83–100.

Merchant, W. Moelwyn. "Timon and the Conceit of Art." *Shakespeare Quarterly* 6 (1955):249–57.

Midgley, Graham. *"The Merchant of Venice:* A Reconsideration." *Essays in Criticism* 10 (1960):119–33.

Mincoff, Marco. "What Shakespeare Did to *Rosalynde." Shakespeare-Jahrbuch* 96 (1960):78–89.

Minor, Andrew C., and Mitchell, Bonner. *A Renaissance Entertainment: Festivities for the Marriage of Cosimo I, Duke of Florence, in 1539.* Columbia: University of Missouri Press, 1968.

Morris, Harry. *"Hamlet* as a *memento mori* Poem." *PMLA* 85 (1970):1035–40.

Muir, Kenneth. *Last Periods of Shakespeare, Racine, Ibsen.* Detroit: Wayne State University Press, 1961.

——. "Shakespeare's Imagery—Then and Now." *Shakespeare Survey* 18 (1965):46–57.

——, ed. *Macbeth,* by William Shakespeare. 9th ed. The Arden Shakespeare. 1962. Reprint. London: Methuen & Co., 1970.

Myrick, Kenneth O. "The Theme of Damnation in Shakespearean Tragedy." *Studies in Philology* 38 (1941):221–45.

Nicoll, Allardyce. *Studies in Shakespeare.* London: Leonard and Virginia Woolf, 1927.

Noble, Richmond. *Shakespeare's Biblical Knowledge and Use of the Book of Common Prayer, as Exemplified in the Plays of the First Folio.* London: Society for Promoting Christian Knowledge, 1935.

O'Connor, Sister Mary Catharine. *The Art of Dying Well: The Development of the Ars Moriendi.* Columbia University Studies in English and Comparative Literature, 156. New York: Columbia University Press, 1942.

Orgel, Stephen. *The Jonsonian Masque.* Cambridge, Mass.: Harvard University Press, 1965.

——, and Strong, Roy C. *Inigo Jones: The Theatre of the Stuart Court.* 2 vols. London: Sotheby-Parke Bernet, 1973.

Ornstein, Robert. *A Kingdom for a Stage: The Achievement of Shakespeare's History Plays.* Cambridge, Mass.: Harvard University Press, 1972.

The Oxford Dictionary of the Christian Church. Edited by Frank Leslie Cross. 1957. Reprint with corrections. London: Oxford University Press, 1958.

Panofsky, Erwin. *Early Netherlandish Painting: Its Origins and Character*. 2 vols. Cambridge, Mass.: Harvard University Press, 1953.

————. *Hercules am Scheidewege und andere antike Bildstoffe in der neueren Kunst*. Leipzig: B. G. Teubner, 1930.

————. *The Life and Art of Albrecht Dürer*. 4th ed. 1943. Reprint. Princeton: Princeton University Press, 1955.

————. "The Mouse that Michaelangelo Failed to Carve." In *Essays in Memory of Karl Lehmann*, edited by Lucy Freeman Sandler, pp. 242–51. New York: J. J. Augustin, 1964.

————. *Studies in Iconology: Humanistic Themes in the Art of the Renaissance*. 1939. Reprint. New York: Harper & Row, 1962.

Paradin, Claude. *Devices heroiques*. Lyons: I. de Tournes, 1551. Translated by P. S., q.v.

Parrott, Thomas Marc. *Shakespearean Comedy*. New York: Oxford University Press, 1949.

Passavant, Johann David. *Le peintre-graveur, contenant l'histoire de la gravure sur bois, sur métal et au burin jusque vers la fin du XVI. siècle. . . .* 6 vols. Leipsig: R. Weigel, 1860–64.

Patch, Howard Rollin. *The Goddess Fortuna in Medieval Literature*. 1927. Reprint. New York: Octagon Books, 1967.

Paul, Henry N. *The Royal Play of* Macbeth: *When, Why, and How It Was Written by Shakespeare*. New York: Macmillan and Co., 1950.

Peacham, Henry. *Minerva Britanna, or a Garden of Heroical Devices*. London: W. Dight, 1612. STC 19511.

Perrière, Guillaume de la. *Le theatre de bons engins*. 1539. Facsimile reprint with introduction by Greta Dexter. Gainesville: Scholar's Facsimiles and Reprints, 1964. Translated by Combe, q.v.

Phialas, Peter G. "The Medieval in *Richard II.*" *Shakespeare Quarterly* 12 (1961):305–10.

————. *Shakespeare's Romantic Comedies: The Development of Their Form and Meaning*. Chapel Hill: University of North Carolina Press, 1966.

Pignatti, Terisio. *Giorgione*. London: Phaidon, 1971.

Pope-Hennessey, John. *An Introduction to Italian Sculpture*. 3 vols. in 5. London: Phaidon, 1955–63. Vol. 1 is *Italian Gothic Sculpture*, Vol. 2 is *Italian Renaissance Sculpture*, and Vol. 3 (in 3 parts) is *Italian High Renaissance and Baroque Sculpture*.

————. *Renaissance Bronzes from the Samuel H. Kress Collection: Reliefs, Plaquettes, Statuettes, Utensils and Mortars*. London: Phaidon, 1965.

Posner, Donald. *Annibale Carracci: A Study in the Reform of Italian Painting around 1590*. 2 vols. London: Phaidon, 1971.

Praz, Mario. *Mnemosyne: The Parallel between Literature and the Visual Arts*. Princeton: Princeton University Press, 1970.

————. *Studies in Seventeenth-Century Imagery*. 2d ed. Rome: Edizioni di Storia e Letteratura, 1964.

Prisian. *Grammatici libri omnes*. Venice: Aldus, 1527.

Rabkin, Norman. "Meaning and Shakespeare." In *Shakespeare 1971: Proceedings of the World Shakespeare Congress, Vancouver, August, 1971*, edited by Clifford Leech and J. M. R. Margeson, pp. 89–106. Toronto: University of Toronto Press, 1972.

————. *Shakespeare and the Common Understanding*. New York: Free Press, 1967.

————, ed. *Reinterpretations of Elizabethan Drama*. New York: Columbia University Press, 1969.

The Rat-trap: or, The Iesvites Taken in their owne Net, &c. London, 1641. Wing R294.

Read, Charles Hercules. *The Waddesdon Bequest: Jewels, Plate, and other Works of Art Bequeathed by Baron Ferdinand Rothschild*. 2d ed. London: British Museum, 1927.

Réau, Louis. *Iconographie de l'art chrétien*. 3 vols. in 6. Paris: Presses Universitaires de France, 1955–59.

Ribner, Irving. *Patterns in Shakespearean Tragedy.* London: Methuen & Co., 1960.

Ribner, Rhoda. "The Compasse of this Curious Frame: Chapman's *Ovids Banquet of Sence* and the Emblematic Tradition." *Studies in the Renaissance* 17 (1970):233–58.

Ripa, Cesare. *Iconologia.* 1593. Facsimile reprint of 1603 illustrated edition, with introduction by Erna Mandowsky. Hildersheim, N.Y.: G. Olms, 1970.

Robertson, D. W. *A Preface to Chaucer: Studies in Medieval Perspectives.* Princeton: Princeton University Press, 1962.

Rose, Mark. *Shakespearean Design.* Cambridge, Mass.: Harvard University Press, Belknap Press, 1972.

Ross, Lawrence J. "Art and the Study of Early English Drama." *Renaissance Drama: A Report on Research Opportunities* 6 (1963):35–46.

————. "The Meaning of Strawberries in Shakespeare." *Studies in the Renaissance* 7 (1960):225–40.

————. "The Shakespearean *Othello:* A Critical Exposition of Historical Evidence." 3 vols. Ph.D. dissertation, Princeton University, 1957.

————. "Shakespeare's 'Dull Clown' and Symbolic Music." *Shakespeare Quarterly* 17 (1966):107–28.

————. "Symbol and Structure in the *Secunda Pastorum.*" *Comparative Drama* 1 (1967):122–49.

————. "The Use of a 'Fit-up' Booth in *Othello.*" *Shakespeare Quarterly* 12 (1961):359–70.

————. "Wingless Victory: Michaelangelo, Shakespeare, and the 'Old Man.' " In *Literary Monographs* 2, edited by Eric Rothstein and Richard N. Ringler, pp. 3–56, plus 20 pp. of illus., nn. on pp. 197–212. Madison: University of Wisconsin Press, 1969.

Rossiter, Arthur P. *Angel with Horns, and other Shakespearean Lectures.* Edited by Graham Storey. New York: Theatre Arts Books, 1961.

Roth, C. "Medieval Illustrations of Mouse-traps." *Bodleian Library Record* 5 (1956):244–52.

Rowan, Donald F. "The 'Swan' Revisited." *Research Opportunities in Renaissance Drama* 10 (1967):33–48.

Rowland, Beryl. *Animals with Human Faces: A Guide to Animal Symbolism.* Knoxville: University of Tennessee Press, 1973.

S., P., trans. *Heroical Devices . . . of M. Claudius Paradin.* London: W. Kearney, 1591. STC 19183. Translation of Paradin, q.v.

Sabbattini, Nicola. "Manual for Constructing Theatrical Scenes and Machines" (1638). Translated by John H. McDowell. In *The Renaissance Stage: Documents of Serlio, Sabbattini, and Furttenbach,* edited by Bernard Hewitt. Coral Gables: University of Miami Press, 1958.

Sarum Missal. 14th ed. Paris: F. Byrckmann, 1527. STC 16206.

Saxl, Fritz, and Wittkower, Rudolf. *British Art and the Mediterranean.* Oxford: Oxford University Press, 1948.

Schmitt, Otto, et al., eds. *Reallexikon zur deutschen Kunstgeschichte.* 6 vols. thus far. Stuttgart: J. B. Metzler, 1937– .

Schuman, Samuel. "Emblems and the English Renaissance Drama: A Checklist." *Research Opportunities in Renaissance Drama* 12 (1969):43–56.

————. "The Ring and the Jewel in Webster's Tragedies." *Texas Studies in Language and Literature* 14 (1972):253–68.

————. "The Theatre of Fine Devices: Emblems and the Emblematic in the Plays of John Webster." Ph.D. dissertation, Northwestern University, 1969.

Schwarz, Heinrich. "The Mirror in Art." *Art Quarterly* 15 (1952):97–118.

Scragg, Leah. "Macbeth on Horseback." *Shakespeare Survey* 26 (1973):81–88.

Seiferth, Wolfgang S. *Synagogue and Church in the Middle Ages: Two Symbols in Art and Literature.* Translated by Lee Chedeayne and Paul Gottwald. New York: Ungar, 1970.

Seltzer, Daniel. "Shakespeare's Texts and Modern Productions." In *Reinterpretations of Elizabethan Drama,* edited by Norman Rabkin, pp. 89–115. New York: Columbia University Press, 1969.

Seymour, Charles, Jr. *Masterpieces of Sculpture from the National Gallery of Art.* Washington: National Gallery of Art, 1949.

Seznec, Jean. *The Survival of the Pagan Gods: The Mythological Tradition and Its Place in Renaissance Humanism and Art.* Translated by Barbara F. Sessions. Bollingen Series, 38. New York: Pantheon Books, 1953. (First published in French in 1939.)

Shakespeare, William. *The Complete Works.* Edited by Peter Alexander. 2d ed. New York: Random House, 1952.

———. *The First Folio of Shakespeare, 1623.* Facsimile reprint edited by Charlton Hinman. New York: W. W. Norton, 1968.

Shapiro, Meyer. " 'Muscipula Diaboli,' the Symbolism of the *Mérode Altarpiece.*" *The Art Bulletin* 27 (1945):182–87.

Shaw, John. "Fortune and Nature in *As You Like It.*" *Shakespeare Quarterly* 6 (1955):45–50.

———. "The Staging of Parody and Parallels in *I Henry IV.*" *Shakespeare Survey* 20 (1967):61–73.

Shirley, Frances Ann. *Shakespeare's Use of Off-Stage Sounds.* Lincoln: University of Nebraska Press, 1963.

Shücking, Levin L. *The Meaning of* Hamlet. Translated by Graham Rawson. 1937. Reprint. New York: Barnes & Noble, 1966. (First published in German in 1935.)

Shumaker, Wayne. *The Occult Sciences in the Renaissance: A Study in Intellectual Patterns.* Berkeley: University of California Press, 1972.

Siegel, Paul N. "The Damnation of Othello." *PMLA* 68 (1953):1068–79.

Smith, Hallett. *Elizabethan Poetry: A Study in Conventions, Meaning, and Expression.* Cambridge, Mass.: Harvard University Press, 1952.

Snyder, Susan. "The Left Hand of God: Despair in Medieval and Renaissance Tradition." *Studies in the Renaissance* 12 (1965):18–59.

Sprague, Arthur Colby. *Shakespeare and the Actors: The Stage Business in His Plays, 1660–1905.* Cambridge, Mass.: Harvard University Press, 1944.

———. *The Stage Business in Shakespeare's Plays : A Postscript.* 1953. Reprint. Folcroft, Pa.: Folcroft Press, 1969.

Spurgeon, Caroline F. E. "A Shakespearean Picture Book." Unfinished MS at the Folger Shakespeare Library. S.d. 51.

———. *Shakespeare's Imagery and What It Tells Us.* 1935. Reprint. Cambridge: Cambridge University Press, 1958.

Starnes, DeWitt Talmage, and Talbert, Ernest William. *Classical Myth and Legend in Renaissance Dictionaries: A Study of Renaissance Dictionaries in Their Relation to the Classical Learning of Contemporary English Writers.* Chapel Hill: University of North Carolina Press, 1955.

Steadman, John M. "Falstaff as Actaeon: A Dramatic Emblem." *Shakespeare Quarterly* 14 (1963):230–44.

———. "Iconography and Renaissance Drama: Ethical and Mythological Themes." *Research Opportunities in Renaissance Drama* 13–14 (1970–71):73–122.

Sternfeld, F. W. "Shakespeare and Music." In *A New Companion to Shakespeare Studies,* edited by Kenneth Muir and Samuel Schoenbaum, pp. 157–67. Cambridge: Cambridge University Press, 1971.

Stewart, Stanley. *The Enclosed Garden: The Tradition and the Image in Seventeenth-Century Poetry.* Madison: University of Wisconsin Press, 1966.

Stirling, Brents. "Bolingbroke's 'Decision.' " *Shakespeare Quarterly* 2 (1951):27–34.

Stoll, Elmer E. *"The Tempest."* *PMLA* 47 (1932):699–726.

Strong, Roy C. *The English Icon: Elizabethan and Jacobean Portraiture.* London: Routledge & Kegan Paul, 1969.

———. *Holbein and Henry VIII.* London: Routledge & Kegan Paul, 1967.

————. *Tudor and Jacobean Portraits.* 2 vols. London: Her Majesty's Stationery Office, 1969.

Styan, J. L. *Shakespeare's Stagecraft.* Cambridge: Cambridge University Press, 1967.

Summers, Montague. *The Geography of Witchcraft.* 1927. Reprint. New York: University Books, 1965.

Sutton, Christopher. *Disce Mori: Learne to Die.* 5th ed. London: Widow Burby, 1609. STC 23478.

Sypher, Wylie. *Four Stages of Renaissance Style: Transformations in Art and Literature, 1400–1700.* Garden City, N.Y.: Doubleday & Co., 1955.

Tervarent, Guy de. *Attributs et symboles dans l'art profane, 1450–1600: Dictionnaire d'un langage perdu.* Geneva: E. Droz, 1958.

Thieme, Ulrich, and Becker, Felix. *Allegemeines Lexikon der bildenden Künstler von der Antike bis zur Gegenwart.* 37 vols. Leipzig: W. Engelmann, 1907–50.

Thorp, Margaret F. "Shakespeare and the Fine Arts." *PMLA* 46 (1931):672–93.

Three Chapters of Letters Relating to the Suppression of the Monasteries. Edited by Thomas Wright. London: Camden Society, 1843.

Tillotson, Geoffrey. *"Othello* and *The Alchemist* at Oxford in 1610." *The Times Literary Supplement,* July 20, 1933, p.494.

Tillyard, E. M. W. *The Elizabethan World Picture.* 1943. Reprint. London: Chatto & Windus, 1967.

————. *The English Renaissance: Fact or Fiction?* London: Hogarth Press, 1952.

————. *Shakespeare's History Plays.* London: Chatto & Windus, 1944.

————. *Shakespeare's Last Plays.* 1938. Reprint. London: Chatto & Windus, 1964.

————. "The Trial Scene in *The Merchant of Venice." Review of English Literature* 2, No. 4 (October 1961):51–59.

Tindall, Gillian. *A Handbook on Witches.* New York: Atheneum Publishers, 1966.

Topsell, Edward. *The Historie of Foure-Footid Beastes.* London: William Jaggard, 1607. STC 24123. Facsimile reprint of 1658 edition. New York: Da Capo, 1967.

Trapp, Joseph B. "The Iconography of the Fall of Man." In *Approaches to Paradise Lost,* ed. C. A. Patrides, pp. 223–65. London: Edward Arnold, 1968.

Traversi, Derek. *Shakespeare: The Last Phase.* New York: Harcourt-Brace, 1955.

The Tudor Constitution: Documents and Commentary. Edited by Geoffrey R. Elton. 1960. Reprint. Cambridge: Cambridge University Press, 1972.

The Tudor Period, 1599–1603. Edited by Ralph Edwards and L. G. G. Ramsey. The Connoisseur Period Guides, 1. London: Connoisseur, 1956.

Tuve, Rosemond. *Allegorical Imagery: Some Medieval Books and Their Imagery.* Princeton: Princeton University Press, 1966.

————. *Elizabethan and Metaphysical Imagery. Renaissance Poetic and Twentieth Century Critics.* Chicago: University of Chicago Press, 1947.

————. *A Reading of George Herbert.* London: Faber & Faber, 1952.

————. "Spenser and Some Pictorial Conventions. . . ." In *Essays by Rosemond Tuve: Spenser, Herbert, Milton,* edited by Thomas P. Roche, Jr., pp. 112–38. Princeton: Princeton University Press, 1970.

University of London: The Warburg Institute. London, 1960.

Ure, Peter. "The Looking Glass of *Richard II." Philological Quarterly* 34 (1955):219–24.

————, ed. *Richard II,* by William Shakespeare. 4th ed. rev. The Arden Shakespeare. Cambridge, Mass.: Harvard University Press, 1956.

Vaenius, Otho. *Amorum emblemata.* Antwerp: Otho Vaenius, 1608? [STC 24567b–University Microfilm, Reel 602.] Facsimile reprint. Hildesheim, N.Y.: G. Olms, 1970.

Velz, John. *Shakespeare and the Classical Tradition: A Critical Guide to Commentary, 1660–1960.* Minneapolis: University of Minnesota Press, 1968.

Venezky, [Griffin], Alice Sylvia. *Pagentry on the Shakespearean Stage.* New York: Twayne, 1951.

Vergil, Polydore. *Anglica historia.* Basel: J. Bebelium, 1534.

Verlet, Pierre, and Salet, Francis. *The Lady and the Unicorn.* Translated by R. D. Chancellor. London: Thames, 1961.

Virgil. *Aeneid.* Translated by Thomas Phaer. London: N. England, 1562. STC 24800.

Waddington, Raymond B. "Antony and Cleopatra: 'What Venus Did with Mars.' " *Shakespeare Studies* 2 (1966):210–27.

Waith, Eugene. *The Herculean Hero in Marlowe, Chapman, Shakespeare, and Dryden.* New York: Columbia University Press, 1962.

Walker, D. P. "Kepler's Celestial Music." *Journal of the Warburg and Courtauld Institutes* 30 (1967):228–50.

Watson, Arthur. *The Early Iconography of the Tree of Jesse.* London: Oxford University Press, 1934.

Weiss, John. *Wit, Humour, and Shakespeare: Twelve Essays.* Boston: Roberts Brothers, 1876.

Welsford, Enid. *The Court Masque: A Study in the Relationship between Poetry and the Revels.* 1927. Reprint. New York: Russell & Russell, 1962.

Wenzel, Siegfried. *The Sin of Sloth: Acedia in Medieval Thought and Literature.* Chapel Hill: University of North Carolina Press, 1967.

Wertheim, Albert. "The Treatment of Shylock and Thematic Integrity in *The Merchant of Venice.*" *Shakespeare Studies* 6 (1970):75–87.

Whitaker, Virgil K. *Shakespeare's Use of Learning: An Inquiry into the Growth of His Mind and Art.* 1953. Reprint. San Marino: Huntington Library, 1964.

White, Helen C. *English Devotional Literature, 1600–1640.* 1931. Reprint. New York: Haskell House, 1966.

———. *The Tudor Books of Private Devotion.* Madison: University of Wisconsin Press, 1951.

Whitney, Geffrey. *A Choice of Emblemes and other Devices.* Leyden: Christopher Plantin, 1586. STC 25438. Facsimile reprint. New York: Da Capo, 1969.

Wickham, Glynne. *Early English Stages, 1300–1660.* 2 vols. in 3 thus far. London: Routledge & Kegan Paul, 1959– .

———. "From Tragedy to Tragi-Comedy: *King Lear* as Prologue." *Shakespeare Survey* 26 (1973):34–48.

———. "Hell-Castle and Its Door-Keeper." *Shakespeare Survey* 19 (1966):68–74.

———. *Shakespeare's Dramatic Heritage: Collected Studies in Mediaeval, Tudor, and Shakespearean Drama.* London: Routledge & Kegan Paul, 1969.

Willet, Andrew. *Sacrorum emblematum centuria una.* Cambridge: John Legate, 1591–92? STC 25695.

Wilson, John Dover. *What Happens in* Hamlet. 3rd ed. Cambridge: Cambridge University Press, 1951.

———, ed. *Richard II,* by William Shakespeare. New Cambridge Edition. Cambridge: Cambridge University Press, 1939.

Wilson, Thomas. *The Arte of Rhetorike.* 7th ed. London: John Kingston, 1584. STC 25805.

Wind, Edgar. *Bellini's Feast of the Gods: A Study in Venetian Humanism.* Cambridge, Mass.: Harvard University Press, 1948.

———. *Giorgione's* Tempesta, *with Comments on Giorgione's Poetic Allegories.* Oxford: Clarendon Press, 1969.

———. *Pagan Mysteries in the Renaissance.* 1958. Revised reprint. Baltimore: Penguin Books, 1967.

Winter, William. *Shakespeare on the Stage* [first series]. New York: Moffat-Yard, 1911.

Wittkower, Rudolf and Wittkower, Margot. *Born under Saturn: The Character and Conduct of Artists—A Documented History from Antiquity to the French Revolution.* 1963. Reprint. New York: W. W. Norton, 1969.

Wixom, William D. *Treasures from Medieval France.* Cleveland: Cleveland Museum of Art, 1967.

Woodman, David. *White Magic and English Renaissance Drama.* Rutherford, N.J.: Fairleigh Dickinson University Press, 1973.

Worsley, Alice F. "Medieval Manuscript Illuminations." *Computers and the Humanities* 7 (1972–73):295–96.

Wright, Louis B. *Middle-Class Culture in Elizabethan England.* 1935. Reprint. Ithaca: Cornell University Press, 1958.

Wynman, Nicolaus. *Hercules cum Antaeo pugnae allegorica ac pia interpretatio.* Nuremberg: Jo. Petreius, 1537.

Yates, Frances A. *Giordano Bruno and the Hermetic Tradition.* Chicago: University of Chicago Press, 1964.

Zeeveld, William Gordon. *Foundations of Tudor Policy.* Cambridge, Mass.: Harvard University Press, 1948.

Zerner, Henri. "L'Art au morier." *Revue de l'art* 2 (1971):7–30.

————. *The School of Fontainebleau: Etchings and Engravings.* Translated by Stanley Baron. New York: H. N. Abrams, 1969.

Zetter, Jacob de, trans. *Speculum vertutum.* Frankfurt: Jacob de Zetter, 1644. Translation of Haechtanus, q.v.

Zupnick, Irving L. "The Mystery of the Mérode Mousetrap." *Burlington Magazine* 108 (1966):126–33.

Index